LifeManual

A Proven Formula to Create the Life You Desire

BY PETER H. THOMAS

LifePilot

A LifePilot® Publication

"My purpose is to love, share my light, be a world leader, enjoy the experience of life and the journey — and to lead, educate and inspire wherever I go."

Peter H. Thomas

We all need a purpose in life! As you embark on your journey through *LifeManual*, please write your life's purpose:

My name: ....

My purpose in life: ....
....
....
....
....
....
....
....

Signed: ....

Other publications by Peter H. Thomas

Never Fight with a Pig: A Survival Guide for Entrepreneurs

Windows of Opportunity: 21 Steps to Successful Selling

The Peter Thomas Sales Course

This book is dedicated to my son, Todd Thomas (1964-2000)

This book is for you, Todd, in honor and celebration of your life. You once said, "The most difficult thing to do is see the world through other people's eyes or walk the world in other people's shoes." Through your words and your art, you depicted a world where we could live to the highest destiny of the human spirit. You always saw that all humanity, at its deepest level, just wants to give and receive love.

As the poet John Donne wrote, "When one man dies, one chapter is not torn out of the book..." Your inspiration lives on in every chapter of this book and through the lives of people throughout the world who have learned to live with passion and strength through LifePilot.

On this journey, I am not alone. You are and always will be my co-pilot.

Peter H. Thomas
Victoria, BC

Contents

Flourish

> "When once you have tasted flight, you will forever walk the earth with your eyes turned skyward, for there you have been, and there you will always long to return." *Leonardo da Vinci*

Prologue

When Leonardo da Vinci wrote the words above, he had never flown in an aircraft except in his dreams. Though he lived in the 15th century and knew nothing of the mechanics of flying, he was ahead of his time, creating intricate plans for flying machines, including a helicopter and a hang glider. We can only imagine what he would have given for one flight in an airplane.

Today, it is possible for any of us to get on an airplane; some of us are even lucky enough to have piloted planes. As many a great pilot will tell you, the key to successfully piloting an aircraft is made up of two elements: understanding how to operate your craft and gaining mastery of the most important airspace of all — your mind.

LifePilot, the philosophy of living detailed in *LifeManual*, isn't about flying real aircraft. It's about piloting your own life with mastery: learning to read your internal navigational instruments and conquering the mental blocks to achieving a more fulfilling life. In choosing to read *LifeManual*, you've taken the first step toward living a more meaningful, balanced life by bringing how you live into alignment with what you believe in — your values.

I grew up with a firm set of values instilled in me by my mother, Trude, a strong woman who inspired me to believe in my sense of worth. For years, I lived by the values I learned during my childhood and youth. They got me through numerous tricky situations. It wasn't until I was in my 30s, however, that I became aware of the real power of consciously living in alignment with my values.

ADAPTABILITY

could be
actual tower

Honor your values

priorities values

The year was 1974, and I was attending my first Young Presidents' Organization (YPO) University in Hawaii. As an enthusiastic entrepreneur, the idea of meeting new people, expanding my horizons and attending some of the lectures fascinated me. The workshop offered by Red Scott, who was then chairman and CEO of Activa Group, won my vote. Someone told me Red had 17 companies that all surpassed the YPO membership criteria for strong financial performance. With the one company I owned at the time, I barely qualified, but I was an avid learner. "This man can teach me a lot," I thought to myself. Red came into the classroom with a big smile, looked around at the group of 15 of us, and said, "It's far too nice outside. Let's go down to the beach." Out the door he went, and we followed along like puppies.

At the beach, we sat around campfire-style and Red talked about values. "Are you living lives that honor your values?" he asked us. To demonstrate what he meant, he gave us each a pad of paper and asked us to write down what we felt our values were. We worked away for about 10 minutes. Then Red asked us to list all of the priorities in our lives on another page. That took me longer, but after about 20 minutes I had a full page. "Now, check your priorities against your values," Red told us, "and see if each priority aligns with one of those values." Well, big surprise! Probably half of the things taking up my days were not related to *any* of my values.

The philosopher Aristotle said, "We are what we repeatedly do." I was *doing*, all right, but my priorities were all over the place and didn't always align with my values. I realized then and there that some major changes were in order for my life. I had what I now call an epiphany, which *Webster's Dictionary* will tell you is "a sudden, intuitive perception of, or insight into the reality of, the essential meaning of something, often initiated by some simple, commonplace occurrence." To put it more simply, I was hit over the head by a universal two-by-four.

Because of that epiphany, I left the Young Presidents' Organization in Hawaii early and flew straight to California to check out an incredible business opportunity. That led to the creation of Century

21 Canada, which years later I would sell for millions of dollars. Within 90 days of seeing Red Scott, I had moved from Alberta to the West Coast of Canada, launched Century 21, and literally started my life over. By reaffirming my values and matching my priorities to them, I gave myself permission to change my life. From that point on, I became intent on making sure everything that came into my life was first measured against my values.

I have lived my life for the last 40 years according to the lessons I learned on that beach in Hawaii. When I have gone off track — as we all do from time to time — my values always pull me back to what is right for my life.

I learned that day on the beach to be alert for experiences that have the power to enrich and change my life for the better. I also learned the truth of what writer Albert Camus meant when he wrote, "But what is happiness except the simple harmony between a man and the life he leads?"

This approach to life has carried me through the best of times and the worst of times. When I was 60, I had to deal with the most tragic event of my life. I lost my only son Todd to suicide. Todd had suffered from a major sleep disorder. On Tuesday, February 1, 2000, Todd took his life by jumping from the 14th floor of the New York Plaza Hotel. He was 36 years old. With the support of my family and friends, I worked my way through the loss of Todd. I learned that you must get past tragedies like this but you never get over them.

After I lost Todd, life didn't hold much wonder for me. I felt empty and disconnected. For the first time, I had encountered something I was powerless to fix. No matter what I did, I couldn't bring my son back. I felt unmotivated and seemed to sleepwalk through my days without the spark, desire and excitement I had always possessed. I did not discuss these feelings with anyone else in my family — I felt they each had their own pain.

Instead, I put on a show but the inner laughter and joy of life were just not there for me. The only times the old Peter Thomas seemed to come back was when I became involved in anything that honored Todd.

During that time, I was on a planning committee for an upcoming event for the World Presidents' Organization (WPO). We decided to have a meeting on my yacht, so during the summer of 2003 all members of the committee came aboard the *Thomas Spirit* for a three-day work/play session. One of the WPO members, Paul Robshaw from Austin, Texas, noticed my thick three-ring binder with Peter Thomas' *LifeManual* written on the cover.

"What is that?" he wondered. I told him it was the binder from which I basically ran my life.

"Do you mind if I take a look?" he asked.

"Well, it's personal stuff, but I don't mind," I said. He took the binder and disappeared downstairs for some time. When he came back up, he asked if he could make a copy and study the book further. Very easily, in an instant, I made the decision that he could make a copy if he thought it would help him. Some people have found it unbelievable that I would share my innermost life with someone so quickly, but in the past I had shared my life plan with a few other special friends. I knew Paul well and had a lot of respect for him. Besides, I didn't feel I had any deep dark secrets.

After that WPO session, Paul returned to Texas. I didn't hear from him until about two months later when he called and asked me to come down to Austin to teach him and a group of his associates how to create their own *LifeManuals.* "It's not something I teach," I explained. "It's just my own way to keep my life on track."

Nevertheless, Paul was very enthusiastic. "We'd like you to share your journey," he insisted. How could I turn down a request like that?

"I'd be honored," I told Paul. We booked a time and I traveled to Austin with my binder. I met with Paul and his friends in a very simple room. I sat on a stool and easily walked everyone through my *LifeManual*, explaining the philosophy I used to guide my life. I told them about my system of ensuring everything I did aligned with one of my values. "It's critical," I explained, "for each of you in this room to recognize what your values are." As I spoke, it became apparent from the questions and enthusiasm that everyone really enjoyed the session.

Paul and I talked soon after my trip to Austin. "Why don't you put your *LifeManual* into a formal training program and teach it all over the world?" he asked me. He felt the money I raised through this program could be given to charity in honor of my son Todd's life. It just seemed so easy and so right to make the decision that this would become my main purpose.

LifePilot truly began at that point. Since then, not a day goes by that I do not involve myself in the LifePilot program in some way. It has given me a purpose in life again and I am my old self — full of happiness, drive and fun.

The educator and poet Patrick Overton writes, "When we walk to the edge of all the light we have and take the step into the darkness of the unknown, we must believe that one of two things will happen. There will be something solid for us to stand on or we will be taught to fly."

Through LifePilot, and through remembering my values and how to navigate by them, I have learned to fly again, and I feel my son is my co-pilot in this venture. Todd was always supportive of my quest to live true to my values and to pass that knowledge on to others. He was a very spiritual and artistic young man who believed in all of the principles outlined in this book. He has been the motivating force and angel in ensuring its completion. I know Todd would be very proud of LifePilot and what we are doing. He is part of it every day.

Todd's life may have ended early but his legacy continues in the work I do through LifePilot. The Thomas Foundation raises awareness of the magnitude of mental illness and its effect on individuals as well as society, to erase the stigma associated with it and to search for effective treatments. So far, the organization has helped raise several million dollars for mental health initiatives, including development of a model Crisis Response Unit. The first such unit is located at Royal Jubilee Hospital in Victoria, British Columbia. It is aimed at providing timely, appropriate, and dignified care for people living with mental illnesses.

* *

Today, I still have my three-ring *LifeManual*. So do thousands of people throughout the world who have taken part in LifePilot workshops. Now, through the publication of this book, that message will continue to spread. By living true to my values, my life has changed. I live at a deeper level now, and have become even more empathetic due, in part, to the compassion so many people have shown to me after I lost Todd. My purpose is to love, share my light, be a world leader, enjoy the experience of life and the journey — and to lead, educate and inspire wherever I go.

I have learned that living a life of fulfillment is more about the way we see the world than the way the world sees us. To illustrate this, I'll share a story with you that I often tell in LifePilot workshops.

Once upon a time a tired father came home from work, slumped into a chair, turned on the TV and tried to rest after a particularly tiring day. Just as he was almost asleep, his six-year-old son came running downstairs. Spying his Dad in the chair, he ran up to him, shook him and said, "Dad, read me a story, please read me a story!"

The tired father tried to say no, but his son was very persistent. Finally, the father picked up a magazine lying by the chair. On one page, he noticed a map of the world. He ripped the map up into small pieces and gave the pieces to his son.

"When you paste all of the pieces together, I'll read you a story," he said. Confident this would keep his son busy for quite some time, he leaned back to grab some more shut-eye.

In just a few short minutes, his son was back at his side. "OK, Dad," he said excitedly. "I've put the map together — read me a story!"

The father was surprised. "I can't believe you put the picture together so quickly," he said. "How did you manage that?"

"Well," said the boy, "I just looked on the back of the map and there was a picture of a man's head. When I put the man together, the world turned out perfect."

I love this story because it's the perfect metaphor for how we often struggle to figure out the world when all we really need to do is figure out ourselves. As you'll discover in *LifeManual*, when you identify and live by your values, the world around you falls into place.

Life is a wondrous and incredible process. Each of us is filled with inner genius and the potential to take flight. You can take any number of shots at the runway, but whether or not you get airborne is all a matter of attitude. Hockey great Wayne Gretzky had it right when he said, "You miss 100 percent of the shots you never take."

So take your best shot at living the life you deserve to live. Become the pilot of your own destiny and, as Frank Sinatra so famously sang, "Come fly with me."

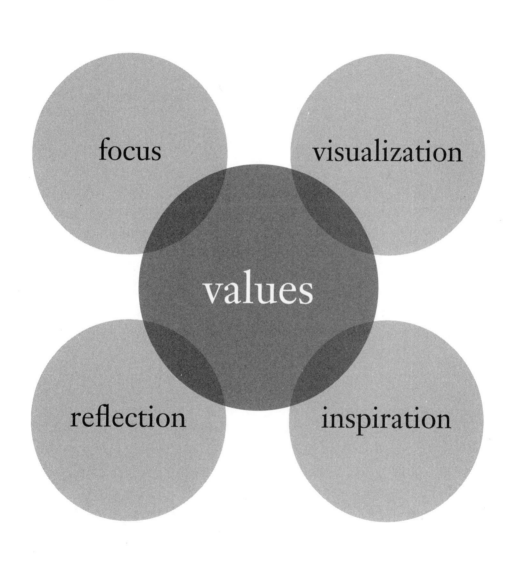

learn to like being a beginner

SECRET 1

You Become What You Value

Computers, cars and airplanes come with operating manuals. Human beings don't. Most of what we know is based on trial and error, and how much we are willing and able to learn from others. When we first enter the world, much of our focus is spent on just staying physically upright, and satisfying our basic needs for food, love, comfort and warmth. We feel our way through our early years, guided by a combination of nature and nurture.

As we grow, our needs become far more complex. Before we know it, it's not about keeping our balance as we learn to walk or ride a bike — it's about trying to cope with balancing our entire lives. But coping is not the same as thriving. So we begin to endure, but according to English writer Elizabeth Bibesc, endurance is frequently a form of indecision. Coping and enduring may get you off the runway, but they won't keep you in flight.

With no operating manual to guide us, it's not surprising so many of us wind up feeling off-balance, unfulfilled or just plain lost. We rush from one task to another. We reach for success, only to achieve it and discover it isn't as satisfying as we hoped it would be. And it seems there's never enough time for all the things that really matter to us.

While it's true you aren't born with an operating manual, you *can* create your own *LifeManual* by applying the philosophies and techniques of the LifePilot program to your life. You'll discover what you truly value and how to bring everything you do into alignment with your core values. Creating your *LifeManual* will put you in touch with your personal navigation system that will guide you to new heights of happiness and success. You will gain:

* the tools to identify your personal values and recognize where improvements may be necessary to live in alignment with these values

* a blueprint to set and achieve your goals

* a system for expanding your vision while keeping your focus

* a progressive yet permanent record of your past accomplishments and ongoing plans, with a focus on future achievement.

I believe we are all born with untold potential. *LifeManual* will help you create your operating manual to tap into your potential and live life to its fullest, with integrity, focus and self-determination. You'll discover a sense of purpose, inner strength and freedom you never imagined possible. You'll become more aware of where you are going and how to get there. Life will cease to be something that just happens to you as you sit back passively. Instead, you'll learn to file your own flight plan and take flight. If this sounds beyond your reach, tell yourself, as I always do when I'm faced with a challenge, "It will be easy — a piece of cake." You'll be amazed at how well this works. If you say it enough, you'll begin to believe it.

Flight Simulation

Imagine you are piloting an aircraft. (Don't worry, you don't actually need to have flown one to do this exercise!) How do you navigate your craft and keep it from crashing? An experienced pilot will tell you that you need to look at the control panel in front of you and read your instruments.

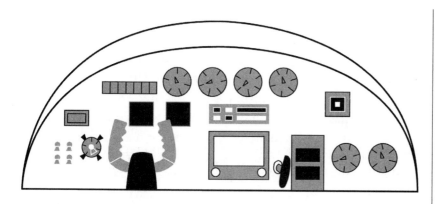

In an aircraft, these instruments tell you which direction you are heading in, and the state of your engine, altitude, speed and fuel. As a human being, your instruments are *your values*. These values tell you when you are on course, when to make adjustments, when to re-fuel and how to remain in flight. They also tell you when to land and wait for better weather.

I remember flying in a helicopter over Whistler Ski Resort in the Coastal Mountains of British Columbia. From a clear day at the base of the mountain, we were suddenly surrounded by clouds so thick it seemed as though we were flying through milk. I've thought back to that experience many times, because life is like that. You might be flying along quite happily when suddenly you hit rough weather, or the fog of uncertainty curls in around you and blocks your vision. Life feels chaotic. This is the point where many people wing out of control. Maybe you get fired or someone you love leaves you. Perhaps your finances plummet or your health is in jeopardy.

As you struggle to regain your bearings, it's vital to check your instruments — your values. According to the advice of the old US Navy magazine, *Approach*, "Instrument flying is when your mind gets a grip on the fact that there is vision beyond sight." Knowing and understanding your values will help guide you until the rough weather calms and the fog clears.

In All Kinds of Weather

Navigating by your values isn't just for bad times. Checking in with your values will give you confidence and a sense of direction at every stage of your journey through life. Dru Narwani, an aviator who has flown his single engine Cessna from New York to Australia and was personally commended by the Canadian prime minister, says even when there's not a cloud in the sky, it's easy to become lost if you don't check your instruments, especially if you are in places with few discernible landmarks. Starting a new job, entering a relationship or experiencing loss are some examples of this. If you know your values, you can use them to guide you through this unfamiliar territory. You'll be better prepared to deal with chaos or uncertainty when they arise.

Dru has not only learned how to navigate the skies, he has learned to navigate his own life by living in tune with his values and mentoring others to do so as well. Five years ago, Dru was at the height of a very successful banking career as the president and CEO of Standard Chartered Bank in Thailand. At that time, he and his family were living what can only be described as a luxurious life in Bangkok. But Dru felt something was missing. That epiphany hit him one evening as he sat down to dinner with his family. As usual, he was the last one at the table, as his work usually kept him late. Even during dinner, the demands of phones and faxes meant constant interruptions. This night was no different. But for some reason, Dru paused long enough to realize his children were very subdued.

"Why are you so quiet?" he asked them.

"Mom asked us not to share things about our school because you're so busy," they told him. He realized it was true, and that realization had a profound effect on him.

"I was so disconnected and so busy," he recalls. "My values included family, health and integrity but I had lost track of that. I said, 'It's time to follow my values.'"

Though still a young man, Dru opted to retire. He and his family returned to Canada after ten years away, and began to build a new life that honored their values. Dru and his wife have journeyed far and wide in their Cessna, and have just finished writing a book about their travels.

Value Celebration

Tapping into Values

"Values are essential to living and to human happiness," said Pope John Paul II. This idea is not unique to Catholicism. It is echoed throughout the works of the world's greatest philosophers and leaders, from Socrates to Gandhi, but they didn't invent values anymore than the Wright Brothers invented gravity. That knowledge has always been within us. Some of our best-known parables, fables and works of art are based on human beings' struggles to live true to their values. Even children's books, such as the *Harry Potter* series, contain the subtext of living true to values.

My own journey into discovering my values and living in alignment with them isn't something I invented either. I firmly believe a wise person learns from experience — and a wiser person learns from other people's experiences. As Sir Isaac Newton said, "If I have seen far, it is by standing on the shoulders of giants."

LifeManual draws on the work of history's great thinkers and many of the successful people I have met, to help you access a powerful structure and philosophy by which to live your life and achieve your dreams. Many of these remarkable people credit the establishment of — and commitment to — objectives and values as a fundamental basis for their success. Benjamin Franklin, one of our greatest inventors, understood the importance of weighing his actions against his values, just as we do in *LifeManual*. Franklin developed a list of 13 virtues that he considered essential to his life. Each day, he would check his actions against those virtues.

Make Your Commitment to a Better Life

If you are ready to create a more balanced, fulfilling life, I'd like you to fill out and sign the *LifePilot Personal Commitment Contract* on page 7. You may share this contract with others if you like, but it's more important that *you* look at it from time to time to remind yourself of your dedication to creating the life you desire.

Signing this contract isn't just a whimsical notion — it's a way to make your intentions clear and help you visualize living the life of your dreams. As we'll discuss later in the book, what you visualize becomes your future. So please take a moment to fill out and sign your contract before reading on.

When you commit to LifePilot and creating your own *LifeManual*, you are committing to a life-friendly system of living that is adaptable to your unique personality and lifestyle. You won't feel like you are constantly trying to fit a square peg into a round hole or trying to follow someone else's plan for your life. Your *LifeManual* belongs to you alone. I recommend that, once you have completed the initial work in this book, you review your *LifeManual* at least weekly. This will remind you of what you value, and inspire you to remain on track. I also recommend you revisit the major components annually. Making the effort to incorporate the lessons of *LifeManual* into your life offers lasting rewards.

As the poet and dramatist Johann Wolfgang von Goethe once said, "Seize this very minute…what you can do, or dream you can, begin it. Boldness has genius, power and magic in it. Only engage, and then the mind grows heated. Begin it, and the work will be completed."

PERSONAL COMMITMENT CONTRACT

The power to identify and clarify your values, and live in alignment with them, generates inner peace and personal effectiveness. Committing to LifePilot enables you to discover a clear sense of purpose and direction.

Congratulations for taking this significant step; you are embarking on a more fulfilling life. Enjoy the journey.

Pilot

date

address

telephone

email

signature

CHAPTER REVIEW

* Values are your personal principles. They represent your priorities and what is most important to you.

* When you live in alignment with your values, you'll experience a life filled with happiness, passion and achievement.

* Use your values as navigational instruments. This will keep you on track and help you avoid chaos and uncertainty.

* To experience an epiphany in your life, you must navigate around chaos when you can, and use your instruments to fly safely through it when you can't go around it.

* Signing your *Personal Commitment Contract* will make your intentions clear.

* Seize the moment and remind yourself of your commitment to a more fulfilling, balanced life. Don't wait any longer to create the life you really desire.

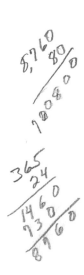

Navigate By Your Values

There is a well-told parable about a bank that deposits $86,400 into your account every morning. This bank allows no balance to be carried over to the next day, and it offers no savings account, so whatever you don't spend wisely is lost forever. No matter how much you beg to get that money back, you can never retrieve it. If you were wise, you would draw out every cent, every day of your life, and spend freely. You would leave no crumbs for the bankers to reclaim.

It's a great fantasy, isn't it? But what if I told you that you really *do* have such a bank account in your life. It isn't filled with money — it's filled with time to spend on the things you value. Each morning, this bank deposits 86,400 seconds into your account. Each night, it reclaims whatever you failed to spend on what you value most.

All of the seconds we are given every day add up to only 700,000 hours in the course of a typical lifetime. Upon hearing this, many people feel a sense of melancholy as they ponder how much time they have let drift through their fingers. They talk about what they *should* have done, the things they *wished* they'd said, and the people they *would* have treated better, forgiven or apologized to if only they could have some of that time back.

The stark truth is that there is no way to reclaim that lost time but there is a way to start living a more meaningful, balanced life.

The answer is simple — spend time on what you value and weed out time-wasters that take you away from what matters most. Giving your time to what you value frees you from hours of indecision and worry, and brings you clarity of mind and purpose. You'll begin to feel an authenticity to your life that many of us so easily lose as we try to change ourselves to satisfy the expectations of others. "We are what we pretend to be," says Kurt Vonnegut, author of *Slaughterhouse Five*, "so we must be careful about what we pretend to be."

Even as you read this, you may be coming up with all kinds of reasons why the LifePilot approach won't work. The biggest one usually is, "I don't have time to focus on me and my values." I'm going to ask you to suspend your disbelief until you've finished this book, because reading *LifeManual* will change your life. You'll begin to see that by focusing on what you value, you'll discover who you really are.

Getting Deeper into Values

Your values represent what matters most to you. They also satisfy the deep inner longing for meaning, and influence every aspect of the way you interact with the world around you. You gain your prevailing values over the course of your lifetime, and you continue to develop these values as you pass through various stages of life. Most of your values were instilled in you during your childhood, teenage years and early adulthood. These values are further shaped by experience, temperament, role models, mentors, parents, teachers, friends and cultural icons.

"In the early stages of life we are often focused on pleasing others…," writes self-development expert Suzanne Zoglio, PhD. "In an effort to get our needs met, we learn to play by other people's rules. But as we mature, we become more competent, independent, and able to meet our own needs. We are then less motivated to do what others want us to do. We tire of keeping up appearances, and care much less about what other people think. We no longer want to chase someone else's dream; we want to live our own dreams."

This is the part where most of us get hung up. How do we break out of patterns that keep us living up to other people's dreams and expectations, and not our own? Sometimes the answer is simple, but we can't see it because we're so focused on figuring out complicated solutions to seemingly complex problems. My wife Rita and I saw this so clearly on a trip we took to Thailand. There, we had the fascinating experience of learning how the Thai people train elephants. In this centuries-old practice, a young elephant is chained by one of its legs to a post. The elephant soon discovers he can only move a few feet away from the post. After two or three years of being chained, the elephant no longer needs to be tethered to the post. As long as the chain remains around his leg, the elephant will not stray or even attempt to escape. He believes, out of habit, that he is still chained to the post.

As humans, we like to think we know better than animals, but we are also tethered by our habits. All we have to do is pull away. It's so simple but our habits often blind us to the possibilities.

File a New Flight Plan

I remember my first solo flight during helicopter training. As I prepared to take off, I pulled up on the stick. The helicopter rose straight up into the air. As I continued to hang onto the stick, the helicopter began moving from side to side, then shuddering and rocking. It was a frightening moment. My mind slowed, as the mind seems to do in such situations. Finally, something told me to let go of the stick. As soon as I let go, the helicopter stabilized. A guy on the ground later told me if I hadn't let go when I did and stopped fighting the machine, I would have crashed. The machine, he said, wanted to fly. I just had to let go and trust my intuition. Breaking away from unproductive or unhealthy habits is a similar process.

We often come up with amazingly tangled reasons for not letting go of negative habits, people and situations. If we hang on to negativity long enough, eventually we risk crashing. This tendency is sometimes called the "Yes but" syndrome. If you've ever played this game with someone who is determined to remain in a negative situation, you know the frustration of seeing the solution clearly only to hear, "Yes but" from the person who can't pull away from the post or let go of the stick.

Learning how to break away from negative patterns and habits begins with getting to know yourself better and consciously identifying what you really value. After all, what you value is what you become. Watch your thoughts, for they become words. Choose your words, for they become actions. Understand your actions, for they become your habits. Study your habits, for they become your character. Develop your character, for it becomes your destiny.

Your values may range from down-to-earth values such as family, financial security, career and health to universal values like harmony, world peace, and ending poverty. When you are truly in touch with your values, they tell you when to say yes, when to say no, and what to do under extreme stress.

Here's an example of how my values guided me through one of the most fog-ridden times of my life. Back in the late 1970s, the North American real estate market boomed. Then, in 1981, the bottom dropped out. One minute I was on top of the world, living a jet-set lifestyle and suffering fairly heavily from what I call King Arthur's Disease — the feeling that I was invincible. The next moment everything changed: interest rates rocketed to 22 percent and property values fell dramatically.

I was happily in the midst of delivering a workshop to the Young Presidents' Organization in Texas when, miles away, back in Vancouver, Canada, my business partner unexpectedly announced to a ballroom full of people at the Bayshore Hotel and a national TV audience, that he was bankrupt. Suddenly, my world tilted on the edge of chaos. Before my eyes, my fortune of $150 million plunged to minus $70 million. At that point, I'm sure many people would have understood if I had gone to the nearest bar and drowned my sorrows. They also would have understood if I'd given up and said, "I guess if my partner's bankrupt that's the end of me too."

I didn't do any of those things. Instead, I took a deep breath and checked my navigational instruments — my values. Health has long been one of my core values, so despite the chaos I found myself in, I decided to go running rather than drinking myself into a stupor. I remember one night in California, when my business partner and I found ourselves awake and sitting in the kitchen at 3 a.m. We were discussing our problems and turning solutions over in our minds. Suddenly, he stood up and said, "Let's go for a run."

We went out into the California night and ran like two horses through the dark, with the moon shining overhead. At one point, he veered off through a field because he knew the route. I figured there would be gopher holes in the field but I followed him anyway. As I ran, I discovered I wasn't thinking about my problems (which were enormous to be sure), I was focused on the moment. I began to gain perspective and reconnect with what I valued most. When we finally got home, I fell into bed and slept until noon the next day. It was the best sleep I'd had in months.

For several years it was touch and go as to whether or not I would lose everything I had earned. Frankly, I was feeling pretty sorry for myself. When I was in the deepest end of the situation, I had a very good talk with myself and evaluated where I stood. I picked up a pencil and a pad of paper and wrote down my assets. They were: health, freedom, family, friendships, reputation, relationships, self-esteem, wisdom, good work ethic, success (at least up until that time!), integrity, being a mentor, being a leader, lots of love — and on and on. In fact, the only thing that I could not put on the list was MONEY.

When I saw in writing all the assets I *did have*, I suddenly felt like a very lucky man. At that moment, if God would have told me I had to give away one of my assets, the reality is I would have chosen to give away MONEY. I could always make more money but I could never have regained most of the other assets once I lost them. As pastor Billy Graham says, "When wealth is lost, nothing is lost; when health is lost, something is lost; when character is lost, all is lost."

Appraise Your Assets

Take some time to think about your assets — your strengths, talents and the people in your life as well as your material assets. This list will help you when it comes time to identify your values as I'll ask you to do later in this chapter. List your assets in the chart below:

What are my assets?	8.
1.	9.
2.	10.
3.	11.
4.	12.
5.	13.
6.	14.
7.	15.

In creating your list, you may have discovered, as I did, how "wealthy" you really are. Many people find money is likely the first thing they would give away if their values were threatened.

In a sense, that's exactly what happened to Kevin Foster, the former vice president of IXL, an Internet company. During his very successful career, Kevin made millions of dollars and traveled the world. In September 2000, he went to his daughter's school for parent-teacher night. All of the children had colored pictures of what they had done over the summer. Kevin walked around the room, searching for his daughter's picture. He finally found it. She had drawn a picture of her and her sister playing on their swing set in the backyard with their Mom. Up in the sky, she had drawn a plane with the word "Dad" written on it. An arrow pointed up at the plane.

At that moment, Kevin realized his values were so out of balance he had to change his entire life. The next day he walked into the president's office at IXL and resigned. The epiphany he had experienced at his daughter's school brought his values into sharp focus. He knew he could get another job; he could never regain the precious time with his daughter.

Be Mindful of Your Values

Sometimes you may receive big signs that your life is out of synch with your values; other times the signs are as small as a child's drawing. These signs show up in different places and point the way; all you have to do is recognize them and act on them.

This reminds me of an old fable about a truth seeker. After years of searching for the truth, the seeker was told to go to a cave, in which he would find a well. "Ask the well what is truth," he was advised. "The well will reveal it to you." When he found the well, the seeker asked that most fundamental question. From the depths came the answer, "Go to the village crossroads: there you will find the truth you are seeking."

Full of hope, the seeker journeyed to the crossroads only to find three rather dull shops. One shop sold pieces of metal, another sold wood, and the third sold thin wires. Nothing and no one there seemed to have much to do with the revelation of truth.

Disappointed, the seeker returned to the well to demand an explanation, but he was told only, "You will understand in the future." When he protested, all he got in return were the echoes of his own shouts. Indignant for having been made a fool of — or so he thought at the time — the seeker continued his wanderings. As the years went by, the memory of his experience at the well gradually faded until one night, while he was walking in the moonlight, the sound of sitar music caught his attention. It was wonderful music, played with great mastery and inspiration.

Profoundly moved, the truth seeker moved closer to the sitar player. He looked at the fingers dancing over the strings. He became aware of the sitar itself. Then suddenly he exploded with a cry of joyous recognition: the sitar was made out of wires, pieces of metal and wood just like those he had once seen in the three stores and had thought unimportant.

At last he understood the message of the well: *we have already been given everything we need.* Our task is to assemble and use the pieces in the appropriate way. Nothing is meaningful so long as we perceive only separate fragments. But as soon as the fragments come together into a synthesis, a new entity emerges, whose nature we could not have foreseen by considering the fragments alone.

Most of us are not so very different from the seeker in the story above. Often, we are unaware of what we really do possess; we continue to believe the answers to our deepest questions are "out there."

What Do You Really Value?

Deciding what you value is a highly personal process. No one can do it for you. There may be values you *want* to have because everyone else tells you that you *should* have them. But are they your values? Can you live up to them if they aren't yours? Do you listen to your heart, or to those who may want you to ignore your values in favor of theirs?

Many people discover themselves by rebelling against the values their parents and others try to instill in them. "I wouldn't turn out the way I did if I didn't have the old-fashioned values to rebel against," says Madonna. Now, you might not agree with Madonna's values but the fact is that most generations rebel against the values of previous generations. It's a natural and important part of discovering who we are, a way of testing the waters. As we grow older and learn more, we may eventually incorporate some of these values back into our lives if we find they are right for us.

Many years ago, I learned an important lesson about the vast differences in the way each of us perceives value. I love buying, selling and trading cars. I've been doing it since my teenage years. Every weekend I would buy the *New York Times* just to read the

"Classic Cars For Sale" section. One particular Sunday, I was relaxing at home and reading my car section when an ad leapt out of the paper at me. It went something like this, *"For Sale: a 1958 Green Thunderbird Convertible in perfect condition, power steering/ brakes/top. Fully serviced, must be seen to be appreciated. Price $900."* This price was about 50 percent of the market value of the car!

At that time I was living in Edmonton, Alberta and the seller lived in New York, miles away, but the car was worth any transport fee, so I picked up the phone and dialed the Big Apple. A man answered and confirmed the car was still for sale. We talked a lot about his perfect car. Finally I said, "Look, if your car is as you say, I will buy it on one condition — I want you to deliver it to me in Edmonton and I will pay the gas plus $200." He agreed on the spot and said he would schedule the time and call me to confirm.

"Are you absolutely sure the car is as perfect as you say it is?" I asked him.

"I wouldn't be fool enough to drive it all the way from New York to Edmonton in the dead of winter if it weren't," he said. It made good sense to me so I awaited his call.

Three weeks later, at 6:00 p.m. on a freezing winter night, there was a knock at my door. I answered it and there stood a short man wrapped in so many clothes I could hardly see his face. He introduced himself as Mr. Kilthorpe and said he was delivering my 1958 Thunderbird. I could not believe it! There had been no confirmation phone call — nothing.

"Wait there," I told him. "I'll be right back." I went inside and pulled on my coat and boots, then out the door I went. There at my curb sat a green 1958 Thunderbird. It was the worst looking car I had ever seen. It actually had a rust spot on the front bottom fender that was big enough to stick your fist through. In addition, the car had rust spots all over it. You couldn't even see into the car because of the sheets of ice all over the windows. I didn't know what to say, but I couldn't let this go on any longer.

"Are you seriously expecting me to purchase this car?" I asked Mr. Kilthorpe. "It's the biggest pile of junk I've ever seen!"

He looked at me like I was absolutely crazy. "This car is perfect," he said. "It's just come trouble-free from New York in five days of straight driving." Clearly, we had a very serious difference of opinion as to the value of the car. I went back into the house and took a couple of moments to clear my mind and talk with my wife. Then I took $200 out of my wallet and went back outside.

"I absolutely do not want the car," I told Mr. Kilthorpe, "and I'm very angry you misrepresented its condition the way you did. Upon my signal, my wife will call the police and they'll be here in a couple of minutes if there's any trouble. I feel sorry for you, so out of the goodness of my heart, I'll give you this $200 to help you get back to New York."

I gave him the money, turned around and went back into the house. The next morning, I awoke and looked outside. There, under the snow, was the Thunderbird. It continued to sit there until spring when the city came along and hauled it away. To this day, I do not know what happened to Mr. Kilthorpe.

This story illustrates how different people's values can be. What I saw as a rusting bucket of bolts was obviously something Mr. Kilthorpe saw value in. I'm sure he would never have driven the car all the way from New York to Edmonton unless he thought I would buy it.

Find out for yourself what you value, and do not let others pass, sell, lend or force their values on you. "If you don't set a baseline standard for what you'll accept in life," says author and peak performance expert Anthony Robbins, "you'll find it's easy to slip into behaviors and attitudes or a quality of life that's far below what you deserve."

Once you identify your personal values and begin consciously living by them, they will guide you through every decision you make in your life and bring you peace of mind. Instead of worrying about how to stay in the air, you'll start to really enjoy the flight, confident in your ability to read your navigational instruments.

It's All Relative

But what if you aren't sure what you truly value? Perhaps you feel lost, alienated or that something is missing in your life? If you look deeper, you may realize what you are really craving is a strong connection with your values.

Read the following poem, and then take the time to think about what matters to you. See if you can tap into your core values by looking at the events and benchmarks of your life:

> To realize the value of ten years:
> Ask a newly divorced couple.
> To realize the value of four years:
> Ask a graduate.
> To realize the value of one year:
> Ask a student who has failed a final exam.
> To realize the value of nine months:
> Ask a mother who gave birth to a stillborn.
> To realize the value of one month:
> Ask a mother who has given birth to a premature baby.
> To realize the value of one week:
> Ask an editor of a weekly newspaper.
> To realize the value of one hour:
> Ask the lovers who are waiting to meet.
> To realize the value of one minute:
> Ask a person who has missed the train, bus or plane.
> To realize the value of one second:
> Ask a person who has survived an accident.
> To realize the value of one millisecond:
> Ask the person who has won a silver medal in the Olympics.
> Time waits for no one. Treasure every moment you have.

Author Unknown

This poem takes us back to the story of the bank that deposits 86,400 seconds into your account each day. Ask yourself again: how will I spend those seconds before the bank tries to reclaim the ones I have neglected to spend on what I value?

Identify Your Values

It's time to write down what you value most in life. To help you develop your personal inventory of values, explore the list on page 21 for ideas. If you don't see all of your values there, don't worry — you can add your own.

As you review your list of values, ask yourself the following questions:

* Is this value something that is important to me?

* Do I feel good about this being important to me?

* Would I feel good if people I respect knew this value was important to me?

* Would I stand up for this value even if others ridiculed me?

* Does this value complement my vision of my life?

Select no more than 15 values, and no less than five. Choose wisely, for the values you select will guide you toward your destiny. Later, you may want to pare those values down, but for now, select as many values as you need.

What do I value most?	8.
1.	9.
2.	10.
3.	11.
4.	12.
5.	13.
6.	14.
7.	15.

Some Examples of Values

Achievement	Generosity	Physical Challenge
Adventure	Grace	Pleasure
Arts	Gratitude	Power
Change	Growth	Public Service
Choice	Happiness	Recognition
Community	Harmony	Relationships
Compassion	Health	Religion
Competence	Honesty	Reputation
Competition	Independence	Responsibility
Cooperation	Insight	Security
Creativity	Integrity	Self-Esteem
Diplomacy	Knowledge	Serenity
Enlightenment	Leadership	Sophistication
Environment	Love	Spirituality
Ethics	Loyalty	Status
Excellence	Mentorship	Success
Excitement	Merit	Travel
Faith	Money	Truth
Financial Security	Nature	Volunteering
Forgiveness	Patience	Work
Freedom	Perceptiveness	Wisdom

Live With Greater Clarity

Now that you've written down your values, you have your navigational instruments to live your life by. You'll be amazed at how this will help simplify your life by making your choices so much clearer.

"When your values are clear to you, making decisions becomes easier," says Roy Disney, executive and son of Walt Disney's brother, Roy Oliver Disney.

Disney would likely agree with Lou Marinoff, PhD., author of *Therapy for the Sane: How Philosophy Can Change your Life*. Marinoff said narrowing our options actually opens us up to more, not less, freedom and happiness.

"Every human being suffers, sooner or later," Marinoff writes, "so the operational question is not whether you will suffer, but what you will suffer from. By far a more important question still is how you will seek to alleviate your suffering. The answer you arrive at will determine whether you increase your own suffering (and that of those around you), or diminish it. Unfortunately, there are many ways to increase suffering. Fortunately, there are comparatively few ways to alleviate it. Why fortunately? Because limited options make your way much clearer."

It seems like a paradox that narrowing our options gives us more freedom, but in the case of our values, it's true. When we know our values, we become less concerned with *quantity* to fill the emptiness within. Instead we experience the fulfillment of a *quality* life.

Beyond Chaos

Knowing your values will help you better manage chaos — to expect it, embrace it, but not get caught up in it.

The key is to trust in your values to get you through it and not lose sight of those values.

Losing sight of what matters is seldom a sudden occurrence. It's a process of erosion. Who hasn't heard the story of the successful business owner who started a venture in the hopes of making his family wealthy and happy, only to end up divorced and unsatisfied? Even as he told everyone that family was what he valued most, his family was slipping away from him because *his reality wasn't in line with his values*.

Experts say that when we do not live in tune with our values, we encounter psychological pain. Often, it's because we've got on the wrong track, but sometimes we just give up, perhaps because we let others impose their values on us or we choose to ignore what we know is right. Eventually we lose our direction.

"It takes great strength to live consistently with integrity, honesty and dignity," writes Christina Felman in her book *Silence*. "We are so often tempted into pathways of living and acting that compromise our integrity and leave behind harmful residues of regret and guilt. These, in turn, can trigger further compromising behavior."

I've discovered through the LifePilot process that *it is possible to achieve success and retain your values*. In fact, when you retain your values and use them to navigate by, the success you achieve is far more satisfying because you haven't sacrificed everything you believe in to get it.

When you live in alignment with your values, you'll be amazed at how people around you begin to respond and eventually respect your principles. You'll begin to attract people and opportunities that complement your values. Life will seem to move forward more smoothly. This doesn't mean that you won't ever experience problems, but now you have a system to navigate by.

Act in Alignment

John Papaloukas was born in the small coastal British Columbia town of Prince Rupert to hard-working Greek immigrants. John and his brother started Villages Pizza, one of the top two pizza businesses in Victoria, British Columbia. This is no small feat in a city that loves its pizza. Known affectionately as "Pappy," John is a founding member of the Young Presidents' Organization. He's a respected member of the community and he's generous with his time.

With his business growing, everything seemed to be going right for John, but he wasn't looking after himself. His weight ballooned to over 500 pounds. By his own definition, he was unhealthy, "stressed to the max" and caught up in a conflict with his brother over the business. His life started to change when he began his LifePilot journey.

"LifePilot made me look at my longevity, and my family and children," says John. "What LifePilot really said to me was, 'If you're really serious about living true to your values, then why aren't you doing anything about it?'"

Today, John weighs in at 320 pounds, he's a devoted exercise buff, training regularly in Core Ball, and is the sole owner of Villages Pizza after buying out his brother. He also has a wife, Marvalee, whom he adores, and two sons, Alexander, one, and Lucas, three. Not only is John living his values, he's incorporating his values into his work.

"Through LifePilot, I identified health as one of my core values and I began to live that value," he says. "As I realized the benefits of better health, it was something I wanted to pass on to my customers." In keeping with that, John brilliantly launched what he believes was the first low-carbohydrate pizza, created with soy-protein-based dough. The low-carb offering gained him international media coverage. This year, John announced his pizza crusts would no longer contain trans fats. He made the move to extra virgin olive oil in the pizza crust.

"When you go through something like LifePilot," says John, "you realize some things aren't as important as you thought they were, and some things are more important than you could ever imagine. You learn that 'I'm only here once and I've got to make the most of it.' You've got to make time for yourself, your family, and your children. You can still do everything you did in the community but I think if you take care of yourself first, and take care of your home base, then it's really easy because you come from a position of strength."

Like John, more and more people are making value-based decisions about their careers and their businesses. When Oprah Winfrey changed the format of her talk show to move away from what she called "the trash pack," she made a values-based decision. In interviews she said, "I cannot listen to other people blaming their mothers for another year. We're not going to book a show where someone is talking about their victimization." Since doing this, Oprah has set a new standard in positive television programming that inspires people to change their lives and live by their values. It's interesting to note that as she did this, her personal life underwent dramatic changes as well. Like John, Oprah also embarked on a fitness and weight loss program. Today, she is a shadow of what she once was in weight, but her light shines all the brighter for living by her values.

Your Values, Your Priorities

Once you have decided on your personal values, I'd like you to take some time to prioritize them. This will go a long way toward helping you achieve balance in your life. Deciding on your priorities is not a one-time task that will lead to ongoing balance. To achieve this, you must continually adjust the weight of your values and priorities against your behaviors and actions.

How do you decide on your priorities? Here's an example: Let's say that your values are financial freedom, career, independence and family. Which things in life deserve the highest priority? You may find that unless you find ways to honor your need for independence, you are unhappy. Yet the demands of working in a competitive corporate environment and living up to family obligations are smothering your need for independence. What do you do?

First, I would ask myself, "Are there ways to attain financial freedom that complement my need for independence and still provide a source of income for my family?" For example, many entrepreneurs love working for themselves because it gives them a great sense of freedom. They feel like the captains of their own destinies. Being an entrepreneur, while it certainly has its risks, also offers the potential of uncapped income, which contributes to greater financial stability. No longer are you locked into a monthly paycheck and the whims of an employer who may or may not value your need for freedom and your sense of family.

In terms of dealing with limitations placed on you by family, it often helps just to know you'll have time to express your love of freedom. One man I know has arranged with his family to take time off twice a year by himself. During these times, he heads to the hills and hikes on his own for periods of 10 to 14 days. He returns from these trips refreshed, and his family finds he is more centered when they allow him his time alone.

Another way to successfully manage your values is to do activities that touch on as many of your values as possible. I was jogging the other day on a path overlooking the ocean. It was a beautiful day, with the sun shining and lots of families out with their children. I stopped to enjoy the view for a few minutes and along came an interesting sight: a woman in jogging gear pushing an pram with a very young baby, and her husband jogging beside her with a small boy in the child carrier on his back. I could not help but think that this family was sure hitting all of their values that day: health, happiness, family, relationships, and on and on.

It may take some experimentation to get your priorities right, but eventually this will become second nature to you. As you are prioritizing, it may help to remember these words of wisdom by Henry David Thoreau: "The price of anything is the amount of life you are willing to pay for it."

To help people attending LifePilot workshops to grasp this idea, I hold a values auction where participants must bid against others in the room for the things they value most. Using a budget of $3,000, they have to decide which values to spend it on and how much to allot to each.

Some people try to spread their budgets around to cover everything — because they want it all — only to find they are consistently outbid. Others throw all of their money in one pot. In the end, the ones who spread their money around too readily find they didn't bid enough on any one value to win it, and they are left with lots of money in their accounts.

"What can you do with that money now that the auction is over?" I ask them. "There's nothing left to spend it on. What's the value of hanging on to all that money?" Their answer: "The money has no value; it's worthless. I should have spent it while I had the chance."

For those who put all their money in one pot, I ask what they've had to sacrifice for bidding such a heavy price to obtain their value. Let's say someone bid all their money on the value career success — and they won their bid. "That's wonderful," I tell them, "but you realize there's nothing left for anything else in your life like family, health or friends." By now, I can see awareness beginning to dawn as they discover that they've symbolically sacrificed everything for career success.

Think back to the 86,400 seconds we discussed earlier in this chapter. You can see that the values auction is another way of coaching the mind into understanding that we only have so much time to live. Yes, the values auction is only a fun game, but when you think about it, it's also a pretty good simulation of the way we live our lives. The lesson in this is to enjoy your life every day — don't save up to have a great time later or when you retire, and don't blow it all on any one thing. As Ernest Hemingway said, "It is good to have an end to journey toward; but it is the journey that matters in the end."

Prioritize your values:	8.
1.	9.
2.	10.
3.	11.
4.	12.
5.	13.
6.	14.
7.	15.

Set Value Boundaries

Some people may not support your new desire to live by your values. A rare few may try to sabotage you, but usually you sabotage yourself first by not setting and respecting boundaries that protect those values.

Take the example of a young professional man who had just started out in his career. He had recently married and was expecting his first child. Finally, he received the call from home that every expectant father waits for — his wife was ready to give birth and needed to leave for the hospital immediately. His elation turned to dismay when the very next call he received advised him that the big deal that he had been working on for six months was coming to a conclusion.

The client requested that he come to New York immediately to give a presentation. *What to do? Go to New York or not?*

One year later it was his little boy's first birthday celebration. A similar phone call came. *What to do? Go to New York or not?*

Five years later, the little boy was going to his first day at school. A similar phone call came. *What to do? Go to New York or not?*

Eighteen years later, the boy was graduating from high school. A similar phone call came. *What to do? Go to New York or not?*

Twenty-two years later, the young man was graduating from university. A similar phone call came. *What to do? Go to New York or not?*

Twenty-five years later, the now-grown son was going to get married. A similar phone call came. *What to do? Go to New York or not?*

There will *always* be phone calls from New York or somewhere else requiring your presence elsewhere. Very early in your career, you need to decide how you'll handle these situations. Would you go to New York or not? Sometimes urgent issues are unavoidable, but most of the time, if family is one of your core values, you'll find you can restructure your work demands to honor that value.

Even if you aren't just beginning your career, you can still make changes and set new boundaries. An old truism says, "If you always do what you've always done, you'll always get what you always got." Once you've committed to living by your values, maintaining your boundaries is far easier than you ever thought possible.

Treasure What You Value

Many of us may spend our lives trying to fill the emptiness within. We realize, as aviator Dru Narwani did at the height of his banking career, that something is missing. We often search and search but fail to recognize something of value even when we're actually touching it, or we settle for a quick-fix solution.

One story that always reminds me to pause and recognize what I value is called "The Touchstone." A young man was out walking one day and met an old wise man. The wise man said, "If you can find a touchstone, I will buy it from you for $1,000,000."

"Where can I find one of these stones?" the man asked.

"Oh, they are just lying on the beach," the wise man told him. "They look like any other stone only they are almost too hot to touch. That's how you'll recognize one when you find it."

The man walked down to the beach and started sifting through the rocks in search of the touchstone. He did this for days, then months, then years. Eventually, he became an old man. Even so, he still went to the beach every day in search of a touchstone. One day, as he was picking up stones and throwing them over his shoulder, he actually reached down and picked up a touchstone. So absorbed was he in throwing stones back in the water, he didn't notice the warmth of the touchstone. In fact, he didn't even glance at it twice; he just threw it over his shoulder and continued picking up stones and throwing them away.

Contrast this with the story of scientist Alexander Fleming, who in 1928 found his "touchstone" in a culture of the bacteria *Staphylococcus aureus* left under the microscope for too long. Some mold spores had landed on the culture and begun to grow. Fleming was about to throw the culture away when he noticed the mold had actually begun to kill off the bacteria. He explored further and found that, while the mold was deadly to bacteria, it wasn't harmful to humans. The culture Fleming did not throw away turned out to be one of humanity's biggest touchstones — the discovery of antibiotics.

What do you value in your life, and can you recognize it? What do you throw away every day without a second glance?

Navigate By Your Values

Now that you've identified your values, ask yourself: *Is there a gulf between what I value on the inside and the way I actually live my life?* For many people, there is. When this kind of imbalance occurs, we continually fall short of our own expectations, sometimes without even realizing why. Working to bring our inner and outer lives into alignment creates the dynamic for success. Suddenly, what we feel is what we manifest — and what we manifest nourishes our deepest longings.

Robert Oppenheimer is often called "the father of the atomic bomb." But before he began working for the US military effort during WWII, Oppenheimer was a respected professor at the University of California in Berkeley, and worked on theoretical physics. By all accounts, he was a genius who valued exploration, learning and freedom of thought. In 1943, General Leslie Grove recruited Oppenheimer to lead a team of scientists to design the first atomic bomb. The bomb actually became two bombs, which were dropped on Hiroshima and Nagasaki, effectively ending the US-Japan War. But the "success" of the project broke Oppenheimer, by all accounts. He had surrendered his values.

A rare few of us will ever have our values tested on the scale of Oppenheimer, or on the level of prime ministers, presidents and generals, but our values *will* be tried and tested. "It's like, at the end, there's this surprise quiz: am I proud of me?" writes Richard Bach, author of *Jonathan Livingstone Seagull.* "I gave my life to become the person I am right now! Was it worth what I paid?"

The Time is Always Right

For those of you who think there may be too much water under the bridge to make values-based changes in your life, it's important to remember what writer George Eliot said: "It is never too late to be what you might have been."

It's true. Life may take a few rounds out of you, but the essence of who you are is always there, as is the opportunity to realize your inherent potential by aligning your life with what you value.

I once heard the story of a speaker who started off his seminars by holding up a $20 bill. "What is this and is it worth anything?" he asked the audience.

"It's a $20 bill," called out one of the participants. The speaker crushed the bill in his hands, wrinkling it into a ball. He unfolded it and held up the now very-wrinkled bill.

"Is it still worth $20?" he asked. The participants agreed that it was still worth its original value.

"Well," he said, "what if I do this?" He dropped the bill on the floor and ground it with the heel of his shoe. When he picked it up, it was dirty, crumpled, defaced and not easy to recognize anymore.

"Is it still worth its original value?" he asked the audience. They debated, but in the end they agreed it was.

"There's an important lesson in this exercise," said the speaker. "Even when I crumpled, stomped on and defaced the $20 bill — no matter what I did to it — you still upheld its worth because you were sure in your minds that my actions did not actually decrease its value. It was still a currency note worth $20."

"We all go through times in our lives," he continued, "when we feel as if we are crumpled, ground into the dirt, and scarred by the decisions we make or the circumstances that come our way. We may feel as though we are worthless, and others may see us as worthless as well. But no matter what has happened or what *will* happen, please remember that you never lose your 'value.'"

* Pause to recognize what you value most in life. Don't be too quick to throw it away in search of a seemingly magical solution.

* Spend time on what you value and weed out the time-wasters. Giving time to what you value frees you from hours of indecision and worry, and brings you clarity and purpose.

* Learning how to break away from negative patterns and habits begins at a fundamental level — get to know yourself better and consciously identify what you really value.

* Once you identify your personal values and begin consciously living by them, they will guide you through every decision you make. They will tell you when to say yes, when to say no, and what to do under extreme stress.

* To achieve equilibrium in your life means continually adjusting the weight of your values and priorities against your behaviors and actions.

* Working to bring your inner life and outer life into alignment creates the dynamic for success.

* What you feel is what you manifest — and what you manifest nourishes your deepest longings.

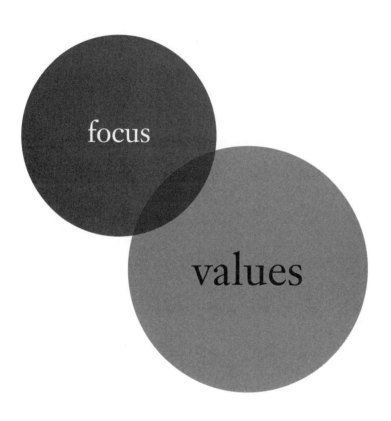

SECRET 3

Focus on Your Future

"Only one thing has to change for us to know happiness in our lives," says former NBA player Greg Anderson, "where we focus our attention." Could it really be so simple? Could one thing change our lives for the better? If you listen to some of the most successful people, from sports stars to business greats to outstanding social leaders, you'll find that the single-minded pursuit of that one thing has been critical to their success.

"One hundred percent of the successful people I know understand how to pick a focus and take the noise out of life. If you can accomplish that with strong values, the better off you are," says Dr. Steven Funk who turned his own ability to focus into major success. He has overseen the construction of the largest underground parking structure in Shanghai, built the largest car park management business in Canada and the fourth largest in North America, and he manages nearly 100,000 acres of sustainable development and environmental custodianship in the Belize rainforest.

Your Focus Becomes Your Reality

Steven has known me for years, first as my employee and then as an associate and friend, so he knows I consider my ability to focus critical to my success. This ability to focus often set me apart from many of my peers, who became distracted. They would start the day with lists of things they needed to do but would not prioritize their lists. They found themselves carried away by things that just "came up." Many of these people were no less talented or dedicated than I was.

As a young man in the Canadian army, I learned at an early age to focus on doing what needed to be done. There was no choice. You just did it, no questions asked. If you were on the shooting range and the sergeant yelled, "Drop," you didn't turn around and ask why — you just dropped or you might end up dead. If you focused on what the army wanted and gave them what they asked for — arriving on schedule, having your clothes and shoes cleaned, being on parade on time, and attending classes punctually — the benefits were wonderful: great weekend passes, a fantastic car and so on. You started to get into trouble, however, if you lost focus and disobeyed the rules.

My former employer Ken Marlin will tell you I brought a lot of focus into my sales career once I left the army. That's true, but I don't think I truly appreciated the power of focus until, at age 24, I went to work for Ken as a mutual fund salesman at First Investors Corporation in Edmonton, Alberta. At that time, many of the company's sales people used to go to a coffee shop each morning. It was kind of an honor to be asked to join them, so when they invited me along, I went. I had fun doing this for about a month, but I silently wondered about all the time this wasted. Most of them would head to the coffee shop around 10 a.m. and stay there until 11:30 a.m. Then they would head back to the office just to check their messages before taking off for lunch.

One day, I had some work to finish so when the other salesmen went for coffee I stayed behind at the office. I planned to join them later. I finished my task and was about to leave for the coffee shop when I happened to glance over at the number one salesman in the company, Don Slater. He sat there behind his desk in his shirtsleeves with his impeccable jacket on the hanger beside him. He always looked as if he had just stepped out of *Gentleman's Quarterly*. I gently knocked on his door.

"Would you like to come for a coffee with us?" I asked him.

"Why would I go there?" he replied. "*They* aren't going to buy any mutual funds from me." That statement hit me like a ton of bricks. He was right — I was absolutely wasting my prime time at the coffee shop and it wasn't furthering my career.

I *did* go to the coffee shop that morning, but I wriggled and squirmed and was so uncomfortable I returned to the office after only ten minutes. From that day on, I decided I would no longer spend time on unproductive coffee breaks.

I also realized the importance of learning from people who were successful, like Don Slater. I made it a principle to study successful people, to ask questions whenever I could, and to mimic what they did to achieve success. I firmly believe in what Socrates said: "We are what we repeatedly do. Excellence, then, is a habit."

Insight into Intensity

Successful people focus with intensity on what they need to do to achieve their aims — then they do what they say they are going to do. James Allen, author of *As a Man Thinketh*, describes this as "a process of diverting one's scattered forces into one powerful channel."

The power of focus isn't a new notion by any means. In the early part of the century, American clergyman Henry Emerson Fosdick said, "No steam or gas ever drives anything until it is confined. No Niagara is ever turned into light and power until it is funneled. No life ever grows until it is focused, dedicated, disciplined."

People with a strong ability to focus understand the power of clearing away distractions and friction. "What this power is, I cannot say," wrote inventor Alexander Graham Bell. "All I know is that it exists...and it becomes available only when you are in that state of mind in which you know exactly what you want...and are fully determined not to quit until you get it."

For those of you who've had the pleasure of sledding down a snowy hill, you know that you must clear away unnecessary snow mounds, tree branches and other obstacles that will slow your progress. The first few runs are tough, but the more you go down the hill, the smoother your ride becomes and the faster you go. Soon, you're flying down a sleek path. You're not worrying about obstacles — you're able to focus entirely on the joy of the ride. Each time, you push more snow out of the way. Each time, you go further.

Achieving focus means directing your energy to a defined purpose. This is something well understood by Zen monks and martial arts experts. In his article "The Power and Techniques of Focusing," Aikido sensei Hoa Newens writes, "We can see because light rays focus in a specific way inside our eyes. If these light rays are out of focus we do not see well. You can lift an object with your arm because you direct your energy into the motion of grabbing and lifting. Anything that interrupts your focus, such as a startling noise, may cause you to drop the object. You can converse meaningfully with someone at a party full of people because you focus your attention on what your interlocutor says. If an old friend passes by and catches your attention, then you may lose your focus and the thread of the conversation. In fact, we generally see only what we focus on, we hear only what we focus on, we feel only what we focus on, we smell only what we focus on and we taste only what we focus on. It can be said we live the life pattern that we focus on."

Alan Cohen, a syndicated columnist and contributing writer for the bestselling series *Chicken Soup for the Soul*, would likely agree. "The universe always gives you more of what you are focusing on," he says.

Tune Out Distractions

The better you become at focusing on specific challenges, the more quickly you can get them off your plate and make room for other activities. But how do you achieve this focus in a multi-channel universe that seems designed for distraction? After all, most TV sets have 50-plus channels. Some TVs even allow you to watch one program while monitoring several more in the corners of your screen. We are barraged by emails, text messages and phone calls. Many people feel scattered and unable to concentrate. They strive for results but are unable to produce them. Some of them feel completely overwhelmed by the tension of being pulled in too many directions. "I can't stand to make one more decision," is a common refrain.

The comedian George Carlin wrote an eloquent piece that I think sums up why we have such trouble achieving focus:

> "The paradox of our time in history is that we have
> taller buildings but shorter tempers, wider freeways,
> but narrower viewpoints. We spend more, but have less;
> we buy more, but enjoy less. We have bigger houses
> and smaller families, more conveniences, but less time.
> We have more degrees but less sense, more knowledge,
> but less judgement, more experts, yet more problems,
> more medicine, but less wellness. We drink too much,
> smoke too much, spend too recklessly, laugh too little,
> drive too fast, get too angry, stay up too late, get up
> too tired, read too little, watch TV too much, and
> pray too seldom.
>
> We have multiplied our possessions, but reduced our
> values. We talk too much, love too seldom, and hate too
> often. We've learned how to make a living, but not a life.
> We've added years to life not life to years...."

No doubt about it, multi-tasking has become the rallying cry for getting things done and achieving success, but its advantages are far overextended. Some people call what they do multi-tasking when they are really just giving in to distractions. The best multi-taskers actually have incredible focus. A busy receptionist is intent on answering 30 phone lines, screening calls, typing memoranda and handling walk-in clients. If she is effective at her job, she is not also trying to run a technology department. An emergency room physician certainly requires the ability to multi-task, but he or she also needs to be able to focus intently when making a life-or-death diagnoses. Journalists rely on the ability to multi-task while meeting often-insane deadlines. But here's some strong advice from one of the best, Emmy-award winning journalist Diane Sawyer, who was the first woman to break into *60 Minutes* in the 80s and today is the star anchor at ABC. "I think the one lesson I have learned is that there is no substitute for paying attention," she says. No doubt, it's impossible to reach the levels Diane Sawyer has reached without a strong ability to focus on what's really important and cut out the noise.

The Sense of Simplifying

Developing the ability to focus allows you to simplify your life. When that happens, as Henry David Thoreau wrote, "The laws of the universe will be simpler." Studies have borne out what Thoreau wrote over a century ago. The happiest, most successful people selectively narrow the choices they face so they are able to focus only on those things that represent their priorities and passions. As we discussed earlier, living in alignment with your values may seem limiting at first, but ironically, taking steps to eliminate unnecessary distractions actually means your life expands in meaningful ways. As Abraham Zaleznik of Harvard Business School writes, "Keep focused on the substantive issues. To make a decision means having to go through one door and closing all others."

It's Never Too Late

If you doubt your ability to focus, keep in mind that you *can* learn this skill, providing you are willing to work on it. Neuroscientist Dr. Michael Merzenich, one of the world's leading neuroscience experts, says we retain our brain's plasticity and ability to change and create new habits throughout our lives. Doing something over and over develops into a habit, and this in turn creates lasting changes in the brain that, in the case of highly trained specialists, show up on MRI scans. That, says Merzenich, is why flute players have "especially large representations in their brains in the areas that control the fingers, tongue and lips." The same phenomenon can be seen in MRI scans of sports stars, CEOs and anyone else who has developed an outstanding ability to focus.

Picture the Results

Later, we'll take an in-depth look at the power of creative visualization, but for now just keep in mind that visualizing the outcomes of achieving your goals is critical to your success. When you visualize the end result, you'll begin to believe it. More importantly, your brain will believe it — it doesn't know the difference between external visions and internal ones. "What the mind can conceive," wrote Napoleon Hill, author of *Think and Grow Rich*, "the mind can achieve."

Olympian Bruce Jenner says, "To me, the definition of focus is knowing exactly where you want to be today, next week, next month, next year, then never deviating from your plan. Once you can see, touch and feel your objective, all you have to do is pull back and put all your strength behind it, and you'll hit your target every time."

Florence Chadwick was a champion swimmer who wanted to set the record for swimming the English Channel. Chadwick felt as prepared as she would ever be on the day she stepped into the cold waves of the Channel, her body greased to provide insulation against the biting cold. The Atlantic was unusually rough that day, but Chadwick wasn't bothered — she had trained for it. Besides, she had the support of her trainers who rowed alongside her, feeding her soup and talking to her.

The only thing Chadwick hadn't counted on was the heavy fog. It soon engulfed her. She began to lose her bearings. As the fog grew denser, she felt less able to cope with the cold and the high waves. Her limbs began to cramp. Finally, she was forced to quit. When the media later asked her why she had given up when the shore was so close she said, "I lost sight of my goal. I'm not sure I ever had it firmly in mind."

The story of Florence Chadwick points to the essential need to remain focused on what you want to achieve, even when life tosses in unexpected surprises. Her story isn't one of failure because she learned from that experience. She went on to become the first woman to swim 23 miles across the English Channel in *both* directions.

By practicing the principles of LifePilot, you will strengthen your ability to screen out the distractions that prevent you from achieving your dreams. This will happen on a macro level, by spotlighting which values to focus on, and on a micro level, by focusing on goals and activities that are stepping stones to your dreams. Everything else is a distraction.

Decide What You Want

My primary focus, for instance, is to devote myself to LifePilot and raise funds for charitable causes. In order to make time and space for this, I'm no longer looking for real estate deals, which was once my focus. This doesn't mean I won't listen to someone who presents me with a great opportunity, but I am not actively looking. Someone can still knock, but whether I open the door or not depends on my priorities at the time.

My wife Rita has watched me adjust to this change in priorities. "When I first met Peter," she says, "he was very driven and passionate about his work — his real estate deals. I wondered if he could ever leave this part of his life behind. However, once he retired from the real estate world, there was no looking back. He has found new things to be passionate about, and new mountains to climb."

Achieving Focus

In the following chapters, I'll show you how to develop your sense of focus, and share with you the LifePilot method to help you do this. You'll learn how to set goals, visualize success, keep stress in perspective and live life to its fullest.

CHAPTER REVIEW

- ⋆ Successful people know how to focus with intensity and screen out anything that doesn't relate to their values and priorities.

- ⋆ They have developed techniques for clearing away distractions and friction.

- ⋆ Eliminating unnecessary distractions in your life means your life will expand in more meaningful ways.

- ⋆ Remember, we are what we repeatedly do, as Socrates said.

- ⋆ It is possible to learn how to strengthen your focus through practice.

- ⋆ What you focus on should align with your values.

> "What you get by achieving your goals is not as important as what you become by achieving your goals." *Johann Wolfgang von Goethe*

> "In the absence of clearly defined goals, we become strangely loyal to performing daily acts of trivia." *Author Unknown*

SECRET 4

Define Your Destination

You've identified the values you will navigate by and learned about the power of focus. Now it's time to define your destination. Mark Caine, author of *The S-Man: The Grammar of Success*, writes, "There are those who travel and those who are going somewhere. They are different and yet they are the same. The success has this over his rivals: He knows where he is going."

One of the best ways to know where you are going is to set goals. Many books exist whose primary focus is on goal setting. *LifeManual* isn't one of them. While I firmly believe the ability to achieve predetermined goals is a major success factor, I know that unless those goals are aligned with your values, you may end up at a destination you don't like.

As you go through the following chapters and begin to set goals, remember to check back frequently with your values. Do your goals and values align? If they don't, you may need to change your goals or go back and better define your values.

The Value of Dreams

Napoleon Hill wrote, "A goal is a dream with a deadline." He's right — and dreams are wonderful things. If you look deep enough you'll find your dreams almost always arise from what you truly value in life. Goal setting is the alchemy that turns those dreams into reality.

Gary Hall, a doctor who lives in Arizona's Paradise Valley, is a graduate of the LifePilot workshop. "After having fallen asleep at the wheel for the last five years of my life, you suddenly woke me up," he writes. "What have I been missing?! In the middle of the [LifePilot] workshop, I realized that when I stopped writing down my goals is precisely when things started taking a turn for the worse. It is amazing to me how the simple task of writing these goals down and periodically reviewing them enables one to accomplish them."

Here's why goal setting is so powerful. If you've ever tried to light a fire by directing sunlight through a magnifying glass, you know you need a defined target and directed energy. If you are patient, committed and focused on your target, eventually you'll start a fire. In your life, when you direct your focus, energies and actions at a defined target, you stand a far better chance of realizing success.

According to author and motivational speaker Diane M. Eade, setting goals programs our minds for success. "The goals we set direct our mental focus. Subconsciously, the mind works continuously to satisfy the expressed need."

Goal setting yields many benefits beyond the achievement of the goals themselves. It decreases stress by providing you with a clear direction. When other people see the clarity of your goals and vision, they become more willing and motivated to help you reach your destination. This, in turn, increases your energy and confidence to reach higher. It's cause and effect.

Keith Ellis, author of *The Magic Lamp: Goal Setting for People Who Hate Setting Goals*, writes, "Life teaches us that we have to put wood in a woodstove *before* we get heat; we have to make a deposit before we can make a withdrawal; we have to plant seeds, water them, weed them, and nurture them *before* we can harvest our first ear of corn or pick our first tomato. Too often we don't apply this knowledge to the way we run our lives."

"If you desire a specific effect in your life," he continues, "whether it involves a relationship, or a job, or an important project, you must first set in motion the cause of that effect. Whenever the cause is missing, the effect will be missing as well. Whenever the effect is missing, you can be certain that you have neglected to set in motion the appropriate cause."

When you set goals and put them into action, you actively determine the way you will live your life rather than just allowing life to happen to you. When you think about it, that's a very powerful concept — and no one possesses that power in your life except you. It's all yours if you choose to use it.

Find Your Way Beyond FUD

Knowing what we now know about goal setting, why would anyone choose not to exercise that power? From what I've observed, it's often due to what I call FUD — Fear, Uncertainty and Doubt. These three things are key factors that we allow to prevent us from reaching our goals and our potential. In essence, by giving in to FUD, we set ourselves up for failure. Read on and take some time to ask yourself these vital questions:

Is FEAR holding you back? Some people avoid setting goals because they fear failure. Often, that fear becomes a self-fulfilling prophecy. Still others fear the changes that may result from actually achieving their goals. For these people, "dreams that do come true can be as unsettling as those that don't," says comedian Brett Butler in her bestseller *Knee Deep in Paradise*.

An example of this is Maya who dreamed for years of returning to university to finish her Master of Business degree. But Maya refused to turn her daydream into an actual goal. "Then I would have to do it and I don't know how I'd feel about being a 50-year-old with all of the 20-somethings," she says. "Also, my family would have to fend for themselves more and my husband wouldn't be too happy with that."

Maya's "yes but" list goes on and on. She doesn't fear failure; she expects it. What she really fears is success because it will change her life and take her out of her comfort zone. In Maya's mind, giving up on her dream is a small price to pay for maintaining family harmony. The question is: can a family be truly harmonious if one member has to pay such a high price?

There are many "what ifs" that might happen when we set goals, but that's all they are. Everything we do in life is cause and effect, after all. I believe if my intentions are good and my goals are aligned with my values, I will accomplish my goals. I can't let fear of what might happen stop me. "In order to succeed," says comedian and actor Bill Cosby, "your desire for success should be greater than your fear of failure."

It's important to put fear into perspective, which is exactly what world champion cyclist Lance Armstrong did when he was diagnosed with cancer. In his book *It's Not About the Bike*, he writes:

> "I thought I knew what fear was, until I heard the words, you have cancer. Real fear came with an unmistakable sensation; it was as though all my blood started flowing in the wrong direction. My previous fears, fear of not being liked, fear of being laughed at, fear of losing my money, suddenly seemed like small cowardices. Everything now stacked up differently: the anxieties of life — a flat tire, losing my career, a traffic jam — were reprioritized into need versus want, real problems as opposed to minor scares. A bumpy plane ride was just a bumpy plane ride, it wasn't cancer."

Hopefully, you will never have to deal with a serious illness to truly put your own fears in perspective. Even so, thinking about mortality really does help you see life in a new way. In LifePilot workshops, in the hope of sparking personal epiphanies, I often use a measuring tape as a prop to illustrate just how short life is. You can do this yourself. Take a measuring tape out of your toolbox.

Extend it to 75 inches, which is the average life span of a typical American. Now count off how old you are today, using one inch for every year. Look at the time you have left. What are you going to do about it and when are you going to let go of the fears that prevent you from living life to its fullest? If you're lucky, you will have a nice, long life ahead of you, but be aware that the measuring tape can retract suddenly, as measuring tapes often do.

Where does your UNCERTAINTY come from? If your uncertainty isn't just about achieving a goal, but goes deeper into the core of who you are, you need to raise your self-esteem. Psychologist William James believed that to improve your chances of attaining your goals, you could do one of two things:

* lower your goals to meet your low self-esteem

* raise your self-esteem to meet your goals.

I've never been one to lower my goals. As an example, even though I never set out with the lofty dream of becoming a multi-millionaire, I always set myself a goal of reaching higher than wherever I was. To do that, I had to believe in my ability to achieve the next stage of success. I never for a minute considered lowering my goals. I chose growth and believed that I was equal to my aspirations. I encourage you to think of the things you value about yourself. Often, you'll find what you value about yourself most complements the values you chose as the guiding principles of your life. Don't just focus on your accomplishments to date; look deeper and you may uncover assets that are sleeping within you and only need to be awakened. Many people have written to me after our LifePilot workshops to say they discovered parts of themselves they had ignored or felt uncertain about.

An example of this is Sean who came to the LifePilot workshop as an overstressed CEO with dangerously high blood pressure and anxiety so heavy that he often fantasized about walking away from everything. When I asked the audience to list their values, Sean began a journey that helped him remember why he had started his business in the first place. It wasn't to sit in highly-politicized boardrooms all day. It wasn't to become what his investors, his staff and his clients thought he should be. It was to make a difference in the world and help people. Years of working in an environment that constantly grated against his core values had worn down his belief in himself to the point where he felt powerless to make a difference any longer.

Following the LifePilot workshop, Sean started to feel the spark of inspiration again — not for his business but for his *life*. He began taking solitary walks for up to two hours a day, his weight dropped, his sleep patterns improved, his relationships with his family started healing, and he began to feel more certain about his future. He has discovered the person he really is beneath the corporate politics and constant demands of meeting payroll. Today, Sean is not sure he will continue to run a company, but he *is* certain about who he is. He is gaining more clarity around his quest to make a difference in the world.

Sean not only delved deeper into himself, he also opened his mind to the people who loved him and were only too happy to tell him about his positive attributes. He began moving away from relationships that shattered his belief in himself, and set boundaries around the kinds of behavior he would accept from others. "Looking at my values and goals was a wake-up call to me," he says. "I was on a collision course, just sort of flying blindly through the fog Peter talks about. There was a mountain in front of me. Fortunately, I learned to take the controls and pull up. Through goal setting, I've begun to articulate what I *do* want, not just what I don't want. It feels good."

Do you DOUBT your ability? When you doubt your ability to achieve a goal, you dramatically lower the odds of reaching it. First, check to see if the goal is truly realistic. If you have trouble deciding, seek the advice of trusted friends, mentors or experts.

When you doubt your abilities, try using my favorite motto, "It's easy; it's a piece of cake." There's not a day that goes by that I don't remind myself of this sentence. For some reason, this helps me accomplish things I cannot normally imagine myself doing. For instance, I travel a lot and always want to be connected. I have my computer and my Treo 600. It can be challenging to get all of this technology working at once. "Piece of cake," I tell myself, and quite often I'm able to repair my own problems. In fact, I may be getting *too* good at it — my wife now refers to me as her computer guy.

When doubt sets in, you may need to set an intermediate goal or two before you tackle the larger goal. In other words, break your goal down into bite-sized pieces.

I learned an excellent technique for this when I was just starting my career selling mutual funds. My manager, Lawrence Henninger, told me about the 18-3-1 rule, which basically said that I needed to make 18 calls and deliver three presentations to make one sale.

"I've trained hundreds of salesmen and the only ones who failed were the ones who did not follow this simple rule," he told me. I liked Mr. Henninger and I believed what he said. In my mind, if that's what it would take for me to be successful then that's what I would do. On the first day, I took 18 paper clips from my desk and put them in the left pocket of my suit jacket. Each time I made a call, I moved a paper clip over to my right pocket. I told myself I couldn't go home until I had moved all the paper clips into my right-hand pocket. Was I successful at selling mutual funds? You bet.

Setting up rules like this for yourself — even if it's crossing items off a list or marking days off a calendar — is a great motivator. Once you set the rules, it's important to develop the self-discipline to follow through. That kind of discipline is another trait I often see in very successful people.

Perhaps you don't just doubt your ability to *achieve* goals, you doubt your ability to actually *set* goals. Maybe you see goal setting as too structured, impeding your ability to "go with the flow." I believe that when you fail to set goals, you fail to use an important tool in determining your future.

If you find yourself unable to set big, lofty goals, start small. Late night talk show host David Letterman's goal is at once ambitious and humble. "I'm just trying to make a smudge on the collective unconscious," he says. And he does.

Document Your Goals

Not only do successful people set goals and discipline themselves to achieve them — they also document their goals in lists, letters, pictures or whatever medium suits them best. They know if they don't have a plan, they'll soon become part of someone else's plan. My longtime friend Ken Marlin is a founder of many successful companies including First Investors Corporation and Marlin Travel. Ken spends his "retirement years" mentoring people to achieve financial freedom. He is a great believer in writing things down and setting goals for the day. "When you do this," says Ken, "you are in control of your time, and it is not in control of you."

In fact, Ken took this goal-setting practice beyond the personal: he applied this philosophy to motivate his team at First Investors. Every day, Ken held a 45-minute morning meeting which every team member was required to attend. When people achieved their goals, they received a round of applause. No recriminations were delivered during those meetings to those who didn't reach their goals. They simply didn't get the positive reinforcement of applause.

Brian Scudamore is a well-known North American success story. In 1989, Brian left Grade 12 and began searching for employment. While in line at a drive-thru restaurant, Brian saw a truck full of junk drive by. "I can do that," he thought to himself. He purchased an old, beat-up Ford, used the $700 he had in his bank account to buy tools and marketing materials, and launched what became a wildly successful company, 1-800-GOT-JUNK, which in 2004 opened its 100th North American franchise.

Like many of the world's most successful people, he's a strong believer in setting goals. That view was only enhanced when Brian attended a LifePilot workshop. He left the workshop that day with the idea of creating what he calls his "painted picture." This picture sets the direction for his company and his personal life.

Brian always had his list of "101 personal goals," and he gets everyone in his company to create their own lists as well. "Checking those goals off the list once they are achieved," says Brian, "adds to the feeling of accomplishment. One of my goals was to appear on *Oprah*. I got to check that one off!"

One of Brian's favorite inspirational stories is about Jim Collins, author of *Good to Great*. In 1978, Collins, an avid climber, became obsessed with climbing *Genesis*, a "100-foot slab of red rock in Colorado's Eldorado Canyon." No one had ever free-climbed this rock — most people thought it was impossible. Free climbers rely on ropes only as the ultimate safety devices; they prefer to climb under their own power. Collins felt he was strong, but *Genesis* intimidated him. He became determined to overcome his fear. In *Good to Great*, he writes:

> "In studying climbing history, I noticed a pattern: Climbs once considered 'impossible' by one generation eventually became 'not that hard' for climbers two generations later. So, I decided to play a psychological trick on myself. I realized that I would never be the most gifted climber or the strongest climber or the boldest climber. But perhaps I could be the most futuristic climber. I did a little thought experiment. I tried to project out 15 years, and I asked myself, 'What will *Genesis* seem like to climbers in the 1990s?' The answer came back clear as a bell. In the 1990s, top climbers would routinely [free climb] *Genesis*, viewing it as simply a warm-up for even harder routes. And less-talented athletes would view *Genesis* as a worthy challenge but hardly impossible."

Collins embarked on an interesting exercise by projecting himself into the future, from 1979 to 1994. He bought a personal organizer and changed all of the dates in it to 1994. Then he visited the canyon and began to imagine *Genesis* the way a climber 14 years in the future would see it.

"With that change in psychology," he writes, "I managed to climb through to the top of the route. It caused quite a sensation and confused many of the best climbers of the day. They were still climbing in 1979, whereas I had psychologically transported myself to 1994. And, indeed, by the early 1990s, these same elite climbers climbed *Genesis* routinely, no longer thinking of it as particularly hard. One climber from England — a much stronger lad than me — even climbed it in his tennis shoes!"

Discover Your Power

Jim Collins' climbing story shows how much power we actually have to achieve our goals. By changing his thinking, he changed the outcome. To demonstrate how much control you have in your life, I'd like you to do the following exercise which Diane M. Eade describes in her article "Goal Setting: Strategies for a Balanced Life."

On a blank piece of paper, list the past five years of your life vertically down the left side of the paper, e.g. 2004, 2003, 2002, 2001, 2000. Next to each year, list the most important event that occurred in *your* life during that year. Now look over the list and try to estimate the amount of influence you had on those events.

"After using this exercise with numerous groups," writes Eade, "I've observed that most people exert a significant influence over at least 80 percent of the most notable developments in their lives. Too few, however, take the time to reflect on their influence, allowing themselves to drift into believing that external forces really chart the course. Seeing how much control you personally exert over your life helps you to realize that you really are in charge, and that you can chart a course to success."

As you do this exercise, it's important not only to look at major business or career accomplishments. Explore your life holistically. Was there a new sport you learned last year? Did you take a vacation with your family? Were you able to assist someone in a way that had a positive effect on your life? Once you've done this exercise, fast forward to the future and try Jim Collins' strategy to accomplish something considered difficult or impossible.

Tips for Setting Goals

Now it's time to start setting your goals. Not sure if you're ready yet? As the 19th-century Russian writer Ivan Turgenev said, "If we wait for the moment when everything, absolutely everything, is ready we shall never begin."

So let's begin. First, make a list of the goals you hope to accomplish during the next year. At this point I don't want you to think of your goals for life, just your goals for the next 12 months. This will help you focus on what you can achieve now. Later, you can explore long-term goals.

Keep your goals specific. If they are too abstract you will lessen your chances of achieving them. As Eleanor Roosevelt said, "Happiness is not a goal; it is a by-product." What she wisely knew was that abstract goals like happiness, peace of mind and success are only achieved by setting and accomplishing concrete goals.

My goals for the coming year are:	

Everyone who knows me knows that health is one of my core values. My goals surrounding health include maintaining my weight, getting at least seven hours of sleep a night, and exercising regularly. They are meaningful goals to me, just as your goals should be meaningful to you. After all, your goals are expressions of your potential. They should be realistic but not unimaginative. For instance, it's unlikely you can become a medical doctor in one year; it *is* likely that you can enroll in medical school and complete a semester.

Scott Adams is a prime example of someone who set realistic, achievable goals that ultimately led to bigger and bigger goals. At 30, Scott was a middle manager, sitting in a cubicle and dreaming of becoming a cartoonist. Scott began to realize he would never fulfill his dream unless he set goals for himself. He decided he would start by just trying to get published in one place before his life was over. He created a package of cartoon strips about a middle manager lost in the corporate maze. A decade later, everyone knows the cartoon strip *Dilbert*. It's published in over 1000 newspapers in more than 30 countries. It all began with Scott Adams' goal to publish just one cartoon strip before he died.

Like Scott Adams, I set achievable goals. I had been a runner all my life until my back started aching so badly I could no longer do it. Thirty years of running had done its damage. All you runners out there know what kind of a sentence this is after a lifetime of running. As I started to gain weight, I realized I had to do something. I turned to the exercise bike with horror.

All of my life, I had wondered how anyone could ride those bikes while it was so great outside — the air, the weather, the freedom! There was no way I wanted to ride that exercise bike inside a gym or at home, but it was obvious I had a decision to make. If I kept on doing what I was doing — nothing — I knew I wasn't going to like what I saw in the mirror. I decided that instead of setting a goal to ride the bike for 30 minutes at a time, I would only ride it for five minutes a day. This was something I could do whether I liked being on the bike or not. Well, very quickly my five minutes expanded to 10, and then 20 and 30 minutes. Now I can't imagine not riding my bike for 30 minutes a day.

By starting out with a smaller goal, I didn't set myself up for failure but for victory. I now do this with any project I find difficult to get excited about. The only thing you have to do is show up dressed and committed — your natural momentum will take over. Trust yourself and get out of your own way. START NOW, no matter how daunting the task may seem.

Be Ready to RUMBA

To help you clearly articulate your goals, I want to share with you the RUMBA method of writing your goals, motivating yourself and focusing your energies. I believe "if it RUMBAs you can do it." To really RUMBA, your goals must be **Realistic**, **Understandable**, **Meaningful and measurable**, **Believable**, and **Agreed upon**.

Realistic: Your goals must have some basis in reality. Make sure you have a clear idea of what you want to achieve and what is required to do this. Do you have the prerequisites, or is there preparation that needs to take place? If so, you may need to readjust your goals to include the various steps you need to achieve before targeting your big goal. Also, it's important to take into account how much time and energy you can realistically devote to your goals.

Understandable: Describe your goals using specific language so you are very clear about what you want to achieve. For instance, saying that you will save money for a trip isn't as clear as saying you will set aside $400 a month for the next 12 months to reach your goal.

Meaningful and Measurable: Your goals should be important to you. They should not be things others think you should do — they are what you choose to do as part of your commitment to a better life. When you set your goals, be as specific as possible. Whenever you can, create timelines, benchmarks for achievement, and deadlines.

If you plan to lose 40 pounds, break the amount down to weekly or even monthly goals. After all, what gets measured gets done.

Believable: If you don't believe you can reach your goal, you won't be motivated to attain it. A prime example is the smoker who promises to quit out of guilt but doesn't really believe she can do it. Without the inner belief that she can triumph over addiction, is it any wonder she is sneaking cigarettes within a matter of weeks of quitting?

Agreed Upon: If you set personal goals and don't share them with anyone, you often lose the benefits, encouragement and fun of involving stakeholders in your success. A surefire way to help yourself stay focused on your preset goals is to share those goals with people who are important in your life — your spouse, your employer, your friends, your mentors, and anyone else who will be affected either by your drive to accomplish your goals or by your success.

When you tell others about your goals, you create partners in your journey towards accomplishment. For example, if you are in sales and your goal is to sell one million dollars worth of products, enlist your family's support by planning for a vacation you will all take when your "team" reaches its goal. Get brochures with pictures of your destination to help them envision the outcome and get excited. By enlisting this kind of team support, you are not alone, and when the going gets tough for any reason, you have others to boost your spirits on your journey.

Telling others about your goals broadcasts your intentions. Here's a funny story about the power of making your intentions known. Years ago, when I was living in Calgary, Alberta, I joined a few friends at the Calgary Stampede, the world-famous rodeo known as the "greatest outdoor show on earth." We headed to a popular bar, but when we arrived we discovered a line-up of several hundred people. It seemed impossible to get inside. One of my friends surveyed the situation and immediately ran in front of the crowd, yelling, "Make way for Mr. Thomas, make way for Mr. Thomas!"

Then the seemingly impossible happened — the crowd began to part. With me in the lead, my friends and I started walking towards the door. When we were just about there, someone in the crowd yelled, "Hey, that's only Peter Thomas." Before the crowd could react, I grabbed the door and we all ran inside the club, just in the nick of time.

Just as the crowd parted for me on that crazy night in Calgary, people will move to help you achieve your predetermined and stated goals if you make your intentions known.

CHAPTER REVIEW

* Effective goal setting is a common practice among the most successful people in the world.

* Beware of FUD (fear, uncertainty and doubt).

* Take time to list your goals for the coming year.

* Write your goals in a positive voice, with optimism and confidence.

* Make your goals specific and measurable, with clear dates and quantifiable milestones. Do they RUMBA?

* Ensure your goals are achievable or at least possible!

Secret 5

Align Your Goals With Your Values

You have now listed your goals for the coming year. Congratulations on taking this major step. Now it's time to check your goals against your values, prioritize your goals and put them into action with a personalized action diary. First, use the chart below to list your values down the left side of the page. Then look at your goals for the coming year and try to assign each one of them to a corresponding value.

Values	Goals
1.	
2.	
3.	
4.	
5.	
6.	
7.	
8.	
9.	
10.	
11.	
12.	
13.	
14.	
15.	

If any of your goals do not clearly align with your stated values, you may want to re-evaluate the goal or discard it. First, explore ways you can reshape the goal to align it more closely with the value. That's exactly what happened to pizza entrepreneur John Papaloukas, who you met earlier in the book. Two years ago, John and his wife Marvalee had an opportunity to travel to Russia, something they had been planning for some time.

"Because we were going through all of these issues with business, we literally had to sit down and say, 'OK, we just took the LifePilot workshop that taught us to look at things like this.' We had made all the arrangements but in the end we changed our plan because it just didn't fit our values. Family, health and financial security were part of our values and this trip would have jeopardized these values by me being away from my business for two weeks and incommunicado at a critical time. It just wasn't giving the right message."

For John, keeping his goals in line with his values is a philosophy he lives by. Last year, he attended a conference in Boston at MIT. "It's a big one," says John, "but it was over Father's Day. I said to the organizers, 'I don't understand you guys. That just doesn't make any sense — many of us are parents. If you want us to come back next year, make sure it's not on Father's Day.'"

The next year, when John received his conference agenda, he noted that it was once again scheduled for Father's Day. "I said, 'No offense, but I'm not attending. Why? A group of us asked you not to have it on Father's Day. I've got two children at home, my wife was mad last year, so no, I won't be coming this year. I want to spend Father's Day with my family.'"

Grade Your Goals

Once you've finalized your goals and assigned them to your values, I'd like you to go back to the chart on page 63 and rate each goal as an 'A', 'B' or 'C' priority based on the impact it will have, its importance and its urgency. Prioritizing your goals in this way helps you to further focus your energies and avoid letting others chart your course for you, which can leave you feeling frustrated. For example, perhaps your partner schedules an important business dinner on the day of your hair appointment — you feel guilty so you cancel your appointment. Maybe your employer demands that you work late every second night to finish projects, so you miss spending time with your children. These are examples of the way we put our own values and goals aside to service the needs of others, often out of guilt, fear, or a need to please.

By setting your priorities, you'll begin to create order in your life and give yourself permission to make choices that align with your values. Sure, you may still occasionally have to deal with other people's needs and demands, but now you have the tools to make conscious choices about the way you spend your time, from a position of strength and awareness, not from uncertainty and guilt.

Nancye Miller of Dallas, Texas built a successful career as a growth and brand strategist and consultant. Today, she is the dynamic CEO of the Entrepreneurs' Organization, which has 6,000 members throughout the world.

Last winter, Nancye, a huge believer in executive education, attended the LifePilot workshop in Beverly Hills. She says the most valuable lesson she learned through LifePilot is about how she allocates her time.

"I used to criticize myself greatly over how much I had to do. Going through and checking things off my list, I was hard on myself if I didn't get everything done. But after going through the LifePilot workshop, I'm less concerned about the daily results as where the results are taking me."

Today, Nancye is less focused on the quantity of what is on her calendar and more focused on the quality of how she spends her time. "I'm more contemplative and likely to ask, 'Are my thoughts getting me where I want to go?'"

"Life," she says, "is a marathon, not a sprint to the finish. Yet we're constantly sprinting…and in a last-minute rush because we didn't take the time to plan. I think it's a real sign in our society that we have things like interest-only mortgages because we know we won't stay with a home long enough to ever pay it off. Everything is temporary because we are moving so fast."

Nancye recalls a time in her life when, as the single mother of two children, she would spend all weekend cooking and preparing meals for the coming week in an attempt to be the way she thought a mother *should* be, always ready with a home-cooked meal. "I related that to nurturing my children, so I couldn't seem to break the cycle."

One day it dawned on her that the home-cooked meals didn't matter if she was spending the free time she had on weekends cooking instead of just being with her son and daughter. She decided she didn't need to be the kind of mother her mother had been. By looking more deeply at her time and what she really valued, she realized take-out was fine if it meant she could spend more time really focusing on her children.

Nancye's children are now 18 and 21 and pursuing higher education. Nancye continues to live the life of a busy executive with enormous pressures on her time. Despite that, she remains focused on quality over quantity. "I think exploring transitional change is important," she says. "We tend to focus on organizational change when we really need to focus on changing our thinking about how we do things."

Journalist Katie Couric once interviewed a 24-year-old breast cancer survivor. "What personally changed for you from this experience?" she asked the young woman. "I've learned to prioritize my life so I now only spend time on things I am passionate about," the young woman replied.

Often, we wait until our lives are in crisis before we begin to make adjustments to our priorities. Wherever you are in life, and whatever situation you're in, it's important to make changes, starting today, that will lead you to a more streamlined way of living.

Step 1: Reflect on your priorities. What types of things consistently draw your attention? Where do you spend the majority of your time? What issues tend to make you drop everything and cancel plans in order to address them? Try to imagine yourself in a variety of situations. What might pull you away from an important project at work or time with your family?

Step 2: Consider your priorities in light of your values. Do these priorities reflect what you truly believe to be most important to you? Keep your list of priorities handy so you can refer to it again as you define goals and plans for each of your values.

Step 3: Remain flexible enough to adjust your course occasionally when life warrants it, but avoid the "candle in the wind" approach, where you always allow circumstances to blow you this way and that. If you continually allow this, you'll soon find your light dimmed or extinguished.

By recording your values, prioritizing your goals, and checking in with them on a regular basis, you'll begin to notice patterns. It may be that a certain person in your life is always asking you to adjust your priorities.

It may also be that you are cramming too much activity into your life and constantly running up against impossible deadlines that force you to compromise. Learning from these patterns will yield enormous benefits.

Chart Your Progress

Setting your values, goals and priorities them is only the beginning. To make them a reality you need to focus your energy and track your progress.

Daily: Do something every day that supports each of your values. Plan activities that touch multiple values. Since my own values are health, happiness and freedom, I try to set goals and plan activities that combine these values. I might exercise with a friend because exercise is crucial to maintaining my health, and being with friends contributes to my feelings of happiness. Sometimes I invite friends and business colleagues on a dinner cruise with on-board musical entertainment. This boosts my happiness quotient, because I enjoy being around friends and listening to music. It also gives me the opportunity to get to know my business colleagues better. Since relationships are key to business success, and business success is essential to achieving financial independence, this supports my value of freedom.

Weekly: Every Sunday, I take the day off and spend part of it reviewing my *LifeManual*. I note the progress I've made and make my plans for the week ahead. This process allows me to impose my own meaning and expectations on my life instead of feeling vulnerable to outside forces.

Quarterly: Every three months, I spend time refocusing, celebrating my accomplishments and making adjustments in my flight plan.

Annually: Once a year, I look back, review my successes and reflect on areas for improvement. I always make it a point to celebrate my overall success. To really celebrate, try doing something you've always dreamed about. It's very motivating.

Activate Your Action Plan

Now that you've defined and prioritized your goals, it's time for action. Look at each of your goals and list all of the activities you must complete in order to achieve those goals. This step sends people who aren't detail-oriented into tailspins when they first hear of it, but rest assured, you'll eventually come to enjoy this step once you experience how critical it is to your success.

"Desire becomes intention when action is taken," says success coach Isabel Parlett. Creating your action plan is like connecting the dots in your life. How will you get from one dot to the next in order to complete the big picture? Start by exploring the gap between where you are now and where you want to be. Add detail, including timeframes, to each of the activities or steps in the plan to the degree that this will help you define a clear map for achieving your goals.

As you complete the remaining exercises in this book, you'll likely identify additional goals you wish to accomplish. After reading each section of the book, you might want to return to your goals and add in new ones.

Do Your Daily Diary

The next activity is very valuable for discovering where your time and effort really go, and for gaining a further sense of control over your life. If you've ever created a spending diary to discover where all your dollars are really going, you know that this exercise can yield some surprising results.

If this feels overwhelming, remember that from a distance a forest looks impregnable — you can't get through it. As you get closer, you start seeing the tree trunks, branches, and the pathways. It's exactly the same with LifePilot. As you examine what you do every day, you'll begin seeing things more clearly. Then you can start deleting those items that don't align with your values and adding things that do.

First, create a daily diary for the next two weeks. In your diary, write an hour-by-hour account of your activities. Once you've completed your two-week practice diary, make a note beside each activity of the value it supports in your life. Don't reach for connections that aren't there. Ideally most of your activities will be associated with at least one value — you've scored a home run if you can link *all* of your activities to at least one of your values. You may argue that mowing the lawn, going shopping, paying bills, and other chores doesn't align with your values, but living your values requires that you look after your basic needs. We can hardly use our values to escape every unwanted chore!

Aligning Goals and Plans with Values

You can use the following chart as an example of how to track which values your activities support.

Values				
1. Health	2. Freedom	3. Happiness	4. Spirituality	5. Family

Activity Diary	DAY 1	Supporting Values
07:00-08:00	Ready for work/school	(5)
08:00-12:00	Work	(2)(3)
12:00-13:00	Lunch with Sally (friend)	(3)
13:00-18:00	Work	(2)(3)
18:00-19:00	Make dinner	(1)(3)(5)
19:00-20:00	Dinner with family	(3)(5)
20:00-21:00	Play/read/bathe kids	(3)(5)
21:00-22:00	Pay bills, clean	(2)
22:00-23:00	Visit with Bob (husband)	(5)
23:00-23:30	Read	(3)
23:30-07:00	Sleep	(1)

If there is less alignment between your goals and values than you would like, don't be discouraged. This exercise is intended to highlight opportunities for change and to allow you to create a more balanced and meaningful life.

Next, ask yourself if there is an activity that is meaningful to you that is not reflected in your values. Do you need to expand the definition of one of your values or add a new value to reflect this?

When you are finished with your two-week practice diary, it's time to create an ongoing daily diary that will help you gain control over your time and leave space for the things you love most. The key to making this diary work for you is discipline. Take it with you wherever you go and keep it current so it always gives you a real picture of the way you spend your days. From time to time, look back over your diary and reflect on which areas of your life need more work, and which areas have improved because of your new practice of setting goals and keeping track of your time.

Choose Your Priorities

Decide what you want to accomplish every day and write it down in your daily activity diary. Set your intentions and make them clear. My longtime method of focusing my day in alignment with my values and goals begins before I go to bed the previous night. At that time, I create my list of priorities for the following day. The list is a focal point for my energies, and it contains things I feel are most important in my life, including business, personal and family priorities.

In the film *What the Bleep Do We Know!?* Joe Dispenza, who has traveled the world lecturing on the close relationship between brain chemistry and physical health, discusses his method of focusing his days. "I wake up in the morning and I consciously create my day the way I want it to happen," he says. "...Now sometimes, because my mind is examining all the things that I need to get done, it takes me a little bit to settle down and get to the point where I'm actually intentionally creating my day. But here's the thing: When I create my day out of nowhere, little things happen that are so unexplainable, I know they are the process or the result of my creation...."

You might say, "That's all fine and dandy when you don't have young children to get ready for school and yourself to get off to work." But I would say that if gaining more focus and happiness in life is important to you, you can find the five minutes it takes to create your list of priorities. It doesn't matter who you are, how much money you have, where you live or what you do.

The success of your day depends on how closely you follow your list of priorities. Don't let distractions get in the way. When I practiced to compete in the New York City Marathon, I had many other pressing concerns. Even so, going for a five-mile run was always number one on my list, no matter what other priorities came up. Once an activity makes it onto my list, it gets done.

Let's say, for instance, that my priority list for the day has 11 items on it, six of which I plan to accomplish for sure. It might look like this:

1. *Proofread new workbook and call A. about printing*
2. *Call A.M. about the university sponsorship for LifePilot workshop*
3. *Call K.S. regarding interview schedules*
4. *Call P.R. about sponsoring a LifePilot workshop in Moscow and Dubai; schedule a meeting tomorrow in Geneva*
5. *Call D.F. about Advisory Committee*
6. *Make calls regarding setting up two workshops*
7. *Call M.S. about recruiting participants*
8. *Pick up newspaper*
9. *Discuss line of credit with the bank regarding investment opportunity*
10. *Order George Jones and Buddy Holly CDs from Amazon.com*
11. *Confirm with A. that the spotlights are in the trunk of the 49 Monarch.*

I begin my day by placing all the calls I need to make. Then I start on the dreaded proofreading job that is my number one priority. To help with self-motivation, I tell myself, "It's easy; it's a piece of cake." Just as I'm getting into the proofreading, I get a call from the bank. They want to be paid out on a loan within two weeks. Now I have a decision to make: do I call them back regarding the bank loan or do I continue with the proofreading? For me, there's no decision — I continue with the proofreading. Nothing is going to happen today if I call the bank. Besides, I know calling the bank has the capacity to suck my day totally away — one call with them often lasts for two hours. Then, of course, I would need to call my team and explain the details. I stick with the proofreading because it's my number one priority, even though it's not my favorite thing to do.

You won't necessarily like doing all of the things on your list, but they may be necessary to help you achieve your bigger goals. It's much like a parent changing a diaper. It's not much fun but because it makes the baby happy and clean the parent lovingly does it. If I have to change some metaphorical diapers to get my priorities completed, I do it willingly because I'm focused on building an organization that has the potential to raise millions of dollars for charity in honor of my son.

Do What You Need to Do

During the course of your day, unexpected surprises *will* arise. It's important to put these in perspective. When these surprises happen to me, I always check them against my values and priorities. In doing so, I can make informed decisions. I remind myself that these unexpected surprises are the things that are out of focus — my priorities remain clear. With some practice, you'll be able to do this almost automatically because you will have come to know yourself so well.

You can't always ignore life's intrusions but living in alignment with your values allows you to put these intrusions in perspective. If you are an employer, for instance, a wildcat strike at your plant will likely take precedence over proofreading. If you're a parent, a sick child is a top priority. If you're an employee, you may be struggling with a sudden rush job for your boss while trying to leave early for a family event. These things happen, but by organizing the major areas of your life, knowing your values and keeping a daily list of priorities, you'll find you can respond more effectively to unexpected events when they occur.

My wife Rita has seen me grapple with these kinds of issues. She says, "Peter puts his values into action every single day. He constantly asks himself, 'Is this going to affect my values?' particularly in regards to work issues. I recall one instance a few years ago when a very large development project he owned was not going well. He couldn't seem to find the right person to make it work. We discussed this over dinner one night. He suggested perhaps he and I should move to Texas for a few months and get the project back on track. It would have been very easy for us to do this as we were available and we could have had that office cooking in no time. But in the same breath, Peter said, 'I'd rather lose the money and let the deal die than do this because we'll be working 24/7 and I won't be living by my values. I want balance in my life, and this would definitely put my life out of balance.'"

Unify Your Life

So many people draw lines in the sand between their work and their personal lives. But the universe doesn't always recognize these lines. I've learned not to either. I do not have a separate business and personal life — I have a *life*. Everything blends together: my work, my family, my friendships, and my personal time. The same lessons I apply to my business life are exactly the lessons I apply to my personal life, whether I'm exploring health-related activities or attending a business meeting.

It's funny how many people make rigorous use of their personal organizers during their Monday-to-Friday working lives. Yet on weekends and holidays their days often turn into free-for-alls. Have you ever heard someone say, "The weekend passed so quickly and I never got to the movie I wanted to see or the gardening I hoped to do. I wanted to spend time with my kids but the house needed cleaning." Chances are, they didn't schedule these things as priorities. If they had put them on their lists or in their personal organizers, they likely would have achieved these things. So we need to readjust the way we think about our personal organizers. Instead of associating them exclusively with work, we need to make them all-encompassing navigational plans for our *lives*.

Only when you see the whole picture of your life — the big picture *and* the details — will you get a true understanding of how you can better manage your time for more balance. Kelly is a frantically busy vice president for a major corporation, and the single mother of two girls. She is a "big picture thinker" who used to feel frustrated when dealing with details. Planning not only overwhelmed her, it frightened her.

"I think I subconsciously worried that if I really started to acknowledge how complex my life was, I wouldn't be able to cope," she says. As a result, even though she earned a large salary, her household bills piled up. "I can't count the number of times my cable was cut off, not because I didn't have the money, but because I forgot to pay."

Kelly literally ran through her weeks, and fell into bed exhausted on the weekends. Because she didn't plan for vacations, she tended to book them at the last minute and ended up paying hundreds of extra dollars, always missing the pre-booking discounts. "That money could have gone into hiring a personal assistant or a house cleaner," she says now, smiling. "I was so dysfunctional."

Then one day, Kelly simply didn't get up for work on a Monday morning. "I literally couldn't. It was all too much: my career, childcare, housework, the friendships I was ignoring, my own health. I was done." She went on stress leave, but she knew that couldn't last for long. She had to get it together.

Finally, she talked to a friend who had attended a LifePilot workshop. "She had many of the same issues in her life as I did," says Kelly, "but she was getting it together and I could see a huge difference. I decided I needed to do this."

Today, Kelly's life is simpler. She still works at her job, but she has learned to focus on what matters most to her. "I no longer work in the evenings or on weekends, plus I've hired someone to help with childcare so I can have some free time to myself and go out to a movie occasionally. I know my values and priorities. This has helped me feel more confident about saying no to what doesn't fit, and it allows me to say yes to doing the things I love."

Bring Your Whole Life Into Focus

You might question the idea of actually scheduling in time with the people you love, but if these people are priorities, ensuring you have time for them actually honors your relationships with them.

One of the things I love doing is going for cappuccino with my daughter Liane and listening to her talk. These times are precious and I know she treasures them as much as I do, so I make it a priority to spend time with her. To keep this top of mind, I write it in my daily goals to review each time I'm in the city where she lives. In this way, each day I'm there I can look at my daily goals and make the conscious decision to make time for Liane.

My relationship with my wife Rita has never been without some form of LifePilot. The second time we met, I shared my *Goal Book* (that's what I called my *LifeManual* back then) with her. We went through every page and I explained to her why this book was important to me and how it worked. Rita loved the concept. She immediately set up her own system and shared it with me.

At that time, I tried to convince Rita her values should be the same as mine; namely, health, freedom and happiness. We had many discussions about this, and I finally agreed it made sense for Rita to have her own values and for me to have mine. I opened my eyes and really explored what Rita's values were and why they were important to her. This was a real turning point in our relationship because I began to honor Rita's values and tried to help her fulfill them.

That's not to say bringing two lives together is always a smooth process. "Initially, we didn't have much interaction with our books," says Rita, "but one year when we were doing our annual reviews, I suggested to Peter that we should each create a list of things that bugged us about each other and add it to our books. Peter agreed so I presented him with my list, which had about 10 things on it. It was actually quite funny because Peter grabbed the list, stormed into his office, slammed the door and stayed there for a couple of hours! He was shocked I could come up with so many things. He then presented me with his *lengthy* list. It was a tough adjustment at first but now we know exactly what we need to do to stay on track."

Rita and I feel LifePilot has helped us create a true partnership. We know what matters most to each other. It's also a great tool for helping us to schedule and plan our lives. We set goals together and help each other reach those goals.

For instance, Rita really values relationships, particularly with her family, so I often organize surprises for her that relate to family and friends. For Christmas one year, I purchased tickets for her, her four sisters and her Mom to go to Umberto's cooking school in Italy. We recently purchased a townhouse in the Okanagan region of British Columbia to spend more time with Rita's family.

At times, our priorities are very different. If this happens, LifePilot comes in handy because it helps us understand each other's decisions. Instead of working at cross-purposes, we are able to work in harmony.

"LifePilot affects me every single day," says Rita. "I'm constantly making decisions on what is important. Living my life with Peter presents so many options, there's the constant issue of choices. On one of our visits to Victoria, we were there for only three days. We spent the first two days with our grandkids, and I wanted to spend the last day packing and getting organized for three months in Europe (which is a big pack). Peter wanted me to spend our last day having dinner with the grandkids. This meant I would have to stay up past midnight to pack. We had a very early morning flight and I was already on the edge of exhaustion, so I took a look at my values, which included relationships and health. I knew there was a good chance if I didn't get enough sleep that night I might end up sick from exhaustion, so the choice was easy. As much as I love my grandkids, I didn't want to make myself sick."

Making a Commitment

Rita and I know what we value, and we plan our lives and our schedules according to those values. We respect each other's values and priorities, and we work together to our mutual benefit.

For relationships to succeed, this kind of mutual respect is important. You and your partner may not share the same values but it's important your values are not so divergent that you can't experience any kind of harmony or common goals. The same is true with other close relationships. Some of you may be as fortunate as I was to find a partner who understands your values. Others may have to work harder to find common ground.

Vance Luetke and Michelle Farver-Luetke met in Las Vegas three years ago. This dynamic young couple quickly discovered a shared passion for life and a commitment to their high-energy careers. Vance is the CEO of Alpine Affiliates, Inc. and Michelle is a membership director for Abercrombie & Kent Destination Clubs as well as the owner of Executive Tans Elite in Scottsdale, Arizona. Both are big sports fans who love travel, good food and adventure. They love surprising each other, like the time Michelle hired a plane on their one-year anniversary to fly over with the message, "One night changed my life. I love you, Vance."

Last year, Vance and Michelle attended a LifePilot workshop in Phoenix. That experience inspired them to take their commitment one step farther. Last summer, they got married in Cabo San Lucas, Mexico in front of 50 friends and family members.

"LifePilot helped us to understand that if we really value what we have, why not take the next step toward a deeper commitment?" says Vance.

"We already shared similar values," says Michelle, "but we were living self-centered lives. I don't mean that in a negative way. I just mean that we were very focused on doing what we each loved. LifePilot reminded us that if we value each other, then we needed to spend time together, doing things we *both* love."

Vance says he used to play golf a lot, but since he and Michelle examined their values, they decided to play tennis together instead because it allowed them to value their relationship.

Exploring their values together has only deepened their passion for each other. "I think that when you share your values with each other," says Vance, "it gives you a stronger understanding of who the other person is. It's important for couples to do that."

Course Corrections

When you make a commitment to LifePilot, your family, friends and the people you work with may be resistant to your new focus. At first, they may try to pull you away from your focus, either consciously or unconsciously. This may be the reason most people fall off their commitment. They feel — perhaps out of guilt, fear or a sense of obligation — that they must abandon their priorities to fulfill other people's needs. Some of your friends, family and co-workers may even laugh at the idea of being "scheduled in," but once they realize the benefit is spending quality time with you, they'll be smiling. Give this a try — you'll be astounded at how well it works.

That's not to say it's always easy (but tell yourself it's a *piece of cake* anyway!). As soon as you try it, it may seem as though everyone is out to sabotage you, and you'll find it hard to focus on your priorities. After all, if you are focusing on your priorities, then you aren't necessarily focusing on the priorities others try to impose on you. This brings to mind a Chinese proverb, "The person who says it cannot be done should not interrupt the person doing it."

Whether you proceed or not with pursuing your focus is a choice you'll have to make for yourself, but I'm here to tell you that you *can* achieve your goals if you focus with intensity. Remember, you only get out of life what you desire and focus on. Sometimes you have to go through a lot of changes and pain to get there. Resetting a broken bone isn't a pleasant experience but it's necessary if you want to regain use of a limb. Ask yourself: *is short-term discomfort bearable if I know enduring it will result in living the remarkable life I was meant to live?*

No Straight Line to Achievement

Achieving your goals won't always be easy. Sometimes you will have to deal with setbacks, but with a positive attitude you will move forward just as inventor Thomas Edison did when his laboratory in New Jersey burned down in 1914. He lost over two million dollars worth of equipment and research. The next day, the inventor toured the site and poked through the ashes. "There is great value in disaster," he said. "All our mistakes are burned up. Thank God we can start anew."

Edison could easily have closed his doors forever, but he chose to take a positive view of an otherwise disastrous situation. He didn't lose site of his goals and neither should you. No matter what, remain optimistic and undeterred. Keep moving forward. To do this, the Taoists recommend that you envision yourself as water. Unlike stone, water does not crack or become stuck when it confronts obstacles. It flows around or over all obstacles, or eventually erodes even the toughest barriers.

One of the most famous jockeys who ever lived was George Edward Arcaro, who *Sports Illustrated* called "the most famous man to ride a horse since Paul Revere." Eddie, as he was known to millions of fans, won 4,770 races during his 30-year career. He was one of only two jockeys to win the Kentucky Derby five times, and the only jockey to have won the Triple Crown twice. Eddie was the leading money winner three times. By the time he retired in 1962, he had won 549 stakes races and over $30 million — both of these were records. What most people overlook about Eddie's extraordinary career is that he actually *lost* 250 races in a row before he ever rode a winner to victory.

It's easy to become discouraged when the path to our goals isn't a straight runway to success. But many successful people will tell you their character was built as much by their so-called failures as their successes. Another example is Babe Ruth. Arguably the most famous baseball player of all time, Ruth holds two records: the most home runs (714) and the most strikeouts (1,330).

When you look at the lives of successful people, you generally find that they have tried more and worked harder to achieve their goals than others. They get the law of averages to work for them. "Of course, the entire effort," writes poet Stephen Spender, "is to put oneself outside the ordinary range of what are called statistics." While a less dedicated player may have quit or slowed down, Babe Ruth just kept swinging his way to success. Michelangelo is often called a genius and his works have been deemed miracles of the imagination. "If people knew how hard I worked to get my mastery," he said, "it wouldn't seem so wonderful after all."

I would not begin to compare myself to Babe Ruth and Michelangelo, but I do know the power of hard work and persistence. When I was 28 years old and just beginning my career, I was appointed as a first-time manager. Now I had to count on my ability to get results from others rather than just doing it myself. On a particularly worrisome day, I shared some of my frustrations with my boss, Ken Marlin. He listened patiently then said some simple and powerful words I've never forgotten: "Peter, keep smiling and leaning."

No matter how bad a day you're having or how many things seem to drive you away from your preset objectives, just keep your head down and plow ahead. With your values identified and your goals set out, you'll be surprised how well you can operate.

When it seems like the odds are stacked against you, it might also be helpful to think of the story about a farmer's old horse that fell down a well. The poor horse neighed for hours as the farmer tried to decide how to get it out. Finally, the farmer reasoned that the horse was old and the well needed to be covered up anyway. He invited his neighbors to help him shovel dirt into the well. When the horse saw this, he began to neigh again. Then, to everyone's amazement, he quieted down. A few shovel loads later, the farmer finally looked down into the well and was astonished by what he saw.

With every shovelful of dirt that landed on top of the animal, he would shake it off and take a step up. After a few hours, the horse stepped up over the edge of the well and trotted away. Sometimes life shovels a lot of dirt on you along the path to achieving your goals. It's important not to give up. Shake off the dirt and step up to your future.

Reach for New Heights

In the major baseball leagues, a hitter's success and salary are measured by the amount of times he hits the ball when he steps up to the plate. A 250 hitter earns about $50,000 a year. At 333, a hitter earns about $500,000 a year. Now, here's an eye-opening fact — the 250 hitter only needs one more hit every three games to move his average up to 333 and increase his earnings by $450,000 a year. So give it your best each time you "go up to bat" in life. As your averages improve — and they will — you'll be inspired to set your sights higher and higher.

Several years ago I had an amazing lesson in setting my sights higher. I took the Concorde from Paris to New York. It was my first and only "faster than the speed of sound" experience. To say I was excited would be an understatement. At the start of the flight, the flight attendant told us all the usual information. We fastened our seatbelts and prepared for what I thought would be an unbelievable experience. At first, the plane soared skyward much like any other plane. When we reached about 35,000 feet, the lights came on and the flight attendant told us we could unfasten our seatbelts. She served us champagne and I wondered, "Is that it?" Needless to say, I had expected a whole lot more but since it obviously wasn't coming, I sat back to enjoy the flight.

After about 15 minutes, the flight attendant picked up our glasses and made another announcement that went something like this: *Ladies and gentlemen, please fasten your seatbelts and prepare for Supersonic Flight.*

Now I was excited again. The engines began to roar, and the plane vibrated as it picked up speed. Then it thrust its nose up and soared towards the heavens. I was ecstatic. I looked at the gauge on the wall in front of me and watched the numbers rushing from 400 up to 1,000. As soon as the gauge read 1,000, the flight attendant came back on the address system. "Welcome to Supersonic Flight!" she said. "We are flying at 52,000 feet." When I looked out the window, I could actually see the curvature of the Earth. I felt excited, inspired and humbled at the same time. I truly had an epiphany. I thought to myself that Concorde flight was a metaphor for my company — we had been cruising at 35,000 feet. Now it was time to take it to MACH 1 and 52,000 feet.

The Concorde experience was about more than business however. It was a lesson in life. On that flight I knew what Isak Dinesen meant in *Out of Africa*, when she wrote: "Every time I have gone up in an aeroplane and looked down, I have realized I was free of the ground. I have had the consciousness of a new discovery. 'I see,' I have thought. 'This was the idea. And now I understand everything.'"

When you've gone as high as you think you can go, set your sights higher. There could be more!

CHAPTER REVIEW

★ Keep an activity diary to monitor how you spend your time. Ask yourself if you are spending it wisely or not.

★ Write your priorities down every night before you go to sleep or first thing in the morning.

★ In order to live a balanced life, your list must include items relating to work, family, spirituality, health, recreation and more.

★ To help with self-motivation, say, "It's easy; it's a piece of cake."

★ When unexpected surprises arise, check them against your values and priorities. In doing so, you will make informed decisions.

★ Realize some people will consciously or unconsciously try to sabotage your efforts to live by your values. Do it anyway.

★ Reward yourself for achieving milestones and benchmarks.

★ Celebrate the ultimate attainment of a goal — you deserve it!

"Do, or do not. There is no 'try'." *Yoda (The Empire Strikes Back)*

"Yes, you can be a dreamer and a doer too if you remove one word from your vocabulary: impossible." *Dr. Robert H. Schuller*

SECRET 6

Put Confidence On Your Control Panel

You've identified your values, and set your goals and priorities. Now it's time to leave the runway. That means building the confidence to believe you can achieve the life you've dreamed about, and trusting your navigational instruments.

In my experience of teaching people how to reach new heights, I've observed basically three types of people and they all take different approaches:

Passive Types tend to sit back and never leave life's runway. Life happens to them; they do not actively pursue their own dreams and passions.

Active Types like to fly and can be motivated to leave the ground and take to the air. Some of them reach the clouds and go no higher. Others may reach the altitude of jets if they are strongly inspired and motivated.

Proactive Types take the controls and decide to soar higher and farther than anyone else. They are eager to ascend above the clouds, and even above the cruising altitude of jets. They seek the supersonic flight of the Concorde.

All of these types possess the same potential, but some are better at pushing past their FUD (fear, doubt and uncertainty) to create the lives they want. If you feel tentative, contemplating all the things that could go amiss as you embark on this new, values-based approach, ask yourself if worrying about "what ifs" is a good reason to ground your dreams? When I think about the energy we waste on worrying, I'm reminded of a story involving the famous Italian conductor Arturo Toscanini.

Once, shortly before a prestigious concert in front of a standing-room-only audience, a member of Toscanini's orchestra approached the conductor in a state of heavy anxiety. "Maestro," the musician said, "my instrument is not working properly. I can't reach the note of E-flat. I'm beside myself with worry and the concert will begin in just a few minutes."

Toscanini smiled and put his arm around the man's shoulders. "My friend," the maestro said, "do not worry about it. The note E-flat does not appear anywhere in the music you will be playing this evening."

Brian Tracy, author of *Create Your Own Future*, writes: "Your greatest limits are not external. They are internal, within your thinking. These are contained in your personal self-limiting beliefs. These are beliefs that act as brakes on your potential. These are beliefs that cause you to sell yourself short, and to settle for far less than you are truly capable of."

If you're sitting there, looking at the runway and wondering if you should leave the ground, I can only tell you that the time is now. It takes an enormous amount of energy to get off the ground, but once you do, flight seems so effortless that you wonder what kept you grounded in the first place.

Learn from Example

The famous aviator Antoine de Saint Exupéry said about flying, "You'll be bothered from time to time by storms, fog, snow. When you are, think of those who went through it before you, and say to yourself, 'What they could do, I can do.'"

This is the way I've lived my life, by making a concerted effort to learn the secrets of success from those who have attained it. Learning from the masters boosts my confidence, especially when I read about their challenges. Many of these people weren't born with wealth. Some had to overcome major obstacles. What separates them from the rest is that they never spent their time worrying about what *could* happen if things went wrong — they kept their eyes on the prize.

During LifePilot workshops, I like to ask participants to guess who the following person is. See if you can figure it out:

* He had to work to support his family after they were forced out of their home.
* His mother died.
* He failed in business.
* He was defeated for the legislature.
* He lost his job and couldn't get into law school.
* He declared bankruptcy, and spent the next 17 years of his life paying off the money.
* He borrowed from friends to start his business.
* He was defeated for the legislature again.
* His fiancé died and his heart was broken.
* He had a nervous breakdown and spent the next six months in bed.
* He was defeated in becoming the speaker of the state legislature.
* He was defeated in becoming an elector.
* He was defeated for Congress.
* He was defeated for Congress again.
* He was defeated for Congress yet again.
* He was rejected for a job.
* He was defeated for Senate.
* He was defeated for Vice-President and got less than 100 votes.
* He was defeated for Senate again.
* He was elected President of the United States.

Most people find it hard to believe that this long saga of so-called failures is actually the blow-by-blow account of the life of Abraham Lincoln, the 16th president of the United States.

Believe in Yourself

In his book *The Other 90%*, Robert K. Cooper shares a lesson his great-grandfather William Downing taught him. He said, "A person should always wear clothes that have two pockets…In one of the pockets, keep a note that says, 'I am nothing but dust and ashes.' In the other pocket, keep a note that says, 'For me the world was created.'"

Life is short. We will all die eventually. But while we're here we have a mission to pursue our ultimate potential. To do this, you need to believe in yourself.

Art Linkletter used to host a wonderful TV children's program called "Linkletter's Kids." Millions of households tuned in to listen to the impromptu things kids would say when Linkletter asked them questions. One day, Linkletter asked a young boy how he got invited to be on the show. The little fellow said, "I'm the smartest kid in my class."

"Did your teacher tell you that?" Linkletter asked.

"No, I figured it out by myself," the boy replied.

I wish I had possessed that kind of confidence in my abilities when I was a young boy. I remember being in grade two art class. My teacher, Miss Belmont, asked everyone in class to draw a picture of a cow. I drew the best cow I could. I was quite happy with it until, for some unknown reason, Miss Belmont came to my desk, took my picture of a cow and held it up for the class to see. They all laughed at my drawing, and I was horrified. Needless to say, I never drew again.

Much later in life, when I was in my early 40s, I went to an art gallery in Vienna and saw one of Picasso's depictions of cows. "My cow is much better than his!" I thought, yet I had let the students' laughter convince me I'd done a poor job. Ironically, years later I read a quotation by Pablo Picasso that said, "Every child is an artist. The problem is how to remain an artist once he grows up."

Some people have asked me if I ever tried to draw again. At one point, my son Todd, who had a natural talent for art, graciously agreed to teach me some of his skills. It didn't take me long to admit that maybe Todd had inherited his artistic flair from his mother, Donna.

The Japanese-American artist Isamu Noguchi, considered one of great sculptors of the 20th century, credited his mother with helping him to believe in his talent. By all accounts, she was a strong and powerful influence on the early development of her son.

We should all be so fortunate to have such strong champions of our potential. But whether you do or don't have support for your talents, you must look inside and recognize that potential we all possess. It's still there, no matter how old you are. Discovering it is an amazing process, a bit like finding a long-lost treasure you buried as a child. When you find it, you'll remember how good it felt, and how right.

When he was a boy, Dr. Steven Funk, who you met earlier in the book, dreamed of becoming a farmer. But somehow the Iowa farm kid ended up pursuing an education in oral surgery. It wasn't until he was well into his post-secondary education that he realized he was moving toward a destination that didn't excite him.

So why did Steven choose a career in oral surgery? "I remember jumping up and down on the bed when I was a little kid," he says. "My Dad was there and he was asking, 'What are you going to be when you grow up?' I said, 'Dad, I'm going to be a farmer' — because my Dad was a farmer. I remember him saying, 'You don't want to be a farmer. Go be a doctor.'"

He did what his father wanted him to do. He studied at the University of Iowa in his home state, then moved to Vancouver, British Columbia for his residency. "I picked Vancouver out of a *National Geographic* magazine," he laughs.

Steven tried to find something that appealed to him about a career in oral surgery, but his heart wasn't in it. "I remember being very inspired by one of my great friends in dental school, Doug Hutchison. I returned to Iowa for Christmas one year, and Doug and I were sitting in front of the fireplace when he said, out of nowhere, 'I really hate this. Yeah, I can't wait until I retire.'"

"You know, it's funny, I don't like it either," Steven told his friend. The thought of an Iowa farm boy with a love of the outdoors spending all his life cooped up in an office was almost unbearable, he recalls.

"If you grow up on a farm, your life is freelance," he says. "If I went into dentistry, I knew how I'd spend all of my days. I'd work 9 to 5 and spend scheduled time playing golf."

Uncertain about the future, Steven returned to Vancouver where I eventually met him. In fact, my business partner and I hired him. One moment he was an oral surgery resident, the next he was working for two fast-moving entrepreneurs whose entire approach to life was full of enthusiasm — and anything but 9 to 5. It was the freelance life he'd dreamed about back in school.

Steven went on to become founder and chairman of a major corporation. True to his farming background, he now oversees nearly 100,000 acres of precious sustainable development and environmental custodianship in the rainforest of Belize — and he owns agricultural farmland in conjunction with his family in his home state of Iowa. He is also a founder and officer of the Presidents' Peace Action Network Chapter of the World Presidents' Organization.

Like so many people, Steven had a potential and a calling he almost denied. Although Steven's father undoubtedly wanted the very best for his son, the father's dream wasn't Steven's dream. By looking deep inside, Steven found the courage to pursue his dream and turn it into a success.

The Gleam of Genius

The world is made up of ordinary people who do extraordinary things every day. People sometimes comment that I live an extraordinary life, but I know I'm not extraordinary. I'm just an ordinary guy who has ordinary fears and an ordinary intelligence. I'm able to live an extraordinary life because I've been able to establish and maintain a personal discipline that allows me to focus on preset goals.

Many years ago, I was inspired by a book by Glenn Clark called *The Man Who Tapped the Secrets of the Universe*. The book had many insightful quotations and writings, but one particular piece of writing changed my life. It went like this: "I believe sincerely that every man has consummate genius within him. Some appear to have it more than others only because they are aware of it more than others are, and the awareness or unawareness of it is what makes each one of them into masters or holds them down to mediocrity. *I believe that mediocrity is self-inflicted and genius is self-bestowed.* Every successful person I ever have known, and I have known a great many, carries within him the key which unlocks that awareness and lets in the universal power that has made him into a master."

Those words changed my life. At the moment I read them, I realized I had genius within me and it was up to me to uncover it, not wait for other people to find it. My success or failure was my choice and no one else's. Wow, what a realization! I was the one who could make anything happen by believing in myself, and staying focused on goals that aligned with my values. I was in charge of my life.

So often, we look at people who are considered to be geniuses and wonder what they have that we don't have. From what I've seen, most geniuses, instead of accepting the status quo, learn how to think out of the box. They take things out of that box and turn them around, upside down and inside out. From the most successful entrepreneurs to the greatest scientists, this ability to look at life from new angles is what results in those "ah ha!" moments we associate with genius.

Leonardo da Vinci believed that. He advocated always looking at problems and dilemmas from different perspectives. For instance, by seeking commonalities in the relationship between the ring of a bell and a stone hitting water, he discovered that sound travels in waves.

Einstein always formulated his theories in as many different ways as possible. While other scientists used mathematical formulas to reach their conclusions, Einstein — a known visual thinker — often drew pictures and diagrams. Numbers did not play a significant role in his thinking process.

You may feel you need an IQ like Einstein's to be a genius, but according to Dr. Martin Brooks, there seems to be "no single recipe" for genius. High IQ doesn't always predict genius, nor does academic achievement.

"Genius, it seems, demands the expression of qualities often denied by traditional schooling and intelligence tests," Dr. Brooks says. "Though exceptional ability may be a key ingredient, you must also throw courage and creativity into the mix. Top that off with a talent for visualizing problems from new and original angles, and you may be getting somewhere towards that elusive formula."

To illustrate his point, Dr. Brooks refers to the case of Tony DeBlois, a musician who could play 20 instruments and had more than 8,000 songs committed to memory. DeBlois also suffered from a form of autism known as savant syndrome. People with this syndrome often have exceptional abilities in one area, and remarkable deficiencies in another area. Think of Dustin Hoffman in the movie *Rain Man*.

In other words, it's not what you've got — it's what you do with it. In 1921, Dr. Lewis Terman of Stanford University launched a decades-long study of 1,528 children who had IQs above the genius level. He wanted to find the correlation between IQ and success. Like Dr. Brooks, he discovered IQ was *not* the most vital component of success. The real success factors, he found, were self-confidence, perseverance and the ability to set goals.

If you have learned to hide your light and reject your ideas, it's time to take a deep look at the person you really are — the genius who was born with the potential and the spirit to realize your dreams. In fact, the root of the word genius is the Roman word that means "spirit." Take a moment to ask yourself, "What would my life be like if I were to allow the spirit of my inner genius to shine?"

Don't wait to feel like a genius before you set off on a journey to a more fulfilling life. "It's easier to act your way into new ways of feeling," the famous educator Susan Glaser once said, "than to feel yourself into new ways of acting."

The time to act is now. You have what you need. It's time to believe in yourself and leave the runway.

Turn Your Possibility Radar On

Steven Funk was fortunate to find the confidence to create the life he wanted. Doing this means stepping back and looking at the possibilities around you rather than staying in situations that make you unhappy, unhealthy, or both. The following story, often told by inspirational speaker John Assaraf, is a good example of the need to do this.

One day a man walked into a room and noticed a fly buzzing frantically against a windowpane. When the man looked again in 10 minutes, the fly was still buzzing away at the window. Three hours later, he walked by the window again and the fly was dead, lying on the window ledge along with several other dead flies. Just across from the window which the fly had been madly buzzing against only hours before, was an open door — yet not one fly had tried to get out through the door.

We sometimes spend a lot of our lives trying to pursue dreams and objectives by "buzzing" against the window of life. We see our goals in front of us and feel if we just "buzz" harder and longer we'll be rewarded. In fact, we should stop our frantic "buzzing," back up and look around for another opening.

That's exactly what Dr. Kumar Shivdasani, a physician at Vancouver General Hospital, did after attending a LifePilot workshop. Since then, he says he has learned to focus on what really matters to him: his values, his strengths, his growth potential and his goals.

"I've been blessed by a number of wonderful experiences," he says, "largely as result of the empowering seeds of ideas planted during your LifePilot workshop. Opportunities have come into my life that I recognized as 'opportunities' because they touched and connected with my values, strengths, and in some ways even what I perceived as weaknesses…I've been able to face many of my fears and overcome those obstacles of, 'oh no, I can't do that!' As a result of walking through my fears, I've done a list of things my mind said I couldn't do: half-marathons and eventually a full marathon, triathlons, and climbing the tallest peak outside of the Himalayas — Mt. Aconcagua (almost 23,000 feet)."

Inspired by the possibilities he now saw in his life, Dr. Shivdasani went on to climb another of the Seven Summits — Mt. Elbrus in Russia, the tallest peak in Europe. He also became involved in a charity devoted to raising money for children's health initiatives.

When I think of people like Dr. Shivdasani, who found the courage to create the life he really wanted, I'm reminded of what theologian Carl Bard said: "Though no one can go back and make a brand new start, anyone can start from now and make a brand new ending."

* There are basically three types of people in this world and they all take different approaches to flying: passive, active and proactive. All have the same potential, but some are better at pushing past their fears to create the lives they want.

* Your greatest limits are not external. They are internal, within your own thought processes.

* We are all born geniuses; some of us are just more aware of our genius than others. Look inside and recognize your inner genius, that pure potential we all possess.

* Most of the people considered to be geniuses simply learned to think out of the box instead of accepting the status quo.

SECRET 7

Set a Course for Success

Let's say you are piloting a plane and, due to unexpected bad weather, you find yourself off course. Do you stay off course once you've discovered your error? This is the time to check your instruments — your values — and do a course correction. In a worst-case scenario, you may be forced to make an emergency landing and reassess. Are your priorities in line with your values? Are you focusing on goals you don't really care about? Remember, the results you obtain are almost certainly the result of your focus.

Certainly, the story of Canadian athlete Terry Fox is a prime example of the power of focusing on pre-determined goals. His story also highlights an outstanding ability to make course corrections in light of seemingly insurmountable obstacles. As a young man, Terry was struck by bone cancer; he had to have his right leg amputated six inches above the knee. His experience inspired him to create the Marathon of Hope to raise awareness and money for cancer research.

In 1980, Terry began his cross-Canada run, from the East Coast to the West Coast of this huge country. Despite having only one leg, he averaged over 26 miles per day for 143 days. Halfway across Canada, with 3,300 miles behind him, Terry was forced to stop the run. The cancer had spread to his lungs.

"I was doing what I wanted," he said, "and a dream was coming true, and that, above everything else, made it all worthwhile to me. Even though it was so difficult, there was not another thing in the world I would have rather been doing. I'm not a dreamer, and I'm not saying this will initiate any kind of definitive answer or cure to cancer, but I believe in miracles. I have to."

Though he didn't survive to see the results of his run, 25 years later his Marathon of Hope has raised over $270 million and his legacy continues.

Ask for Support

Terry Fox knew he needed the support of others for his dream to succeed. To achieve your dreams, build your support team of friends, family, co-workers, employees, mentors and more. If money allows it, think about hiring an assistant to help out at work or at home. You can't do it all. That's why it's important to delegate where you can.

I have no problem empowering people to help me reach my goals. Nor do I have any ego issues about asking for help. In the companies I own, I believe in launching initiatives then turning daily operations over to people I trust. This frees me to focus on the big picture and do what I'm best at. It also gives others a chance to grow. When you talk to people about your values, and trust them to help you fulfill your goals and priorities, you are often able to achieve your aims more effectively, and you are less likely to experience burn-out.

The Perils of Perfectionism

I wasn't always good at empowering others to assist me. In my earlier years, I wanted things to always be perfect. I think back now on how much frustration and stress it caused me and the people around me to achieve that 100 percent. Then I learned that the difference between 100 percent and 87 percent usually wasn't noticeable to anyone but me. The energy needed to attain the other 13 percent wasn't worth it.

With this realization, I adjusted my standards, delegated more, and subsequently gained more free time to do the things I wanted.

Another thing I learned was that many people could do things as well as I could — and in some cases, even better. By delegating more and empowering others to help me, I gained more time and energy for myself.

If you quit being a perfectionist, you will be amazed at the results. You can always save your special projects and demand 100 percent from them, but as a general rule 87 percent is usually just fine. You now have a new rule in your life — The Rule of 87.

In their book *Art and Fear*, David Bayles and Tony Orland share the story of an experiment conducted by a pottery teacher who divided his class of beginners in half. He told half of the class that the more pots they created, the higher their grades would be. He told the other half of the class they would be graded on the quality of their pots. They would only receive A's if they created perfect pieces of pottery. So who won the challenge? Many people would guess that the students tasked with creating perfect pieces of pottery were the winners. Actually, the real winners were the students who were graded on creating the most pottery because they had been allowed to learn from their mistakes.

Throughout the ages, artists have known the power of avoiding perfection. Japanese artists ensured their works contained "wabi flaws." These flaws were considered artistic signatures; experts could identify the artist by the flaw. The miniaturists of India, the carpet makers of Persia, and the silversmiths of Turkey, always put deliberate flaws in their works. We're told that this is because attempting perfection is an insult to God. Similarly, Native Americans typically wove a broken bead into their beaded works. These beads were called spirit beads — reminders that nothing created by humans can be perfect, because only the Creator is perfect.

We should not be afraid of our flaws and our mistakes. They are a natural and necessary part of our lives. By letting go of the quest for perfection, we begin to discover more time in our lives for the things that really deserve our focus.

Pursue Your Passions

Everyone has things they are passionate about, and it's important to put your focus on these things. Sometimes you just need to be reminded about your passions, or to rediscover them. Make a list of five things you are passionate about and find a way to ensure they fit with every task you do. Doing this will bring you closer to realizing the goals you value most. As an old army sergeant used to tell me, "If that doesn't turn you on then you haven't got any switches."

Focus on Your Strengths

Imagine holding a beautiful vase of indigo-colored water. You set it out on your patio and forget about it overnight. During the night, it rains. When you remember the vase in the morning, you find it overflowing; the water is no longer indigo. It is a weak blue, almost clear.

Our lives are like that. Many of us have remarkable strengths that we water down by adding too many elements. Soon, we feel we've lost the ability to do anything well. "Strength is always specific!" says motivational writer and speaker Peter Drucker. "Nobody ever commented, for example, that the great violinist Jascha Heifetz probably couldn't play the trumpet very well."

"You cannot make it as a wandering generality," says Zig Ziglar, another motivational expert. "You must become a meaningful specific."

John Ratey has studied and written about various mental disorders such as Obsessive Compulsive Disorder. In his book *Shadow Syndromes*, he writes, "One of my patients had developed a company that IBM wanted to buy. He had all these people working for him, and he was just 32 years old. But the only thing he was focused on was going back to college to prove to himself that he was smart — he hadn't graduated because he failed math. Here he was blaming himself for this deficit, for not being good at math, instead of enjoying his accomplishments."

Nike is arguably the world's most famous athletic gear company. How did it become the leader? Focus has a great deal to do with it. "We wanted Nike to be the world's best sports and fitness company," says CEO Philip Knight. "Once you say that, you have a focus. You don't end up making wing tips or sponsoring the next Rolling Stones' world tour."

There is a German proverb that says, "The main thing is keeping the main thing the main thing." Most successful people possess a laser-beam ability to focus on the task at hand. "On the day I'm performing, I don't hear anything anyone says to me," says opera great Luciano Pavarotti.

Former world heavyweight champion George Foreman honed his ability to screen out anything that took away from the positive energy he needed to win. "That's my gift," Foreman said. "I let that negativity roll off me like water off a duck's back. If it's not positive, I didn't hear it. If you can overcome that, fights are easy."

Winston Churchill, England's wartime prime minister, was revered for his focus. That focus and determination is clear in this excerpt from a famous speech. "Never give in, never give in, never, never, never, never, in nothing, great or small, large or petty, never give in except to convictions of honor and good sense." With this sense of focus, Churchill inspired the British to withstand years of war, leading them to eventual victory.

Create Space for Spontaneity

John Lennon said, "Life is what happens when you're making other plans." Some people plan their lives away, but despite my encouragement to schedule as much as you can, I also urge you to leave space for spontaneity. Without spontaneous moments of magic, life is a bit like waking up on your birthday and already knowing what's inside every present. It's just not as much fun! So just as you need to occasionally accommodate unpleasant items that come up, you also need to leave enough room in your life to allow for these wonderful moments of spontaneity. For instance, maybe you didn't plan for the sunset to be so spectacular (how could you?) but when you look out your window and see the sky in bloom, you might just need to put aside work for an hour to walk on the beach with your partner. If you get a sudden invitation to a concert that was sold out — and it's your dream performer — why should you say no just because you vowed to cut the grass that evening?

When these things arise, look at your values, evaluate your priorities and decide from there. For example, if your child has an important piano recital, you may have to say no to your dream rock concert. He'll remember years from now that you were absent, probably long after you've forgotten your concert. If taking a dream cruise means losing an important promotion, is it worth it? For some people it might be. For others, who have listed career success as a key value, it might not be.

Recently, my wife Rita and I had to make a decision that meant turning down the opportunity to spend the weekend on a 262-foot boat at the Cannes Film Festival. Although the offer was very tempting, we actually passed on it after examining our values and priorities. We knew we had a lot of work to do on LifePilot that weekend, which is, of course, a real value for us. The time slot to do this work was our last for quite a while, so the decision was an easy one for both of us.

When I set up my calendar, I use a simple structure. If I'm going somewhere interesting or exciting, I build in as much unscheduled time as I can. This gives me the flexibility to expand or contract the windows of time I have in my life. I also structure my time in blocks so I'll have very busy times — fully scheduled — and large blocks of unscheduled time, from a week to a month at a time. This way, I may find myself working like crazy for a week or two, but I am rewarded with total down time during which I can enjoy my passions, such as driving my classic cars, going scuba diving or heading to some destination I want to really explore. For instance, Rita said she has always wanted to go back to Istanbul. We had a "block" of time available so off we went for a fantastic week of discovery in this exotic city.

Some of the habits I've developed over the years allow me to enjoy free time while still doing the things I need to do to maintain my career and lifestyle. For example, instead of going to dinner with one couple, I try to go with two or three couples in an area or city we are visiting. If I go to a movie, I often invite close friends along. That way we get to see the movie and also enjoy each other's company. Perhaps, we'll go for dinner before or after the movie. When Rita and I travel to a new city on business or pleasure, we do a lot of research to ensure we get full value from the time we'll spend there. Rita constantly researches opportunities, and I usually look after the people to see.

After I turned 50, I began to schedule in three months every year in some destination other than the city in which I lived. This takes me out of my usual patterns and I feel a surge in creativity as I meet new people and discover different ways of living.

If you work in the same environment all your life and take one month of holidays each year at the same time, your mind doesn't get a chance to become truly spontaneous — because spontaneity has no room to enter. It's like sending out a message that says "No Vacancy." Try varying your routine and visiting new places near and far. Once in a while, do something on the spur of the moment.

I've already told you about my experience of flying on the Concorde. The dream had been with me for some time, but booking that flight was a spontaneous reaction to having given a successful speech in Toronto. I wanted to celebrate and the Concorde flight was my spur-of-the-moment reward. What I learned from that flight has become one of the driving philosophies of my life.

Keep in Balance

We've established that focus is a vital part of achieving success. Now I want to risk confusing you by telling you to be wary of focusing too much on one thing, and missing the bigger picture. Most people I have observed become so immersed in detail, they wouldn't notice a train speeding towards them until it was too late.

At that point, many of them just shut their eyes and work harder, hoping a miracle will happen and the train will not hit them.

To illustrate what happens when we over-focus, I show participants in the LifePilot workshops a video of two teams playing basketball. One team is dressed in white; the other is in black. "I want you to watch closely and count the number of times the white team passes the ball back and forth," I tell the audience.

As I play the video, the audience's concentration is palpable. They lean forward intently, their eyes darting back and forth as the basketball passes from team member to team member. Then I pause the video. "Ok, how many passes?" I ask them. The guesses come back to me: 15, 16, 17?

"Watch it again and this time *really* focus." I push play and we watch the same scenario.

"How many passes?" I ask again. Once again they call out. Some people have revised their previous answers.

"Let's watch it one more time. Focus!" I press play. Now they are confused. They squint at the screen. They second-guess themselves. They grit their teeth.

"Ok," I say, stopping the video. "How many?" Some of them are very sure. The number is 17. Others are exhausted by the act of focusing so intently.

"You've all focused really hard, but I'm wondering who noticed the big gorilla that walked through the middle of the action as the teams were passing the ball?"

There is a hushed silence. A few people smile knowingly. The rest look dazed. Gorilla? What gorilla?

The majority of people admit they didn't notice the gorilla. I play the video again and there it is, clear as day. Most of the audience cannot believe their eyes when they see a gorilla walk into the video, thump his chest, then walk off the other side of the screen. Some swear the first two videos did not have the gorilla on the screen and demand that I show them the video again.

The lesson in this is that sometimes we become too focused and miss the whole picture, only seeing the portion we are focusing on. Daniel J. Simons of the University of Illinois and Christopher F. Chabris of Harvard University refer to this as "intentional blindness" or "change blindness." They believe the human brain is constantly seeking to create narratives of meaning out of what we see. When something doesn't "fit the script," we wipe it from our consciousness. This *does* help us focus and deal with confusing sensory input, but it also means we can miss vital information. Often, we don't even know what we're missing.

In his paper "Current Approaches to Change Blindness," Simons relates yet another fascinating experiment. "In a recent study," he writes, "one experimenter approached a pedestrian (the subject) to ask for directions. During their conversation, two other people rudely interrupted them by carrying a door between the experimenter and the pedestrian. During the time that the subject's view was obstructed, a different experimenter replaced the first experimenter. Only 50 percent of observers noticed the change even though the two experimenters wore different clothing, were different heights and builds, had different haircuts, and had noticeably different voices."

"You can't depend on your eyes when your imagination is out of focus," Mark Twain wisely wrote.

Remember I talked earlier about achieving a balance in the way we focus. The gorilla watchers became so immersed in the details, they couldn't see the big picture, but some people are so intent on the big picture, they can't see the details.

To illustrate this, let's switch for a moment from gorillas to whales. In my workshops, I often tell the story of the great Blue Whale. Imagine this incredible creature, the largest mammal alive, swimming through the ocean. At 80 feet long and up to 150 tons, this leviathan is so large and so dominant, it doesn't even notice a pod of orcas swimming alongside and biting small chunks out of its blubber. It is, after all, 20 times larger than each of its attackers. Why should it worry? The orcas seem unimportant — until one of them bites deep and slices into a vital organ. At that point, it's too late.

Have you ever felt like you had it all together? Did having it all together feel so great you forgot to check the details? Check your focus and adjust it so that you have a healthy balance between the micro and macro.

The Power of Discernment

In *Life Matters: Creating a Dynamic Balance of Work, Family, Time & Money*, Roger and Rebecca Merrill pinpoint the issue. "If we totally immerse ourselves in a project, we're afraid we'll lose awareness of the people and opportunities around us. On the other hand, if we try to be aware, we can't give projects the intense focus they need for successful completion. As a result, we often live suspended in a mediocre middle world, only moderately aware, essentially unfocused, feeling victimized by the things coming at us and guilty about what's not getting done."

The answer to this dilemma, according to the Merrills, lies in "discovering, calibrating, and regularly using the wonderful gift we have called the gift of discernment. Properly developed, this gift empowers us to constantly scan for, recognize and respond to what is most important, even when we're focused on something else."

By following the LifePilot philosophy, discernment becomes far simpler because you have your values to navigate by. When life becomes overwhelming and you don't know where to focus first, always go back and check goals and activities against your values.

This will streamline your priorities and tell you where you should be putting your focus.

Have you ever seen a movie about a prison, where bright searchlights beaming from watchtowers continuously sweep the prison yard, probing corners to ensure nothing is out of the ordinary? Ideally, part of you is always scanning and taking in information. The more you practice focusing, the better you'll become at directing your searchlight, while keeping part of your mind open to anything unusual.

You *Can* Have It Both Ways

Some people may tell you that you are either a big picture person or a details person. While we certainly may be predisposed to one type or another, it doesn't mean we can't learn to adjust our focus as necessary. Think of stargazers like Galileo and Kepler. Even as they looked out as far as they could see into the universe, they continued to think in terms of the smallest details of astronomy, which is a science that requires an ability to see far, then work out mathematical formulas to support their hypotheses. "Keep your eyes on the stars and your feet on the ground," Theodore Roosevelt said. After all, you would have to be very tall indeed to keep your feet on the ground with your head in the clouds.

To achieve this balance, set aside a regular time each week to step back and review your values, goal and activities — and prioritize them. I do this every Sunday in my *LifeManual*. I look at everything that's important to me — my values, my wife, my children, my grandchildren, my friends, and my business — and I ask myself if they are all receiving their fair share of my attention. Essentially, I check my focus.

Past, Present, Future

Time is elastic. Realizing this is another key to keeping our focus where it needs to be. Some people put the majority of their focus on what's behind them, whether it's pain, pleasure or melancholy that keeps their focus there. We can learn from lessons of the past and grow from them, but we can't stay there if we hope to create the future we want.

Similarly, we should venture into the future to check out the landscape and plant our dreams there. But if we live solely in the future, we will surrender our ability to enjoy where we are in life now and to do the work to make our dreams come true.

John Lennon said, "Be here now." He was talking about living in the moment and experiencing it fully. Malcolm S. Forbes said, "Presence is more than just being there." Donald Trump sums it up nicely: "I try to learn from the past, but I plan for the future by focusing exclusively on the present. That's were the fun is."

I used to live in Trump Tower in New York City, so I've seen firsthand the fantastic results of Donald Trump's ability to focus. Whatever Donald Trump does, he does it big. Like anyone interested in real estate, I've watched Trump rise, fall and rise again. In his book *How to Get Rich*, Trump talks about the role that focus, or lack thereof, played in losing his fortune in the late 80s. Until then, Trump had made money easily; headlines confirmed that everything he touched turned to gold. But he self-admittedly lost focus. "I'd fly off to Europe to attend fashions shows, and I wasn't looking at the clothing," he writes. "My lack of attention was killing my business."

When the market crashed, Trump crashed with it. He recalls passing a beggar in the street at one point and thinking, "That the beggar was worth more than me." Trump learned his lesson just as I did several years before. "I work as hard today as I did when I was a young developer in the 1970s," he writes, "Don't make the mistake I did. Stay focused."

Use Props for Inspiration

When I was immersed in my own economic challenges, which I wrote about in detail in my previous book *Never Fight With a Pig*, I went out and bought a GI camouflage helmet and presented it to my lawyer, John Norton. I needed him to be totally focused on solving my considerable problems. "If we're going to win this war," I told him, "we need to think 24/7 of our strategies. Losing isn't acceptable." John placed the helmet in a very prominent place in his office.

We *did* win that war. It took as long as the real war — five years — but we did it. With the amount of focus we put on winning, there was no way we could lose.

If you ever find yourself in need of motivation to achieve your objectives, find whatever item you can to keep you and your team focused so they never forget how important their support is to you. The reason there are winners and losers is because of focus. To win, stay totally and completely absorbed with the success of your objectives.

So far in this chapter we've talked about humans, gorillas and blue whales, so why not rabbits? An old saying advises, "If you chase two rabbits, both will escape." It's a good piece of wisdom to end this chapter on. Keep your focus and set goals — don't let your dreams escape.

Chapter Review

* Pursue what you love with passion. Ensure that what you love to do is already well represented in your values.

* Successful people know how to focus and screen out anything that doesn't relate to their values, goals and priorities.

* Part of the art of effective focus is also being able to step back when necessary and scan the big picture. Watch for gorillas! At the same time, don't get so lost in the big picture that you don't notice the details.

* Empower people you trust to help you achieve your goals and maintain your focus.

* In your planning, seek balance. This is vital to achieving fulfillment and keeping your stress levels down.

* Leave room for spontaneity in your life.

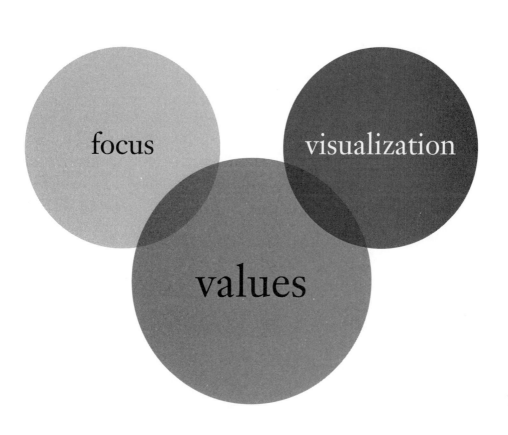

> "What you think about is what you will become." *Earl Nightingale*
>
> "I do believe, and I have seen in my own life, that creative visualization works." *Oprah Winfrey*

SECRET 8

What You See is What You Get

By now you understand the power of focusing intently to create the life you want. The next step is to learn how to direct that energy into reality through creative visualization. Have you ever pictured yourself climbing a podium to accept an award, or giving a speech to a wildly enthusiastic crowd? That's visualization! Successful people tend to focus on a positive picture of the future whereas unsuccessful people often focus on problems and fears.

What we visualize reinforces the way we approach our lives. The world we *believe* we live in is, in fact, the world we *live* in. To discover a successful future, we need to visualize it. For some of us, this might mean we need to change our vision of our lives and ask, "Which movie do I want to star in?"

Sometimes the results are truly amazing. My friend Alfredo J. Molina is owner of Molina Fine Jewelers in Phoenix, Arizona. Alfredo has built a remarkable business with a tradition of excellence that dates back to the Italian Renaissance, but like so many of us, he began with nothing. He remembers arriving in the United States as a young boy and a refuge from Cuba. His family's first American home was in Chicago where the Catholic Diocese took them in and put them up at the Wilson Hotel, which was condemned and torn down just months later.

Somewhere along the way, Alfredo developed the belief that the unconscious mind is a powerful thing. He combined hard work with visualization to realize his success. In fact, the home he ended up living in is the same home he clipped a picture of years ago.

He visualized his Phoenix store out of what had previously been a parking lot. Today, Molina Fine Jewelers is housed in one of the city's most beautiful buildings.

Just Imagine

Credited for centuries as a profound and useful technique, creative visualization can be described simply as using your imagination to create what you desire. Like Alfredo Molina, many other successful people, from Walt Disney to Oprah Winfrey, have used visualization to achieve the lives they want. As far as they're concerned, it's not a matter of "if" they will achieve their dreams — it's a matter of "when." This focus and passion for achieving a goal creates energy to which others respond. This in turn builds momentum. Before you know it, your plane has left the runway and you are in flight.

"The future is simply infinite possibility waiting to happen," according to American futurist Leland Kaiser. "What it waits on is human imagination to crystallize its possibility."

Professional athletes are some of the strongest proponents of creative visualization. "Almost all of the world-class athletes and other peak performers are visualizers," says Steven Covey, author of *The Seven Habits of Highly Effective People*. "They see it; they feel it; they experience it before they actually do it. They began with the end in mind. You can do it in every area of your life." Former Mr. Universe Arnold Schwarzenegger, now governor of California, says that when he has the image of a particular muscle in mind when he's pumping weights, the benefit to that muscle is 10 times that of exercising when his mind is unfocused.

Camille Duvall-Hero, ranked by *Sports Illustrated* as one of the "100 Greatest Female Athletes of the Century," visualized winning water skiing championships. "The morning of a tournament," she says, "before I put my feet on the floor, I visualize myself making perfect runs with emphasis on technique, all the way through to what my personal best is in practice. The more you work with this type of visualization, especially when you do it on a day-to-day basis, you'll actually begin to feel your muscles contracting at the appropriate times."

According to exercise physiologist Elizabeth Quinn, M.S., "Such repeated imagery can build both experience and confidence in an athlete's ability to perform certain skills under pressure, and in a variety of possible situations. The most effective visualization techniques result in a very vivid sport experience in which the athlete has complete control over a successful performance."

Swiss triathlon champion Brigitte McMahon says she visualized the final sprint to the finish in her mind many times before ever coming to the Olympics in Australia. She feels this technique gave her the advantage because she had seen the win in her mind long before she crossed the finish line.

One of the most fascinating stories of the power of visualization is that of Air Force Colonel George Hall, who was captured by the North Vietnamese and imprisoned in a dark box for seven years. For each day of those seven long years, the POW played a full game of golf in his mind. One week after his release from the camp, he entered the Greater New Orleans Open. He shot a score of 76.

It's as Real as it Seems

Visualization isn't just for people who are interested in sports. In the West, medical experts have begun to realize the benefits of creative visualization in their work with critically ill patients. By encouraging their patients to visualize a strong immune system, they found the patients stood a greater chance of fighting cancer. Mark Victor Hansen, who co-created *Chicken Soup for the Soul* with Jack Canfield, recently told writer Mark Litman a remarkable story about the power of visualization.

"First of all," he said, "you've got to figure out what you really want. In my case and in Jack's case, we didn't want a best-selling book. We wanted a MEGA best-selling book, *Chicken Soup for the*

Soul. Beyond that, we didn't really want a best-selling book, we wanted to make a best-selling SERIES.... We cut out the *New York Times Bestseller* list. Then we put our names at the top before we ever got to the top in real life. Then we put it on my mirror and we put one up at Jack's office, on his mirror. So in our mind's eye, when we were shaving, or the ladies were doing cosmetics, we owned the concept that we were best-selling authors before we actually were best selling."

In *Brainstorms and Thunderbolts*, King Gillette, who brought us the Gillette razor, wrote about his experience with visualization. "As I stood there with the razor in my hand...the Gillette razor was born — more with the rapidity of a dream than by a process of reasoning. In that moment I saw it all: the way the blade would be held in a holder; the idea of sharpening two opposite edges on a thin piece of steel; the clamping plates for the blade, with a handle halfway between the two edges of the blade. All this came more in pictures than conscious thought, as though the razor were already a finished thing and held before my eyes. I stood there before that mirror in a trance of joy...I could not foresee the trials and tribulations I was to pass through before the razor was a success. But I believed it with my whole heart."

One of my favorite stories about the power of visualization dates back to when I met my wife Rita, 18 years ago. I'm adept at many things, but at that time, skiing was not one of them. So one day when Rita said, "Let's go skiing!" I found myself in a bit of a dilemma. She wanted us to head up to Whistler, a top-rated ski resort. I hadn't skied since I left home at 15. So naturally, I said, "Sure, let's do it!" And naturally, I didn't tell Rita I barely knew how to ski. I came up with a plan.

I went and bought a video by the French Olympic ski champion Jean-Claude Killy. I decided to watch the video and learn from the master, but I was so caught up in the flurry of life and business that I never found time to look at the tape. The days passed and suddenly the skiing weekend was upon me. I began to wonder how I was going to pull this off.

By the time I was able to watch the tape, I was already in my limo on the way up to Whistler Ski Resort to meet Rita. I put the video in the car's VCR and watched it over and over during the three-hour drive to the ski hill.

The next morning, Rita and I stepped into our skis, hopped on the chair lift and headed up the mountain. Well, I did manage to make it out of the chair okay without falling on my face. Just as I was quietly congratulating myself, Rita tipped her skis to the left and veered off straight down one of the steepest hills I've even seen. I swallowed and took a deep breath. My resolve to show her I could keep up was strong, so off I went. My form may not have been as good as Jean-Claude Killy's or Rita's, but I did make it down the mountain in one piece. I know 100 percent that it was from watching those videos. To me, that's the power of visualization.

When I used to run in marathons, I practiced visualization. I would picture myself running into a stadium full of people, all cheering me on. *I'm in the lead, ahead of the pack, and the crowd is yelling and screaming, "Come on, Peter, you can do it!" I hear the cheering in my head and see the people lining the route.* The ability to see the end results before you begin is a very powerful tool.

A Closer Look at Visualization

The more pragmatic among you may be thinking, "Isn't this the stuff of yogis and mystics? How, in the age of Internet, biotech and reason, can we possibly believe we can create our success by visualizing it? There are many theories about why creative visualization works. What you ultimately believe is up to you. I only know it's worked in my life and the lives of some of the most successful people I know.

Some people approach visualization on a purely pragmatic level — they believe when you visualize an outcome, you naturally devote yourself to making it happen. Your focus and hard work results in success.

Others look to neuroscience for answers. Studies have shown the brain doesn't distinguish between internal and external vision. When we visualize something enough, our body comes to believe the vision is real.

John Assaraf, a former street gang member who broke free of his past to become a multi-millionaire before age 30, writes about the biological foundations of creative visualization. He believes that we build "cells of recognition" in our memory banks.

"When you continuously focus on an image in your mind," he writes, "every cell in your body is involved in that image…it eventually becomes 'fixed' and you automatically attract and move towards that which you desire. The reason athletes do this is because they want to condition their mind in such a way that the body automatically behaves the way they want it to without effort. It is the only way to become 'unconsciously competent.' When you visualize the goal over and over again, your body will eventually automatically do whatever it must to make the image a physical reality."

Still others look to quantum physics for answers. Some scientists now believe reality is affected by the consciousness observing it, and that nothing in the universe exists independent of our perception of it. In short, we create our own realities. Whenever we think of doing something, we typically hold two opposing thoughts in our minds: one is that we can do it, the other is that we cannot. By focusing on what we "can" do, success becomes our reality. The possibility of failure ceases to exist because it does not exist in our consciousness.

Invest in Visualization

Visualization costs nothing but the time it takes to imagine and concentrate, yet the rewards are limitless. That makes it a great investment risk. To visualize, you don't need to meditate or consult any business experts or gurus. You can begin simply by focusing on what you want to become a reality in your life. Do you see your business growing to occupy a full city block and making the

Fortune 500 list? What does it look like? Are there any pictures that exemplify your vision? Cut them out, as Alfredo Molina did, and post them where you can see them every day. Be clear about what you want. Create the space in your life for it. As someone once said, "It's unlikely you'll get a new pair of shoes unless you make room in your life for them." So make room in your reality for success.

Every Sunday, I reserve time to reflect on the week behind me and plan and visualize what I want to happen in the days, months and years ahead. I open my *LifeManual* to the section where I keep photos of my wife, my daughter and my grandchildren. I visualize the happiness I get from spending time with them. I also have pictures of the kind of dog I hope to get one day, and other reminders of the people, experiences, things and ideas I want to be part of my life. As I flip though my collection of pictures, I might picture myself delivering a great LifePilot workshop, mastering a new fitness technique or sitting in a rocking chair years from now, sharing stories with my grandkids of all the wonderful experiences I've had.

Many people will tell you that in order for visualization to work, you must make the transition from wanting something to the belief that you already possess it. Scientist Nikola Tesla said, "When I get a new idea, I start at once building it up in my imagination, and make improvements and operate the device in my mind. When I have gone so far as to embody everything in my invention, every possible improvement I can think of, and when I see no fault anywhere, I put into concrete form the final product of my brain."

For Tesla, the idea came into existence in his mind long before he built anything. He exemplified what Bo Bennet, author of *Year to Success*, meant when he wrote, "Visualization is daydreaming with a purpose."

Focusing on photographs really helps me solidify images in my mind of what I want to achieve. I do this to prepare for public speaking or when planning what kind of car I want to purchase. For me, it's more than idle dreaming. I'm not just wishing — I'm actually there.

Even as a young entrepreneur, I believed in the power of visualization to make dreams come true. One day, when I was a 29-year-old living in Edmonton, I was flipping through a magazine and saw a picture of a Lear jet. I had never seen anything more beautiful in my entire life. I wanted that jet! When I looked at the picture of it, I actually saw myself in it. I clipped the picture out and tacked it on my wall. Six years later I had a Lear jet.

You May Say I'm a Dreamer

"I don't dream at night, I dream all day," says director Steven Spielberg. "I dream for a living."

Like Spielberg, most successful people are incredible dreamers who know how to turn their dreams into reality. Howard Hughes, once known as the world's richest man, also dreamed for a living. But until Martin Scorsese made the Oscar-winning film, *The Aviator*, many people didn't realize the depth and extent of Hughes' ability to visualize and create.

Hughes once held every speed record that mattered. At various times in his life he owned an international airline, an aircraft company, a major motion picture studio, mining properties, gambling casinos, Las Vegas hotels, and a medical research institute.

While it's true that Hughes died as a recluse, locked in the prison of his Obsessive Compulsive Disorder, in his early years he was applauded as a powerful visionary.

Hughes inherited his shares to the Hughes Tool Company fortune after his father died when Hughes was just 18 years old. The company had made millions from the patent of a new oil-drilling bit. The fortune was merely fuel for his passion for flight, which began with his first ride in a plane as a young boy. At 21, he began shooting *Hell's Angels*, a tribute to World War I flying aces. The film cost $250,000 — a staggering amount of money in those days — and took 18 months to film. During the filming, Hughes amassed the largest private airplane collection in the world. Although he went on to make other films, his real interest lay in aviation: to fly fastest, highest and farthest.

In 1934, he broke his first speed record, clocking 185 miles an hour in a converted Boeing pursuit plane. Next, he and his team built the H-1, a plane with the first retractable landing gear. He piloted the H-1 at a new speed record of 352 mph. That same year he founded Hughes Aircraft Company. In 1937, Hughes flew from Los Angeles to New Jersey in seven hours and 28 minutes, setting a coast-to-coast record. In 1938, he flew around the world in three days, 19 hours and 17 minutes, cutting in half Charles Lindbergh's New York-to-Paris record. New York City threw a ticker tape parade in his honor.

During World War II, Hughes aimed to transform Hughes Aircraft into a major airplane manufacturer after winning government contracts for a photo-reconnaissance plane (Hughes crashed the prototype on a test flight) and an aircraft large enough to carry military troops, equipment and supplies over the Atlantic to avoid the German U-boats. Because of a short supply of metal during WWII, the "Spruce Goose" was built mainly of birch, not spruce as its nickname suggests. It had eight engines, a wingspan longer than a football field and weighed 400,000 pounds. It remains the biggest plane ever built. Hughes flew it only once in Long Beach Harbor on November 2, 1947.

He eventually purchased TWA, and fought hard for the right to fly international routes, lobbying against a monopoly by the powerful Pan Am.

"For all of his faults (and there were many of them)," writes author and coach Dr. Phillip E. Humbert, "and for all the craziness in his life (and there was lots of it), Howard Hughes knew the power of focus. He could say a clear, resounding YES! to the things that interested him. Even when it meant ignoring enormous pressures and losing millions of dollars and being labeled 'irresponsible,' he could concentrate on a FEW THINGS and achieve incredible results. He knew his priorities, even when the rest of the world thought he was crazy. We can learn from that."

Who knows what Hughes may have become if he hadn't suffered from Obsessive Compulsive Disorder. Nevertheless, his vision took us higher, faster and farther than anyone else at the time ever dreamed possible. *The Aviator*, starring Leonardo DiCaprio, features a fitting tagline: "Some men dream the future. He built it."

Keep it Real

So why are some people so adept at visualizing their dreams and turning those dreams into reality? In my experience, total dedication is crucial. Some people zigzag from impulse to impulse with no clear, consistent sense of purpose. "All successful men and women are big dreamers," says author Brian Tracy, a leader in human potential. "They imagine what their future could be, ideal in every respect, and then they work every day toward their distant vision, that goal or purpose."

Howard Hughes never doubted his vision. He possessed a "burning desire" to succeed, which Napoleon Hill, who interviewed 500 of the most successful people of all time, said is the one characteristic people who succeed are never without.

Keep it Positive

If you believe your subconscious mind is a powerful tool for creating reality out of imagination, you cannot afford the luxury of a negative thought. If you want a positive outcome, then embody optimism.

"Thought can attract to us only that which we first mentally embody," says Ernest S. Holmes, author of *Creative Mind*. "We cannot attract to ourselves that which we are not."

Another important step, which many people ignore, is the move from vision to action. You may practice visualization, but if you aren't taking action, then it's like passively watching a movie. You may enjoy the movie, but don't expect it to continue to play outside the theatre of your head.

Walt Disney was a believer in creative visualization. One day as he sat on a bench at an amusement park, watching his daughters play, he noticed how dirty the park was. He also noticed that the kids' parents were all anxious to go, even though the kids were having fun. He began to visualize a better amusement park, a clean, safe place that could be enjoyed by children and parents alike. That idea became Disneyland.

Before building the world's largest theme park, Disney traveled the USA. He visited Thomas Edison's Workshop, the Wright Brothers' Bicycle Shop, and the home of dictionary magnate Noah Webster. As he traveled and thought, Disneyland began to take shape in his mind. It then became a reality that has attracted families from around the world. Both kids and parents enjoy it, just as Disney visualized they would. Walt Disney died of throat cancer in 1966, but not before purchasing 28,000 acres of swampland in Florida for what would become his second theme park, Disney World. He never saw Disney World created. But he didn't have to. He had pictured it in his mind enough times.

Rehearse for Success

When I was appointed as a manager at First Investors Corporation, my boss suggested I call a meeting of all my branches to establish the "new regime." I decided we should all meet in Seattle at the Edgewater Inn. I'd never led a meeting before, so I arrived a day early to prepare. On the plane, I wrote each attendee's name on place cards. When I got to the hotel, I went to the room where the meeting was to take place and put these cards on the tables. Then I began to deliver my presentation. As I talked, I clearly imagined each attendee sitting there. One of them talked too much. I moved his card. The other kept ganging up on me with the guy on the left. I moved his card. One guy never said anything. I moved him closer to the front to encourage him. The next day, the meeting went off just as I had visualized it. It was one of the best meetings I've ever given.

Roberta Bondar is best known as the first Canadian woman in space. She is also a distinguished researcher in the field of neurology. Dr. Bondar began visualization at a young age. (It's interesting how naturally visualization comes to children!) She loved chemistry sets and science fiction. She often imagined herself as part of the Flash Gordon stories, and explored her neighborhood, pretending to be an "astronaut." She avidly followed the American space program through pictures and clippings sent to her by an aunt living in Florida. Roberta Bondar wanted to be a real astronaut one day.

In 1983, the National Research Council of Canada announced the formation of the Canadian space program, and invited applications. Dr. Bondar was one of six people, chosen from over 4,000 applicants, who would begin training to become one of the first Canadian astronauts. She was the only female in the group.

Beginning on January 22, 1992, she spent eight days in space on board *Space Shuttle Discovery*. On her return to Earth, Dr. Bondar retired to devote time to her research and to photography. Inspired by her experiences in photographing Earth from space, she photographed all 41 of Canada's national parks. The results were gathered into a book and museum exhibit, appropriately named *Passionate Vision*.

One of my heroes, Elvis Presley, also formed his vision in part from comic books. "When I was a child...," he said, "I was a dreamer. I read comic books, and I was the hero of the comic book. I saw movies, and I was the hero in the movie. So every dream I ever dreamed has come true a hundred times...."

Act the Part

To be successful, you must act the part. Get your life ready to receive success. Dress for it. Think positively. Associate with people you feel good about. Think twice about hanging out with negative people. Be committed to your vision and stay focused on what you want to attract.

One evening, I met with Tom Hopkins, author of the best selling book *How to Master the Art of Selling Anything*. Over dinner and a glass of wine, our talk turned to motivation, and self-motivation in particular. I told Tom that I used to have a small index card hanging from my rear view mirror that said, "This is going to be the best presentation I have ever given!"

"Looking at that card always worked for me," I told him.

"Well, that's pretty good," Tom said, "but here's what I used to do." He told me about standing in front of his mirror every morning, singing his own version of the Frankie Valli song, "Can't Take My Eyes Off of You." Tom's version went like this: "I'm just too good to be true, can't take my eyes off of me...."

Maybe Tom was a little over the top, but he swears this singing strategy helped to motivate him. It's hard to argue with success.

"The people who are crazy enough to think they can change the world are the ones who do," says Steve Jobs, CEO of Apple Computers.

So picture yourself living the life you want to live. Use the following exercises to develop your own visualization techniques; it is amazing what you will manifest.

Visualize a Great Day

What would a great day look like to you? Visualize a time in the near future and include key aspects of what you think would be a fabulous day — from beginning to end, from waking to night time. Where are you? What are you doing? Is it a workday or a day off? If you're dissatisfied with your professional situation, this would be a good time to envision a better one. Where would you work? What type of work would you do? With whom would you have lunch, and where? When would you head home? What would you eat for dinner? Where? With whom? How would you spend your evening?

Take a few minutes now and write down what your perfect day would look like. Remember what Albert Einstein said: "Your imagination is a preview of life's coming attractions."

Visualize Your Potential

Imagine yourself five years from now. Where are you and what are you doing? Who are the people in your life? Where do you live and with whom? What do you do with your time? What do you enjoy?

Now imagine yourself 10 years into the future. Ask yourself the same questions and imagine your life. Once you have done this, imagine your life 25 years from now. How will it be? Write a few paragraphs about what your life will look like in the future.

Visualize "What If"

Michelangelo once wrote, "In every block of marble I see a statue as plain as though it stood before me, shaped and perfect in attitude and action. I have only to hew away at the rough walls that imprison the lovely apparition to reveal it to other eyes as mine see it."

He did not see failure. What he saw were possibilities. What would you shape for your future if you knew you could not fail? What would you do if time and money were not factors? Take some time to explore a life of complete possibility.

What we visualize is real to our brains. Remember my story of tacking a picture of the Lear jet to my wall, and then eventually owning one? That jet was so real to me that I could have flown in it right then and there. When I saw the picture of the Lear jet, *I thought it was mine*! When it actually became mine, all that really happened was my vision leapt out of my imagination onto the tarmac. I have no doubt that visualization works.

CHAPTER REVIEW

* Visualization is a powerful method for focusing on and realizing what you want out of life.

* We use visualization all of the time, without realizing it.

* When you visualize positive things, you get positive results. When your thoughts are filled with worry, fear and doubt, then you picture negative outcomes. If you believe the power of your subconscious mind is fertile ground for planting the seeds of the future, you cannot afford the luxury of a negative thought.

* Cutting out pictures and photographs of what you want your future to look like will serve as a focal point for your visualization.

* Take the time to visualize your future. Who will you be? Where will you be? Are you living your dreams? Of course you are!

> "There has never been another you. With no effort on your part you were born to be something very special and set apart. What you are going to do in appreciation of that gift is a decision only you can make." *Dan Zandra*

> "How you choose to respond each moment to the movie of life determines how you see the next frame, and the next, and eventually how you feel when the movie ends." *Doc Childre*

SECRET 9

The Power of Choice

Did you ever go to the dentist as a child and get to choose from a grab bag of prizes as a reward for enduring the dreaded drill? Do you remember how it felt?

We all knew that as soon as one prize was in our hands, all of the other possibilities were lost to us, at least until the next appointment. Some of us dove right in anyway, restless for our reward. Others hesitated, afraid of making the wrong choice — or any choice at all.

As adults, we may not get prizes from our dentists anymore, but we are still faced with choices. The way you view and manage choice is key to your ability to live a fulfilling and balanced life. Here are some key questions to ask yourself:

* Do you see yourself as a person with choices?

* Do you exercise your power to choose or do you wait for choice to be bestowed on you by those who you feel are more powerful?

* Do you see so many choices that you feel overwhelmed?

* Do you reward yourself with choices or punish yourself with limitations?

It's amazing how many people feel they don't have choices or the right to make their own choices. Sure, they may feel they can choose in small areas of their lives, but what about choosing their destinies? It's a nice dream, they'll tell you, but that's all it is. For these people, life just happens. In fact, author Napoleon Hill said that 98 percent of people work in the jobs they ended up in because *they never made a conscious decision about their futures to begin with*.

I think the key word is *conscious*. According to *Webster's Dictionary*, when we are conscious, we "show realization or recognition of something." In the *Passport to Business Success* that I published and handed out to friends and associates several years ago, one of my inspirational motivators was the following: "There are people who have what it takes to make it happen; there are people who worked very hard to make it happen; and there are people who say, 'What happened?' People who consciously make choices never have to ask, 'What happened?'"

Choice is everywhere. Sometimes you'll make the right choice; sometimes you'll make the wrong choice and be forced to learn from your errors. But to simply accept what life throws at you and not become conscious of your options is like locking in a flight plan and flying on autopilot through every storm, unaware that there is a better, easier way. If this is the way you live your life, then a number of things may occur:

1. The journey will be long and straight, but uneventful and unenlightening.
2. You will somehow manage to make it through every storm and over every obstacle by sheer luck, but as a result you will become worn out or even damaged, and unable to fulfill your true potential.
3. You will crash and somehow survive. This often forces a wake-up call. An example of this is a high-level executive who survives for years on the power of ambition, but who ends up grounded by a serious stress-related illness. Because she did not choose, the choice was made for her.
4. You will crash and you won't survive.

Opening Your Life to Choice

I'd like to open your eyes to the power of choice so you aren't forced to experience a crash. To begin, take a moment to do a small exercise. Say to yourself, "I have choices." Can you feel how powerful that is? Try it again. You may not believe it right away but the more often you say it, and act on it, the better you'll become at making choices and following them through to your dreams.

"One of the greatest powers you have in your life is your power to choose," writes Eric Allenbaugh in his book *Wake-Up Calls*. "When you choose to do something, the world around you responds to your choice. Every choice moves us closer to or farther away from something. Where are your choices taking your life? What do your behaviors demonstrate that you are saying yes or no to in life?"

The biggest and most important choice you can make in life is your attitude. There are many things in life you can't control, but you can choose how you will respond to them. When my son Todd died, there were many routes I could have chosen. No one would have blamed me if I had withdrawn from the world, but because I'm a positive person, I chose to honor and celebrate my son's life by creating LifePilot. This choice has spirited me into a new mission in life, and has put me in touch with people worldwide who are craving the tools to make positive choices.

You Don't Need Permission

Have you ever heard someone say, "Well, that's his lot in life"? A generation or two ago, we may have accepted that people ended up with "their lots," powerless to make choices. Often, men did what their fathers did and women did what society expected of them. Today, thankfully, most of us have rejected the notion that we must labor under pre-determined burdens. We can choose who we want to be and what we want for our lives.

It's vital to examine your reasons for making the choices you do. As an example, the inspirational writer Norman Vincent Peale once met two brothers: one was an alcoholic and the other was a teetotaler. He asked the alcoholic brother why he was an alcoholic and the brother answered, "Because my Dad was an alcoholic." He then asked the other brother, "Why are you a teetotaler?" The other brother answered, "Because my Dad was an alcoholic."

"Other people's opinion of you does not have to become your reality," says Les Brown, author and motivator. He's right, but sometimes the choices you'll make require an almost superhuman effort because they mean exerting your power to choose over the power of your history, your family or your peers. It can be hard to pursue your own choices, but the rewards are worth it. As someone once said, "If you hear a different drummer — dreamer, take a chance. The road you choose to travel means the difference in the dance."

Certainty is Seldom Certain

How do you know which route to travel? How do you decide which choice to make? The truth is, there's no way to be 100 percent certain. However, I've discovered that living by my values has helped me make many choices that, looking back, were wise ones.

Think of some choices you're grappling with and ponder them in the context of your values. Just as your values will help you decide which road to take, they can also tell you when to put the brakes on or move to a different path.

When I was about 15, I learned a valuable lesson about standing up for my life and literally choosing which road I didn't want to travel. My story took place one summer when I worked at a grocery store, bagging groceries. As soon as my daily work was done, my three buddies and I would meet up and head out to the lake for a swim before dark.

One evening after work, we were hitchhiking to the lake. As we stood with our thumbs out, a new 1954 Cadillac hardtop came roaring down the road and braked to a screeching halt in front of us. At the wheel sat the town "hard rock," a Fonzie-like character named Rance. He smiled at us. "Where are you heading?" he asked.

"Baptiste Lake," we stammered.

"That's *exactly* where I'm going," he said with a slick smile. "Jump in." Two of my buddies jumped in the back seat and two in the front. I ended up beside Rance. The second we got in the car — and almost before the door even closed — Rance hit the gas and we sped off. The road was good for the first 15 miles and Rance drove fast, the fastest I had ever gone. I was terrified, but I kept it to myself. By this time, it was clear that Rance was more than a little drunk, and he was having a great time trying to scare us.

We had to swing off the highway to get to Baptiste Lake. That meant Rance had to slow down to make the corner at the turn-off. As it happened Rance's window was down, and he drove with one arm out the window and one hand on the wheel. I don't know what made me do it, but as we turned the corner, I reached down, grabbed for the keys, switched off the engine and threw the keys out the window.

Rance couldn't believe his eyes. He swore at me but he had to deal with a car that suddenly had no power steering. He finally managed to stop the car, and my buddy quickly pushed his door open. The four of us flew out of the car and ran away down the road.

I knew if we had stayed in that car, there was a good chance we would have been killed in a crash. I also knew if we had shown any fear, Rance would have driven faster just to get more of a reaction. I did the only thing that I thought I could do. Looking back now, it was the right thing. There wasn't much time to make the choice but that's usually the way opportunities to make choices appear in our lives. I saw the opportunity and I took it.

No doubt you've encountered such turn-off points in your life. It's the choices you make at these junctures that often define your destiny. The choices never end — life is a series of them and it's crucial to look at these experiences as positive reasons to grow, even if they don't seem so positive at the time.

You won't always know what's around the corner. You won't always have empirical evidence to back up the choices you make. Sometimes your choices will take you into uncharted territory, as Robert Frost explored in his famous poem, "The Road Not Taken":

> Two roads diverged in a wood, and I —
> I took the one less traveled by,
> And that has made all the difference.

Choosing Another Route

Cheryl Wheeler is a LifePilot graduate who also chose the route less traveled, and that made all the difference in her life. Today, Cheryl is a burgeoning artist, painting with a passion she once feared. She lives in Mexico, studies Spanish and dreams of all the possibilities the future holds. She enjoys a mutually respectful, deeply loving relationship with a man, her soul mate, who encourages and supports the fulfillment of her dreams. She has a wonderful relationship with her insightful son who, she says, melts her heart and relentlessly challenges her expectations of life.

This is Cheryl today. But for many years, Cheryl occupied a darker place. By her own admission, the future didn't always seem so "ripe with potential." While Cheryl says it's impossible to point to any one event for her entire transition, there were pivotal experiences and moments of clarity. One of those was a LifePilot workshop, which Cheryl describes as "one of those critical coincidences" that ultimately led to her choosing a different, more rewarding path in life.

Here is Cheryl's story. It's so powerful I'll let her tell it in her own words:

"…my childhood and adolescence were littered with enough dysfunction and chaos to keep a bevy of counselors employed indefinitely. Life challenges were inevitable. At the age of nine, I effectively lost my parents to divorce, resulting in the loss of all discipline and structure in my life. I graduated high school with below average marks because I refused to apply myself — and partying became the center of my life.

At the age of 19, a moment of clarity provided me with the courage to enroll in business school. I had seen myself in a boardroom leading what seemed like an important discussion. I thought, 'How am I going to get from here to there?' At that moment I felt inspired; my imagination was alive and I decided I was going to make it happen. I applied the next day and subsequently completed a Business Management and Marketing program with Honors, then started studying for my securities stockbroker's license. This led to employment as Director of Investor Relations at Samoth Capital Corporation where I fortuitously met Peter. Over the next five years I watched and learned how Peter became successful by using his now formalized LifePilot program.

Have you ever had a burning desire to follow your passions and yet somehow found yourself doing everything else but what you desired? Have you ever abandoned your natural talents because it didn't seem practical or responsible to indulge yourself in pursuing them? For 20 years, I had a desire to paint, but told myself that I couldn't make a living as an artist. So, like most other responsible women of my age, I went to business school instead, and created my own success. I made everyone proud. Everyone but me. Only I knew that my heart was aching to express itself in the form of art.

I am grateful to Peter, who saw my yearning and encouraged me to write down my dreams and goals and then commit to creating them in my life. To begin my artistic journey, I took numerous classes and apprenticed with professional artists. In 2000, I painted my first 'real' painting and upon its completion, I was so overwhelmed with gratitude (towards both Peter and myself) that I persisted in setting goals and following my desires.

As if on cue, when I was ready, my teachers presented themselves. Over the years my passion has grown and my talents have unfolded.

In 2003, I was the president of a publicly-traded company that my partners and I were actively selling. I was at an important fork in the road — a moment that I sensed would leave me forever changed. It was a question of truth and faith. Did I have the courage and strength to let go of that which was financially rewarding but emotionally empty?

I took the leap of faith. I trusted my heart and intuition and followed my passion; walking away from a world and identity I had spent my life creating, to enter a new, unknown one. My new path left me both humbled and vulnerable, yet somehow more alive and authentic. Friends and family squawked in fear, but I followed my new direction in earnest. My supportive and loving husband pledged to be my first patron and to bring me light during times of shadow and fear. I also enlisted the love and support of a "mastermind group," a collection of successful women who come together to support each other in creating their dreams.

With my skills, support and commitment I began to follow a newfound path to freedom and passion. I am a different woman today than I was prior to meeting Peter. Today I enjoy a life defined by peace and serenity, and I pursue my passion each day with vigor and grace. When I begin a new painting I experience a brief apprehension, but soon enough life's beauty, love and energy begins to flow through me, leading to inspiration. I experience small miracles with each new day and each new brush stroke.

I remember being in high school and passing by the art room, looking in and wondering what went on in that mysterious room. I closed myself off to a dream of pursuing the arts, like my grandmother, because at the time I had the limited belief that I could not support myself as an artist. Commercial success is still a desired outcome of my commitment to painting, but the deep sense of joy I receive as a result of following my passion far outweighs the fears I once had that I could never possibly support myself with my art.

Peter taught me the value of defining, and committing to, my dreams. As a result of those insights, I now sit in a studio rather than a boardroom. I watch, smell, feel and hear the Pacific Ocean outside my windows in Mexico rather than watch the clouds of November drench Vancouver in liquid sunshine. I study Spanish each day rather than stock trends. My goals and dreams are in alignment with my husband John's and we look forward to bravely embracing a future that we are actively co-creating.

I have spent the last year of my life living in Puerto Vallarta, Mexico painting with passion and faith. I deeply believe that I will attract the teachers, experiences, supporters and customers that are necessary for me to become a world-class artist. I am selling my art, and my clients feel my passion in my work. I still have fears that occasionally raise their heads, but I gently tell them they are unwelcome, an illusion, and untrue. And they listen, and then leave.

Peter and LifePilot provided me with a framework that helped me create my new reality. What I learned during my life-altering weekend, listening to the inaugural LifePilot workshop years ago, has provided insight and guidance ever since. It changed my life, and could change yours as well if you have the courage and desire to create a more enriching and fulfilling experience of life."

The Courage to Choose

Cheryl Wheeler made the choice to pursue her passion. It wasn't a choice most people would consider easy, but the amazing thing about choices is that when they are right, opportunity seems to flow out of them.

"It's challenging," says Cheryl, "to look back on my life and specifically pinpoint the moments and experiences that fundamentally changed who I was as a human being, and as an evolving soul. We're all born into unique situations and we all transform, to some degree, from who we think we should be to who we are destined to become."

Fortunately, Cheryl has the support of a loving family, friends, mentors and teachers who encourage her to live her dreams. Hopefully, you have this kind of support network, but if you don't, you may have to build a network of people who will encourage and support you.

Another painter, Georgia O'Keefe, made a similar choice at one point in her life. Feeling locked in by the demands of others, she said, "I can't live where I want to. I can't even say what I want to! I decided I was a very stupid fool not to at least paint as I wanted to."

With that choice, Georgia O'Keefe became one of the most celebrated artists of the 20th century. Notably, in the end she *did* live where she wanted — in the desert of New Mexico — and she certainly *did* say what she wanted. She became known for her biting wit and outspoken brilliance.

"...I've learned, the hard way," she said, "that some poems don't rhyme, and some stories don't have a clear beginning, middle, and end. Life is about not knowing, having to change, taking the moment, and making the best of it, without knowing what's going to happen next."

Some people feel paralyzed because they cannot predict the outcomes of their choices, but as Stephen Sondheim, composer of film scores for movies like *The Birdcage* and *Reds*, said, "I chose and my world was shaken. So what? The choice may have been mistaken; the choosing was not. You have to move on."

Stand Up for Your Life

Sometimes, you can be your our own worst enemy when it comes to making choices. Instead of focusing on the positive aspects of choice, it's easy to wallow in self-defeating thoughts. You might expect others to be angry about your choices or worry about disappointing people. You might feel small in the face of opposition, or too embarrassed to make waves. Colin Powell, a man who has made many tough choices in his military career, wrote about how he used his power of choice to shape his destiny. "You can't make someone else's choices. You shouldn't let someone else make yours."

Early in life, I saw the power of standing up for myself and making good choices, beginning with my decision at age 15 to join the army. My mother didn't really try to stop me; she knew I was determined When you're that young, it's sometimes easy to get swayed from what you know is right. My courage to choose was put to the test after I finished basic training and was allowed to have weekend and evening passes. Those passes gave me a lot of freedom. I exercised my freedom by heading for the closest town to the base. There, I met lots of people and even managed to attract a girlfriend.

Some of the people I met, however, were definitely not the best friends for me to choose. One night we were all out in a car, just driving around. All of a sudden, the driver stopped the car on a city street and jumped out along with the other guy in the front seat. I didn't pay much attention until I heard the ear-piercing screech of metal. I immediately recognized they were stealing the hubcaps from a parked car. My conscience began to play a movie of me being taken away to jail for stealing, and being kicked out of the army. I chose to get out of there, so I crawled out and ran down the street, away from that car and those people as fast as my legs could take me.

At that young age, I made a choice. I didn't have long to ponder which path to choose — right or wrong — or how to choose. In the blink of an eye, I drew on what I knew to be right and chose to get out of there. As French political activist and author Madame de Stael once said, "The voice of conscience is so delicate that it is easy to stifle it; but it is also so clear that it is impossible to mistake it."

In matters of choice, conscience — which is intricately entwined with your values — is a key navigational instrument. Have you ever pictured a devil on one of your shoulders and an angel on the other, just like in a cartoon? Usually they are pressing you to make a choice. When in doubt, follow your values straight to your conscience. In this way, you won't be forced to live with regret, which Southern author Katherine Mansfield called "an appalling waste of energy."

By the time I was 17, I was well into army life and had gained a little more experience and the self-assurance to go with it. With ten days of leave ahead, I planned to head West from Ontario to see my family for Christmas. A friend of mine knew a famous Canadian who had a younger brother. He asked if this brother could catch a ride with me, and he would pay some of the expenses.

I met the brother. He looked to be about 15 years old and seemed like a great kid. We set out on the appointed date and had our first stop at a gas station right along the highway in Northern Ontario. I went to the pump and filled the car up with gas, paid the attendant and came back to the car. My fellow passenger was missing so I sat for a while and waited. After about five minutes he came racing back to the car, jumped in and said, "Let's go." I didn't think much of it and drove away. A few miles down the road, my friend pulled a few handfuls of paper money out of his pocket and threw it on the seat beside us.

"Now we don't have to worry about expenses," he laughed.

It took about a minute for me to put it all together and figure out that he had robbed the gas station. I felt my blood turn cold. Thoughts of the police and prison raced through my head; I could see no way that I wouldn't be implicated if we were caught. Somehow, my remote control took over. I slammed on the brakes, almost throwing my passenger through the windshield. I leaned over him, opened the door and pushed him out on to the roadside. Then I gathered up the money from the front seat, threw it out after him, slammed the car into gear and sped away. I traveled as fast as the car could go for about a half an hour, always looking in the rear view mirror to see if the police were chasing me. I never heard of "my friend" again and I never heard from the police. But I never forgot the moment when I went into remote control and threw him from the car, threw out his money and drove away.

At that moment, I made an instant choice based on all of my past experience and values — and somewhere inside I found the confidence to follow through. It might have been easier for me to keep driving with my friend in the car and let him out at another gas station. But it might also have resulted in my car being pulled over and me being held accountable as the driver for a carload of stolen cash.

Always make the decision that you know in your heart is the correct one and never knowingly allow others to put you in jeopardy.

Snakes and Ladders

I had no forewarning of what kind of person my travel companion was. He had come to me through the recommendation of a friend whom I had no reason not to trust. But often, we do receive warnings, however subtle. If we listen to our instincts, we begin to pick up on warning signs that should put our power to choose on high alert.

Many years ago, I read a fable about a little girl who was walking down a garden path when she noticed a small snake lying directly in front of her. As she reached down to touch the snake, it spoke to her.

It said, "I am a snake — if you pick me up I will probably bite you, but I'm very cold and would like you to pick me up."

The girl ignored the snake's warning. She picked it up and held it until it got warm. The snake then bit the little girl hard on the hand and she started to cry.

"Why are you crying, little girl?" the snake asked. "You knew perfectly well what I was when you picked me up and I warned you what I would do. I'm a snake. I can't help it. You should have known better than to trust me."

Many times in your life you'll encounter snakes. If you choose to "play" with them, you *will* get bitten. Often, when you look back you'll realize that all of the warning signs were there. Sometimes, it's easy to ignore the signs because the snake is so well clothed, or so well mannered, or seems to hold power over you, but as an Indian proverb says, "The cobra will bite you whether you call it cobra or Mr. Cobra."

Sometimes snakes will appear to offer us tempting choices, when in fact all that happens is we get bitten. As always, check your values and choose wisely. I learned firsthand about this during my early days in real estate. At one point, there was a severe drop in the market but when I got a call from a person I had met socially, I thought things might be looking up.

"A group of my associates are coming into town," he told me. "They want to establish a lending office in this area and they'd like to associate with a successful realtor like you. Would you be interested?"

"Sure," I told him. He said he would give me a call when they came into town. I didn't think any more about it. Then one Sunday morning he called me at about 9 a.m.

"My associates are in town today," he said. "They have to leave earlier than expected but they have time to see you before they go." He asked if I could meet him at a specific hotel in a specific room at 11:00 a.m. It was Sunday morning and I had plans, but I thought this meeting might lead to an extraordinary business opportunity. I knew I'd kick myself if I missed it.

I arrived at the hotel at the specified time, went up the elevator and knocked on the door of the room. Inside the room were three men. We said our hellos, then one of the men walked over to the dresser and turned on a tape recorder.

"Listen to this," he told me. Suddenly, the room filled with the sounds of gunfire, people yelling and screaming, and engines roaring. Confused, I listened quietly.

When the tape was done, the man reached over and shut it off. "What did you hear?" he asked.

I didn't really understand what he was getting at. "I heard a lot of noise," I answered cautiously.

"This is what we do," he said. I still didn't understand.

"What did you hear?" he asked again.

I was actually getting a little tired of the game. "I don't know," I told him.

Then he threw me the punch line. "We finance wars." The room went silent. At that point, I felt the saying " dumber than a sack of hammers" was written just for me because I still couldn't understand what he was driving at.

He went over to a drawer, took out a roll of bills and tossed them to me. "What's that?" he asked me.

I looked at the roll of money and said, "It's a roll of American $100 bills."

"Look at it again," he told me.

I looked again and he asked me once more, "What do you see?"

I still saw a roll of $100 bills.

"Look carefully at the serial numbers on the bills," he ordered me. As I thumbed through the bills it all became clear — the numbers were all the same. These guys were counterfeiters and they thought I would be a good guy to launder their counterfeit money through because of my precarious financial position.

How I could get out of there? Would these guys kill me if I didn't do what they wanted? What should I do next? My mind raced, but my body felt disconnected and numb.

I looked up at the three men and said, "Oh yeah, I now understand what you do. I don't think I'll be able to help you."

I jumped up and headed for the door before any of them could move. I grabbed the doorknob, twisted it and pulled. Thank God the door opened. I sprang into the hall, ran to the elevator, pushed the button and stood there for about one second before I dove frantically for the stairs. I raced down to the lobby and out to my car. As I started to drive home, I wondered if they would find me and kill me. What should I do now?

I called my lawyer and luckily he was at home. "Look," he said, "don't panic. Just go home. They probably won't approach you again."

We considered the options and decided there was no point in contacting the police. "Do you think you could find them again?" my lawyer asked. "Do you have anything that identifies who they are?"

I thought of "my friend," the contact. I didn't even have his phone number.

"Even if you could take the police to these guys," my lawyer said, "at best it would be your word against theirs. Just go home and let it play out."

I never heard from any of those dubious characters again. One day, about a year later, I saw the fellow who had asked me to contact them. He never said a word — he just disappeared as soon as he saw me.

No matter what situation you find yourself in, remember that you — and you alone — control your destiny by your power of choice. No matter what opportunities come your way, they must be measured against your values.

When I look back now, I see making a different decision at any of those critical points could have changed my life, and not necessarily for the better. It might surprise some of you that with so many opportunities for crime, I was never tempted to become a criminal! But for me, there was no question of doing the right thing. I knew what I valued even at a young age. It was an easy choice.

It's Up to You

There is a famous Zen koan — a question posed to stimulate the mind into enlightened modes of thinking — that asks, "When you can do nothing, what can you do?" Some people will tell you that you have no choices. Others will try to control your choices by offering you up the menu of options they have created for you. They'll ask you to decide between the devil and the deep blue sea, or a rock and hard place. As Grateful Dead frontman Jerry Garcia wisely said, "Constantly choosing the lesser of two evils is still choosing evil." Life should not be reduced to the equivalent of a multiple-choice questionnaire.

The same people who talk about choosing the lesser of two evils could well be the people who talk about having to "make hard choices." In my experience, this can be a euphemism for lack of creativity. "If you limit your choices only to what seems possible or reasonable," writes Stephen R. Covey, "you disconnect yourself from what you truly want, and all that is left is compromise."

When you make choices based on your values, you'll find that making the right decisions is easier than you expected. You won't feel compromised or sacrificed because everything you do, every choice you make, will be within the goal posts of your values. How can it be wrong to say no to a risky investment if financial stability is what you value most? How can it be wrong to say no to joining a 7 a.m. business gathering if your daily morning jog is a vital part of valuing your health?

By knowing and abiding by your values, you'll begin to live by your own agenda instead of the agenda of others. You'll also begin to understand how it is really you — and not the people around you — who limit your choices the most. Again, your attitude will determine your options. Keep your attitude positive and your options will open.

Getting Past the Gray Areas

Life gains clarity when we know and live by our values, but even then we may encounter gray areas. Early in my management career, I gained some wisdom about how to handle these gray areas. At that time, I found myself in a sales contest between all the regions of the mutual fund company where I worked. I was the youngest and probably the most aggressive new branch manager. I wanted to win. I had the best salesmen and we were virtually unbeatable — or so I thought.

In the last week of the contest, I found out that two other branches were running neck-and-neck with our branch. What should we do? We had to pull ahead. We had a meeting that Sunday and schemed out a strategy: my group would divide up into working teams for the week. We would head out to any territory in the province where we felt we could get sales. We weren't licensed to sell beyond provincial boundaries.

Early Monday morning, my sales team left on their mission, geared up to sell. In fact, some were so eager they left the night before. When they returned five days later, they had all made sales, but as I went through their paperwork, I found that two of them had written up most of their sales in the next province. These extra sales definitely would have put us over the top and we would have won the contest hands down, but was it right if the sales were out of the province?

There were several things I could have done, all of which were quickly suggested when I brought the culprits in to explain why they had crossed the provincial border. They reasoned that the out-of-province sales would, in fact, qualify because, despite the fact that the clients all lived in another province, their post office boxes were in the province in which we were licensed to sell. Besides, they told me, the out-of-province clients even shopped for all of their groceries and supplies in our province. In all ways except their actual residences, they were qualified to buy the mutual funds we were selling.

Again, what to do? Sure, the lines were a little blurred, but my sales team had a good point. As their manager, should I accept the sales or not?

Whenever "gray" areas come up and I can't quite figure out what to do, I turn for advice to my mentors or other people who I admire. This time I felt that the situation was so specific, the only person who could help me was the president of the company. He listened to what I had to say. Then he paused and said, "Peter, where did the people who your salesmen sold the mutual funds to actually live?"

"They actually live in the adjoining province but…"

He cut me off. "What province are these salesmen licensed to sell in?"

"In this province," I answered.

"So what's your question?" he asked.

The answer was so obvious I actually felt ashamed for seeking his advice. I thanked him for his time and turned to leave. This is when he gave me one of the best lessons of my life, and one that I always think of when there are "gray" decisions to make.

"Usually," he said, "most questions have very simple answers if you think of things in black and white. They only get complicated when you think of them in gray. So if you have a particular issue, think of it in black and white, then draw an imaginary line. Behind this line, draw another imaginary line. The space between the two lines is the gray area. Don't go there, Peter. Stay with the black and white decisions."

"You'll find," he continued "that 99 percent of the time your decisions will be black or white. If they ever feel gray to you then hopefully you have surrounded yourself with mentors who you can go to, like you have come to me today. Ask your mentors to help you define what is black and white, and what is gray. It will be much clearer to them as they have the benefit of objectivity."

I've learned since then that choosing between black and white usually means you are really choosing between right and wrong. You always want to make the "right" decision.

By the way, my sales story had an interesting ending. Despite the fact that our out-of-province sales didn't qualify for the contest, we won the competition, fair and square. Today, I can look back with pride on the work of my team. It's through examining the reasons for the choices we make, after all, that we learn who we really are.

CHAPTER REVIEW

* The way you view and manage choice is key to your ability to live a fulfilling and balanced life.

* Say to yourself, "I have choices." You may not believe it right away but the more often you say it, and act on it, the better you'll become at making choices and following them through to your dreams.

* The biggest and most important choice you can make in life is your attitude. There are many things in life you can't control, but you can choose how you will respond to them.

* When considering your choices, think of them in terms of your values. Your decisions will become easier.

* We've all encountered "snakes." Sometimes they appear to offer us tempting choices, when in fact all that happens is we get bitten. As always, check your values and choose wisely.

> "Our attitudes control our lives. Attitudes are a secret power working twenty-four hours a day, for good or bad. It is of paramount importance that we know how to harness and control this great force." *Tom Blandi*

SECRET 10
Attitude Determines Altitude

If there's one attribute that determines what heights of success you will reach, it's your attitude. The happiest and most fulfilled people I know are the ones who consistently take a positive approach in whatever they do. They have winning attitudes.

One of the most amazing stories about the power of positive attitude involves Roger Bannister, a young Englishman who achieved the seemingly impossible — he broke the four-minute mile, which no one had been able to do in all the centuries of human existence before him.

Bannister wasn't born blessed with money. Since he wanted to study medicine at one of England's universities, he needed a scholarship. His success on the running track was his ticket to a scholarship to Oxford University. There, Bannister's speed drew the attention of the British sports press who were disappointed when he declined to compete in the 1948 Olympics in London, preferring to focus on his training and his medical studies.

By 1951, Bannister had earned the British title in the mile. He felt ready for the Olympics. Unfortunately, a last minute change in the schedule at the 1952 games in Helsinki forced him to run without resting between events. He finished fourth in the 1,500-meter and was scorned by the British media.

He decided to redeem himself by doing what had never been done — breaking the four-minute record for running the mile. Despite being enrolled in full-time medical studies, which left him just 45 minutes a day for training, he was convinced that slow and steady training would enable him to break the record.

His chance arrived on May 6, 1954 at Oxford. On the four-lap course, he completed the first three quarter-mile laps in less than three minutes. Then, as the amazed crowd watched, he threw an internal switch and ran like he'd never run before. He finished the lap in less than a minute and collapsed as the announcer delivered his time to the cheering crowd: 3:59.4. Roger Bannister had broken the four-minute mile.

Within a month, Australian runner John Landy had broken Bannister's record, but Bannister had the satisfaction of besting Landy at that summer's British Empire Games in Vancouver. Today, the four-minute barrier is broken on a regular basis. Why now and not in all the thousands of years previous to Bannister's win? Again, it goes to the power of a positive attitude and not being willing to accept the limits set by others.

Breaking the Self-Esteem Barrier

Mark Horne has never broken the four-minute mile, but he has broken some important personal barriers. Mark is a successful Florida-based entrepreneur who made his fortune by launching a series of phenomenal websites and selling his business for several million dollars. He's a happy, fit and talented guy who is living his dream. In fact, looking at Mark today it seems hard to believe that he spent most of his life struggling with anxiety, low self-esteem and the attitude that he just didn't belong.

Mark was born in Fort Lauderdale, Florida in 1965. He was adopted into a family who raised him and his brother. He was an exceptionally smart kid who was nonetheless labeled as a problem child and an underachiever because he couldn't sit still, no matter how hard he tried. When he was finally diagnosed with Attention Deficit Disorder (ADD) at 16, the pieces began to fall into place. Unfortunately, with the diagnosis the labeling continued.

"You really can get killed with all of the labeling," says Mark. "You are different than the status quo and some people try to make you feel like an outcast. You can get yourself into inner turmoil by believing that you don't fit in or that something is wrong with you. At times, I felt so aberrant to what I was told was normal in society. You learn, of course, that there is no such thing as normal, just different degrees of typical."

Fortunately, Mark had people who did believe in him. "There was my neighbor, Mrs. DiMartino, who sat me down one very memorable day and said to me, 'Mark, believe me, you will achieve great things in life. You are only different because you are exceptionally creative and intelligent.' Hearing that was like breaking the four-minute mile barrier. Once someone tells you that they believe in you, you're able to go further and set new records. However, unless someone points it out to you, you don't know it's possible."

However, no single action made Mark fight harder, or believe in himself more, than his parent's belief in him. "That gave me the inner feeling that someone was betting on me. They never gave up, so I made sure they won."

At 16, Mark graduated from high school and began college. But he soon found that college didn't hold his interest. "I sat down one day and asked myself, 'If I had the ability to have an instant degree, simply by signing my name, what would I be?' I must of thought of 100 professions and not one came to mind. I realized that I wanted to be an entrepreneur."

Mark he set out to become the best entrepreneur he could be. What followed was a meteoric rise to success. Between the ages 17 and 22 he began researching and trading stocks. He became a true follower of investment gurus Ben Graham and Warren Buffett. "Buffettology" became his only thought process for buying stocks. Mark met Warren Buffett at the Aksarben (Nebraska spelled backwards) Coliseum, and even presented a company to Warren and his company Berkshire Hathaway for purchase.

Between the ages of 22 and 28, Mark held a series 7 and 63 (NASD), became a principle of a brokerage firm (NASD Series 24), became the financial operating principle of a brokerage firm (NASD Series 27 – Fin-op) and was part owner of a brokerage firm. He then went on to work with a company that brought other companies public. Next, he started the New York Bagel Exchange, which he took public to complete his goal.

Mark entered the Internet industry in 1998. Three years later, still in his 30s, he launched Nautical Solutions Marketing, Inc., which started sites such as *UsedBoats.com*, *NewBoats.com* and *YachtBroker.com*. He sold the company to World Publications in 2004.

He set out to prove himself in the business world to the exclusion of everything else in his life, including himself. "When you are focused on building a business," he recalls, you don't have time for other things in your life. Family? Marriage? Fitness? I didn't have time for any of those things."

His 100 percent focus on business brought success, but not happiness and meaning. "I remember the day my company went public. I was worth millions upon millions of dollars. Ironically, the two most memorable thoughts that day were: what do I do now and was my dad right by telling me it wouldn't really matter?"

The same year he sold his company, Mark attended his first LifePilot seminar. "When I took LifePilot," he recalls, "I realized I had accomplished so much but there was something missing. I never thought about tomorrow and I lived like tomorrow would never come. For the majority of my life, I felt as though it was me against the world so I always set out to prove myself."

"No matter how much money and power I had," he adds, "it never meant anything until I was able to put it all together by writing my own *LifeManual*, which LifePilot taught me how to do."

LifePilot inspired Mark to take a deeper look at his life." I realized I was working hard but I didn't see where I was going, I had a girlfriend I wouldn't commit to, and I had lost the everyday connection I used to have with my Mom and Dad."

Armed with that epiphany, he set out to make changes." I started with small steps," he explains. "LifePilot is something I couldn't just leap into. I have learned to be somewhat skeptical of any self-improvement program or teaching. Even though I knew it worked for Peter, one of the most successful people in the world, I needed to test the waters for myself. Much to my delight, the LifePilot approach worked. I instantly started to see results! I set goals and did the easiest ones first. For example, I got engaged to Cathy, started calling my parents on a daily basis, and began eating the right foods. Then I moved on to more pressing issues like deciding whether or not to sell my company."

LifePilot's emphasis on focus helped Mark find ways to channel his ADD and defuse his anxiety. "I can't speak from a clinical standpoint as to why it happened, but I can tell you for a fact that my ADD is so much easier to understand now. LifePilot showed me how to structure my life and achieve the kind of focus I needed."

These days, he is less impulsive and more thoughtful about his decisions. "Before I would just jump. Now I still jump, but with a life parachute on."

With more structure in his life and less anxiety, Mark realized something unimaginable. He started to discover all the positive aspects of ADD and how lucky he was to have it.

"...ADD is not a negative thing. If having it gives me the ability to contemplate hundreds of ideas at one time — since the brains of people with ADD can multi-task like you wouldn't believe — how could this be negative? So what if I can't focus on something that someone else wants me to focus on? I focus on what I want. I mean, you can't pay for something as awesome as this, and I was so blessed to be born with it."

"I recall watching TV one night and they were discussing ADD. I was shocked to learn of all the incredibly successful people that shared it with me."

As Mark began filling in his *LifeManual*, he started dropping pounds. Eventually, he lost 70 pounds and reached his ideal weight. "Through LifePilot, I looked at my values. One of them was my love of fitness. I couldn't do those before because I was too heavy and physically uncomfortable. I knew something had to change — and I changed it." Now, I am 40 years old and on a rowing team!"

Today, with his slim physique and positive attitude, Mark is enjoying the best life has to offer, including a strong relationship with his fiancé Cathy, a solid-gold reputation as one of the most astute Internet business model developers in the world, and the fitness and energy levels to really delve into his love of sports, including scuba diving, cycling, rowing, boating and racing. In true LifePilot fashion, he's also a private pilot.

Other key themes for Mark include a focus on spirituality and contributing back to the world. He attends church at least once a week, donates his time through various church organizations and the Make a Wish Foundation. Whenever possible, he works through the foundation to help sick kids fulfill their dreams of flying in small planes, riding in race cars and more.

"LifePilot helped me realize where to put God in my life," he says. "Today, God is number one. Before there was a huge and endless hole in my life. There was nothing that I could do, accomplish or obtain that could fill it. Now, there is no longer a hole that needs to be filled. I'm now on this incredible journey. I have traveled around the world many times, lived in the most beautiful places and have a lot of people who love me. I am so blessed. Whether life presents opportunities or chaos, I handle each on my terms."

Mark Horne is the perfect example of what Aldous Huxley meant when he said, "Experience is not what happens to a man, it's what a man does with what happens to him." Mark is piloting his own life now — and he loves it.

Remember Your AMCs

I've always been interested in what makes people like Mark successful. What traits or attributes do they possess that help them reach their full potential? When I owned Century 21, I observed that 20 percent of the realtors did most of the selling. We decided to ask them what they felt the most successful people they knew had in common. These three attributes emerged:

Attitude — top performers have very positive, can-do attitudes
Motivation — top performers are self-motivated
Commitment — top performers make commitments and keep them.

These three character traits resonated with me. I call them my AMCs and I have used them for years to recruit, advise and mentor people. I truly feel that if you don't get your AMCs in order you have a good possibility of failing in whatever you are trying to do.

The Ultimate Measure

For most people, it's not too difficult to maintain a great attitude when things are going well, but it's when we're not winning that great attitude really needs to kick in.

"The ultimate measure of a man," said Martin Luther King Jr., "is not where he stands in moments of comfort and convenience, but where he stands at times of challenge and controversy."

How we handle life when the chips are down also determines other people's attitudes towards us. For almost two decades, Chris Evert was a tennis champion, ranked number one for seven years. She won 18 grand slam titles including three Wimbledons, seven French Opens, two Australian Opens and six US Opens. Win or lose, she is always remembered as a favorite for her positive attitude.

"If you can react the same way to winning and losing," says Evert, "that's a big accomplishment. That quality is important because it stays with you the rest of your life, and there's going to be a life after tennis that's a lot longer than your tennis life."

We've all met people who always find something to complain about but complaining drains away the energy you need to change your circumstances. "Complaining advertises your fears," writes Rhonda Britten in *Fearless Living*.

Instead of giving in to the impulse to react and complain, focus on putting out positive energy to attract good things into your life. People will respond to that energy. They will admire your willingness to improve your circumstances.

Once, I was watching comedian and actor Bette Midler, one of my favorites, being interviewed on TV. She was her usual bubbly self, excited about her life and career despite the fact that she was going through all kinds of personal and career challenges, as well as handling becoming an older actress in an industry that worships at the altar of youth.

The TV interviewer asked her, "Bette, on a scale of 1 to 10 where would you rate yourself?"

Without missing a beat, Bette looked at him and said "15." None of the issues she was dealing with affected her ability to rate herself as a winner. Bette Midler is a 15 all of the time and so are you — never let anyone tell you otherwise.

Struggle is Natural and Even Necessary

We usually don't succeed in life *despite* struggle but *because* of it. Struggle builds character. It allows us to test our limits and build our strengths. There is a famous story about a man who found a cocoon and kept it. One day, a small opening appeared in the cocoon. The man sat and watched for several hours as the butterfly struggled to force its body through the tiny hole.

Then it seemed to stop, as if it could go no farther. The man, wanting to help, took a pair of scissors and snipped the remaining bit of the cocoon. The butterfly easily emerged but something was wrong. Instead of emerging light and beautiful, the butterfly had a swollen body and shriveled wings. The man kept expecting the wings to expand to be able to support the bloated body but they didn't. Instead, the butterfly spent the rest of its life crawling around with a swollen body and deformed wings. It was never able to fly.

What the man did not understand was that the struggle required for the butterfly to get through the tiny opening of the cocoon was designed to force fluid from its body into its wings. The struggle was necessary for the butterfly to take flight.

The Optimists Win

I once heard a story about a group of researchers who wanted to find out why some people are naturally optimistic while others are naturally pessimistic. In hopes of finding an answer, they selected two boys to study. One was always happy and laughing at life; the other was always, full of gloom and doom. The researchers set up a room full of toys with almost everything a little boy could want. The pessimistic boy went into the room and just stood there. One of the researchers came in and asked him if he wanted to ride on the wooden horse. The boy started crying and said he might fall off and hurt himself. They then brought in the other boy. He rode the horse, played with the balls, colored in the books and had a great time.

For the next test, the researchers put a pile of horse manure and a shovel in a room. The first boy, the pessimist, wrinkled his nose and cried. The researchers came and took him out. Then it was the second boy's turn. The researchers put him in the room. In a few seconds, the little fellow had leapt into the center of the pile of horse manure and started digging as hard as he could. The researchers rushed in and pulled him out. "What in the world are you digging for?" they asked him. The little optimist said, "With all that horse manure in there, I just know there's a pony in there somewhere."

I've been given plenty of horse manure in my life, and by jumping in and digging I've found lots of ponies.

There are several stories that have inspired me over the years and buoyed my optimism. One of them is the story about a man we'll call Bill, who tried and tried to find work. He finally got a job as a garbage man. On his first day on the job, the boss gave him a written list of the addresses he had to go to pick up garbage.

Bill looked at the list despondently. " I can't read," he confessed to his boss. "Well," said the boss, "if you can't read then you can't be a garbage man." He felt sorry for Bill so he handed him some bananas and wished him good luck.

Bill went to the park to sit and think about his life. He set the bananas on the bench beside him. A man came along and asked Bill if he would sell him a banana for five cents. Bill sold him a banana. Thinking about what happened, Bill placed the rest of the bananas on the bench in a more noticeable position. Before an hour had passed, he sold all of his bananas. In fact, the demand was so high he figured he could raise the price to 10 cents for the last two bananas. Sure enough, they sold. At that price.

"Wow, what a day!" Bill thought. He decided to go down to the grocery store and buy as many bananas as he could with the money from his sales. Back to the park bench he went. Every day throughout the summer, he went to the park and sold bananas. Then he started to sell different fruits, and soon he found a place for himself at the gate of the park.

Things just got better and better for Bill. A few decades later, he found himself in the boardroom of a major company to which he was selling his business, which had now grown to be one of the biggest food distribution companies in the US. The company sold for hundreds of millions of dollars. Finally, the documents were ready to sign. The lawyers put them in front of Bill for him to read over.

"I can't read," Bill said, and he slid the documents over to his lawyer. The purchaser couldn't believe his ears. "This is unbelievable," he said to Bill. "Here you are so successful without being able to read. Just imagine what you could have been if you could read."

Bill thought about that for a minute. "Yes, I know what I could have been," he replied. "I could have been a garbage man."

People with winning attitudes don't focus on what they *don't* have or what they *can't* do. They concentrate on what they *do* have and what they *can* do. Don't spend your life wishing you had a better education or that you were taller, smarter or better looking. Be thankful for what you do have and get on with living.

Another story that always inspired me is about a young man working with his Dad on the family farm. One day, the young man's shirt got caught in the tractor's power take-off. He lost his entire arm but that didn't prevent him from getting on with his life. He went back to school and continued to be an outstanding athlete and student, then he graduated with honors, went on to University, competed in track and field, and eventually became a famous lawyer. Later in life, when someone asked him how he could accomplish so much with only one arm, he answered, "When I lost my arm I accepted that fact. From then on I focused on what I had — not what I had lost."

Do It First, Then You'll Feel Like It

During my early days of selling mutual funds, I'd heard the Dale Carnegie course was the best self-improvement course you could take to learn how to sell. I immediately enrolled and became one of many Dale Carnegie graduates. During the course, the Carnegie trainers teach you that if your spirits are low and you need motivation, you should do the following exercise: *Place both of your hands in front of you, make a fist and clasp the other hand over the hand with the fist. Then shake your joined hands vigorously from side to side at the same time loudly proclaiming over and over "Act enthusiastic and you will be enthusiastic."*

Some time after taking the course, I went out on a late sales call. To say I didn't feel like doing a sales presentation at 9 p.m. would be the understatement of the year, but I went anyway. I found myself standing outside the door of an apartment. I knew in the mood I was in I couldn't have sold anything to anyone. Then I remembered the Dale Carnegie Course and the exercise: *Act enthusiastic and you will be enthusiastic*. If I ever needed motivation it was then.

I knocked on the door and couldn't hear anything inside the apartment so put my briefcase down and started to do my exercise, quietly mouthing the words *Act enthusiastic and you will be enthusiastic* and vigorously shaking my arms side to side. It actually felt pretty good.

Soon, I began to really feel recharged. I was really getting into it when, for some reason, I felt compelled to turn around. There, at the apartment door across the hall, stood two nurses, laughing at me. Meanwhile, the people I had an appointment with were visiting across the hall. When they heard the knock, they also came to the door.

Embarrassed, I explained about my need for motivation and the Dale Carnegie exercise. They laughed and invited me to come in and give my presentation to them *and* their neighbors. I made four sales that night. From that point on, I fully believed how we act definitely influences how we feel.

Mirroring Motivation

During my sales career, I learned many often great techniques for keeping my motivation high and my attitude pumped. I used to tape a 4 x 6 card to my rearview mirror. It said, in capital letters, "THIS WILL BE THE BEST PRESENTATION I HAVE EVER GIVEN." I used to take it down when I was off duty but it always came out when I went out on a sales call. When I moved away from sales, I stopped doing this, but I always remembered that 4 x 6 card. Even today, when I'm delivering workshops, I vow to make each one the best presentation I've ever given.

The famous violinist Nigel Kennedy once said he plays every gig like it's the last one he'll ever play. Imagining this always pulls the best performance out of him. It's important to always give your best; never accept a mediocre performance. This is the only way you can improve.

Sometimes, I find my best performances come when it is most difficult for me to perform. "One man gets nothing but discord out of a piano; another gets harmony," said an unknown philosopher. "No one claims the piano is at fault. Life is about the same. The discord is there, and the harmony is there. Study to play it correctly, and it will give forth the beauty; play it falsely, and it will give forth the ugliness. Life is not at fault."

Perception is Everything

Usually, no one starts out at the top of his or her profession. Life is a journey, after all. A positive attitude always makes the journey more meaningful and enjoyable. To illustrate this, I want to share with you the story of three bricklayers busily working at their trade. A man stopped by and asked each of them what they were doing. "I'm laying bricks," the first man said without ever taking his eyes from his work. "I'm putting up a wall," the second man said. But the third man, with enthusiasm and pride, said, "I'm building a cathedral!"

When you rule your mind, you really do rule the world because the world you live in is the world you perceive. "Nothing is good or bad, but thinking makes it so," said a Zen master. When asked to explain, he added, "A man cheerfully observed a religious fast seven days a week. His neighbor starved to death on the same diet."

Negativity Weighs You Down

When you have a hard time staying positive, consider whether or not you are carrying the baggage of negative or detrimental attitudes. You may need to cast off these weights to stay in the air and really soar. This was a lesson I had to learn a number of years ago — and I've never forgotten it.

After several years in business, I began to realize some success. My confidence and notoriety grew. Soon, other business people sought my advice and asked me to speak to various organizations about how I had managed to become successful. I told them the country was going through a great growth period and that I was lucky to be in a business and a niche where I could take advantage of that growth. Lots of people just smiled and reminded me that, while what I said was true, other people were not making it and I was truly wise and special. It was very difficult not to agree with them as they fed directly into my ego. Inside, I think I *did* agree with them — if not wholeheartedly, then pretty substantially.

As I continued on my upward path, my attitude began to change from good to over confident. More and more deals were offered to me, yet I sought advice less and less. Previously, I had always consulted my lawyers, accountants, my wife, and generally anyone else whom I thought could give me input. I felt I didn't need that advice anymore. After all, who was *really* making all of these brilliant decisions?

Some of these deals were remarkably successful. Even when the deals went bad, thank God I had structured exit strategies so I didn't get burned too badly. With so many wins, I opened myself up to anyone who wanted to talk to me about a new deal. I became a deal junkie or, as they sometimes say in kinder tones, "a serial entrepreneur." Sure enough, like 99 percent of the people on this type of path to destruction, the deal that can "kill" you is just around the corner. It did come and it was a miracle that it didn't bankrupt me.

When things slowed down a little, I had time to reflect and ask myself, "What happened?" I realized how far I had strayed from the early business principles that had, in fact, made me successful. In studying a lot of businesses that ended in bankruptcy and lives that were shattered, I began to recognize a definite pattern. In fact, I saw it so many times, I felt I should give this malady a name so others could also recognize the symptoms. I called this malady the King Arthur's Disease.

The disease applies to men and women equally. The unfortunate victim feels as invincible as King Arthur; nothing can destroy him. He feels he can continue to go into battle (business) just like King Arthur and come out victorious. Well, we all know what happened to Camelot in the end.

If you are a successful Type A personality, you are particularly susceptible to developing King Arthur's disease. This disease is as dangerous to your career as it was to King Arthur who rushed into battle without armor, against a foe he knew nothing about, because he had not done his research. Foolhardy, to be sure.

Conquer Conflict

Fortunately, I overcame King Arthur's Disease and began to put my life into perspective. I wrote about this in my book *Never Fight With A Pig*. The title of that book — a metaphor for negative issues we're often tempted to wrestle with — came to me from business and sports icon Herb Cappozi. One day, we were talking about life and Herb said to me, "Peter, my Dad told me a story one day I've never forgotten. He said, 'Never fight with a pig. You get dirty, the pig likes it and you can't win.'"

If you remember that advice, it will guide you through many delicate situations, just as it did for me. After all, when you take into account the time, stress and loss of income from revenue you could be earning, you'll realize that fighting is usually a lost leader.

"Whenever you're in conflict with someone," said Timothy Bentley, a Canadian therapist, "there is one factor that can make the difference between damaging your relationship and deepening it. That factor is attitude."

My relationship with the fellow who later became one of my best friends started out with his bad attitude and my willingness to fight for my dignity. In 1947, I left England and moved with my Mom to the small town of Perryvale, Alberta. On the day after Mom and I arrived, she enrolled me in the local school. The only clothes I had were my English school clothes: a little blazer, a white shirt, a tie and shorts. The first day was a nightmare but somehow I got through it. After school, I told Mom I was the only person in the school wearing the British schoolboy outfit. Mom said there was nothing else to wear.

On the second day, I went off to school again in my little British outfit. I got to school a few minutes early and I met Allan Saunders, who was about my size and who singled me out to make me the laughing stock of the school. He led the "let's make a fool out of Peter laugh parade," goading the other kids on. Finally, enraged, I lost it and dove for him. We toppled over. Luckily, when we fell, I landed on top of him and was able to get in several damaging blows, one of which gave Allan a nosebleed.

With blood running from his nose, it looked to the other kids like Allan had lost the fight. They figured little British Peter with the shorts was not a kid to mess with. I wasn't going to be anyone's doormat. The teachers pulled us apart, gave us both detentions and made us stand in the corner. From that day on, no one made fun of Peter Thomas — and Allan Saunders became my friend. I stood up for myself with Allan, but he wouldn't have become my friend unless we had both put aside our differences and attitudes.

There will be times in your life when you may have to fight for your dignity. I don't mean getting into fist fights — I'm referring to standing up for your rights. If you don't, it might be that nobody else will.

Insist on Dignity

When I was in my early 40s, I had the world by the tail. I had a company that made more cash than I could spend. I had a private yacht, my own jet, and several homes. Life was good. I was giving a speech at The Mansion on Turtle Creek in Dallas, Texas to the Young Presidents' Organization on how to be successful when someone called me off stage for an urgent telephone call. I excused myself, picked up the phone and was advised my business partner had just declared bankruptcy on national TV. I was the guarantor for millions of dollars in loans given to a company we were partners in.

I finished the speech as best I could even though I no longer felt qualified to talk about how to be a success! I then made a few calls to find out the extent of the damage. It was bad — really bad. When I added them up, there were 18 outstanding loans in default that the bank had called us on. Three of the loans were for $10 million or more, and the rest were for $10 million or less. I decided to head back to Vancouver and face the music. Within two weeks, I had sold my jet for 50 percent of its value. I did the same with the yacht. I doubted the bankers would want to deal with me rationally if they felt I was leading the life of the rich and famous.

That entire period of my life became a blur of meetings. At one particularly tough meeting, I faced a group who had given us $25 million. It was invested in various real estate projects all over North America. They were panicking and demanding their money — immediately. Needless to say this was impossible. It took six months but finally we were able to arrange a meeting of all the parties involved. I hoped at that meeting to work out fair repayment terms.

I arrived at the meeting at the appointed time with my lawyer and my accountant. There were about 25 people in the room, including bankers, lawyers, accountants and more. I recognized one of the men and I smiled at him. He looked back at me and, without even smiling, said, "Did you bring the money?" I stammered a bit and said I didn't think that was an appropriate way to begin our meeting. "Does that mean you didn't bring the money?" he retorted.

Well, I actually have a bit of a short fuse when I am confronted. I didn't know how to react to what he said, so I just stood there for a few seconds looking at him, and then made a complete turn and marched out of the room. My lawyer and accountant followed me to the elevator and asked what I planned to do.

"The one thing I'm *not* going to do is sit in that room and be insulted," I said. I told my lawyer to go back and announce that when the group decided to be civil, we would be pleased to reconvene a meeting, but there would be no meeting that very day.

It actually took about two months to set up another meeting. I sent my lawyer and my accountant but I did not attend. At the end of the day, we settled satisfactorily, not only with this loan group but with all of the people to whom I owed money. I never did have to declare bankruptcy.

No matter how bad things look or get, never give up your dignity or your integrity. Everyone gets into trouble at one time or another. If you are out there risking and driving ahead, you are bound to be wrong sometimes.

Remember, when you find yourself weighed down by trouble, you still have the same brains and abilities you had when you were on top of the world. No one can take that away. As Charles Prestwich Scott, the British newspaper editor, said "Eagles come in all shapes and sizes, but you will recognize them chiefly by their attitudes."

"Dignity consists not in possessing honors, but in the consciousness that we deserve them," said Aristotle.

Don't Fear Forgiveness

During my career, I've had many instances in which I could have fed my anger, acted vengefully and refused to forgive the actions of others, but I've learned that when you can't let go and forgive, it's a total waste of your time and you only damage yourself.

I'm reminded of the story about a Native American grandfather who once said to his grandson, "I feel as if I have two wolves fighting in my heart. One wolf is the vengeful, angry, violent one. The other wolf is the loving, compassionate one."

"Which wolf will win the fight in your heart?" the grandson asked.

"The one I feed," answered the grandfather.

What we give energy to is what we feed. Some people might ask, how is it possible to feed forgiveness and not anger? I look to people like Desmond Tutu, who won the Nobel Peace Prize in 1984 for his work to end apartheid and create a just Africa. After all the cruelty he endured, he still found it within himself to forgive. "I must forgive," he explained, "so that my desire for revenge does not corrode my being."

Similarly, I read an article in the paper one day that said, "Unforgiveness is like drinking poison and waiting for the other person to die." I never forgot it.

Mother Teresa once wrote a poem that I think sums up the power of a positive attitude, perseverance and the will to forgive:

> People are often unreasonable, illogical, and self-centered
> Forgive them anyway
> If you are kind, people may accuse you of selfish,
>   ulterior motives
> Be kind anyway
> If you are successful, you will win some false friends
>   and some true enemies

Succeed anyway
If you are honest and frank, people may cheat you
Be honest and frank anyway
What you spend years building, someone could
　　destroy overnight
Build anyway
If you find serenity and happiness, others may be jealous
Be happy anyway
The good you do today, people will often forget tomorrow
Do good anyway
If you give the world the best you have, it may never
　　be enough
Give the world the best you've got anyway.

CHAPTER REVIEW

* If there's one attribute that determines what heights of success you will reach, it's your attitude.

* Three attributes of successful people are: attitude, motivation and commitment. I call these AMCs.

* How we handle negative situations determines other people's attitudes toward us.

* People with winning attitudes don't focus on what they don't have or what they can't do. They concentrate on what they do have and what they can do.

* None of us are invincible. "King Arthur's Disease" is as dangerous to your business and your life as rushing into battle without armor.

* Always consult with people you trust to ensure you are making decisions for the right reasons.

* Don't give other people the power to make you angry. Don't rent, lease or even lend them space in your head.

* No matter how bad things look or get, never give up your dignity or your integrity.

* Remember, when you can't forgive, you can't move on.

* Stay motivated and positive by posting inspirational notes and sayings where you will see them.

* Focus on putting out the positive energy to attract good things into your life.

> "The greatest way to live with honor in this world is to be what we pretend to be." *Socrates*
>
> "Always be a first-rate version of yourself, instead of a second-rate version of somebody else." *Judy Garland*

SECRET 11

Show the World Who You Really Are

When you start living in tune with your values, you will naturally feel more confident and ready to show the "real you" to the world. Personal branding is a way to showcase your positive influence and convey the essence of who you are.

When people meet you for the first time, all of their gut instincts come into play. They either consciously or unconsciously come up with an impression of you based on the way you dress, talk, smile, frown and act. Unknowingly, they are really thinking about your brand and forming an enduring impression. That is why we say, "You will never get a second chance to make a first impression."

Your personal brand is a combination of the way you look, communicate and act. Think of Donald Trump, Princess Diana, Pierre Trudeau, Barbara Walters, Evil Knieval, Elvis Presley — each name brings to mind a different image and sensation based on a combination of what these people look like, act like and what they've done.

We all have a brand or image we project, whether we're famous or not. Remember, none of these people were famous throughout their entire lives. They only became so through a combination of talent and developing their personal brands.

Walk the Talk

Personal branding is especially important when you're in a public position, but even if you don't crave the limelight you need to be aware of branding. Developing a compelling personal brand helps people see you more clearly. When they do, they begin to feel more drawn to you and what you have to offer. The most effective personal branding helps your family, friends, co-workers, peers and employers understand the essence of who you are. You begin to walk your talk and, as a result, you'll find you have to spend less time explaining who you are or justifying your ideas.

In his book *The Brand Called You*, Peter Montoya writes, "Personal branding lets you control how other people perceive you...You're telling them what you stand for — but in a way that's so organic and unobtrusive that they think they've developed that perception all by themselves..."

The Basics of Personal Branding

In his article "The Three C's of Personal Branding," William Arruda, founder of the branding company Reach, says *clarity*, *consistency* and *constancy* are the keys to strong personal brand development.

Clarity: "Richard Branson," Arruda writes, "is clear about being a risk taker. He is not your typical CEO in a blue suit and white shirt. He is a daredevil who dressed in a wedding gown when he launched *Virgin Bridal*, and was not dressed at all when he launched his book, *Virginity*. Among his first big risky ventures was signing the Sex Pistols onto his record label when no one else would even consider them." Branson went on to challenge *British Airways* by launching his own airline, *Virgin*. He even took on *Coke* by launching *Virgin Cola* and went head to head with Donald Trump by launching his own reality show. Despite his fortune, Branson isn't content to rest on his laurels. He continues to take risks, like attempting to fly around the world in a hot air balloon.

Consistency: To achieve brand consistency, you don't have to remain exactly the same forever. Instead, look at common themes surrounding the way you live. Is a particular style your hallmark? Think of famous people like Jennifer Lopez, Meg Ryan and Johnny Depp. Even though they change with the times, they remain consistent in their overall style.

Constancy: Oprah, William Arruda explains, is the perfect example of constancy. "Oprah is the human brand of show biz. She cares for people and is willing to share herself to help people advance. This clarity about what makes her unique is consistent among all of her endeavors. And it is constantly visible to her target audience through her numerous ways of interacting with the public."

First Impressions

You are in charge of your brand, from the clothes you wear to the friends you keep, to the career and clients you choose. Everything you do radiates who you are. On the popular TV show "What Not to Wear," two fashion and image experts work with people in need of makeovers and personal branding. Even though the entire audience can see these people are not showcasing their best attributes, the people themselves usually don't see it at first. Often, they worry that the makeover process will hide who they really are. However, once they've undergone the makeover — no cosmetic surgery here — they generally end up feeling that the person buried inside is finally allowed to shine. On this show, artists don't come out looking like executives. They look like successful artists. Bike couriers don't look like ballerinas. They just make a better first impression and convey more of the essence of who they really are.

"The five to seven second period of making a first impression is critical," personal branding consultant Lesley Everett told CNN. Everett is the author of the book *Walking Tall: Key Steps to Total Image Impact.*

"Research shows that in the next five seconds we can add another 50 percent to that first impression. Research is also showing that it takes another 20 further experiences with somebody to change a first impression. So in those first 15 seconds we have got key clues into how somebody operates, into their business approach, their attitude, their personality. So when we get to 30 seconds, we have really given enough time to make that impression subconsciously."

Hopefully, when you think of Peter Thomas your impression is that I'm enthusiastic, trustworthy, healthy, hardworking and a good leader. That's who I really am and it's the brand I've worked hard to maintain throughout the years. Everything I do and believe in supports these principles. My mother used to tell me to imagine everything I did would one day be written across the sky for everyone to read. I felt I had better do good things if I wanted to see good things up there.

"A brand is a promise, and your personal brand equity is so critical in this day and age where there is no job security," says Praveen Varshney, director of Varshney Capital Corp, a family-run business based in Vancouver, British Columbia, that provides venture capital, merchant banking and corporate advisory services. "The essence of a brand is the mental imprint we plant on the minds of our market and people around us (even people we don't know)."

In delivering on his brand, Praveen likes to use the phrase "setting and managing expectations." For him, that means "saying what you mean and doing what you say." Better still is UPOD, an acronym Praveen came up with which stands for underpromise and overdeliver so you exceed all your promises.

"Most people do the opposite," says Praveen. "They "OPUD" — overpromise and underdeliver. They say the things they think other people want to hear and set them and others up for disappointment. But I don't know a single person that doesn't like a pleasant surprise!"

Authenticity and Integrity

Praveen has enjoyed a successful career but none of the external trappings of success are as vital to him as maintaining his personal integrity. This internal integrity is about acting in alignment with his values and belief systems and having a strong moral compass — being true to himself and always "doing the right thing." He says one way he checks in with his personal integrity is to make decisions and take actions as if his two young impressionable children were sitting beside him.

"Children do what they observe. What kind of role model do I want to be for my kids? An exemplary one," he says.

Praveen recalls a story told by productivity consultant Denis Waitley. A simple motto hung on the living room wall of Waitley's grandparents' small house, where many seeds for Waitley's development were planted. The motto said, "Life is like a field of newly fallen snow; where I choose to walk, every step will show." His grandparents didn't talk about the motto; they lived it. They believed you were either honest or you weren't."

"There was nothing in between, no such thing as partial honesty," says Praveen. "Integrity, a standard of personal morality and ethics, is not relative to the situation you happen to find yourself in and doesn't sell out to expediency."

"A lot of young people," he adds, "...are taken in by media popularity, big talk, expensive possessions and flashy looks. They move through their years convinced that the externals are what count...Relying on looks or status to feel good and enhance the impression they make is not as important as saying and doing the right things, letting their actions speak for themselves. To develop inner value and personal growth, practice being a 'net giver.' Ask 'how can I help you?' versus 'what's in it for me?' Maintain a steadfast adherence to a strict moral or ethical code."

"Other techniques to build your integrity," Praveen continues, "are to practice humility. Do simple things like saying please and thank you. Treat everyone — no matter what class, race, profession or age — with dignity, respect and courtesy."

"Bottom-line success often leads to fleeting stardom and ultimate defeat. There are no degrees of integrity. Just as you're pregnant or you're not, you have integrity or you don't. And like a ball of glass, if you drop your integrity, it will get nicked or permanently shattered."

He says when you focus on creating and having integrity, you create the awareness and perception — which is reality — that you're reliable, dependable and the "go-to-person" everyone wants on their team. Conversely, no amount of exterior polish will help if you are inauthentic because, on some level, people always sense falsity and pull away from it. To attract the right kind of people in your life, highlight your authentic skills, strengths, values and passions.

Assess Your Brand

To begin bringing out your strengths and developing your personal brand, ask yourself:

* What makes me different from everyone else?

* What are my most admirable character traits?

* What do most people identify me with?

* In what ways do I demonstrate my values to others?

* What parts of myself am I totally comfortable with, and which parts make me feel awkward, as though I am wearing a pair of ill-fitting shoes?

* Do I dress for success and confidence, or do I just "throw something on?" Do my clothes reflect my personality in a polished, professional way?

Create Your Personal Mission Statement

To help you focus on what you want to project to the world through your personal brand, I recommend creating your own mission statement. This statement should say who you are and what you want to communicate most to the people you meet.

To assist you, here's one example of a mission statement written by a biologist:

> *I will live a life of authenticity, originality, adventure and discovery. People will identify me with a warm smile, lack of pretension, strong handshake and high fitness level. I will project the courage to go farther than others to make discoveries. I will travel throughout the world in my quest. I will be energized, fulfilled, and inspired.*

Jamesie Bower, a longtime friend, has been in my life for a few important "firsts." She was there when I returned to Edmonton from Hawaii after I'd just purchased Century 21. She was also there for the very first LifePilot workshop and has subsequently "audited" four more. As the owner of Staff Systems, a successful executive recruitment business in Vancouver, Jamesie hardly needs any reminders of how much she has accomplished. Even so, she found a great deal of value in writing her LifePilot mission statement — with some unexpected surprises.

In 2002, Jamesie was driving home from work, thinking about the mission statement she had been asked to write as part of her LifePilot work. "I wanted to write something that highlighted the positive energy I have been blessed with, so I was very excited," she recalls.

As a busy professional, Jamesie typically followed a solid routine to keep her life on track. But that evening, instead of getting changed out of her work clothes and taking off her jewelry before launching into her chores, she plunged right into cleaning her kitchen so she could get straight to her LifePilot homework.

The next morning, as she was getting ready for an early appointment, Jamesie looked on the dresser where she usually kept her rings. They weren't there. They weren't anywhere in the house. At that point she realized what she must have done. Tossing out the garbage the night before, she had somehow thrown away her rings.

"I was absolutely frantic," she recalls, "because those rings had a great deal of meaning to me. That feeling stayed with me on my drive to work, but then, as I was driving across the Lions' Gate Bridge in Vancouver, I suddenly had an epiphany. I thought to myself, 'J.B., there are thousands of women with more diamonds than you will ever possess. Get over it!'"

Jamesie realized that her diamonds did not define her. What glittered most about Jamesie — and still does — is that remarkable, sparkling energy that no diamonds could ever possess. That energy was the focus of the mission statement she had written.

Oddly enough, when Jamesie went to lunch that day with friends, they inadvertently joined a table of people whose business was diamond exploration. She told them her story and they joked about "exploring" the garbage for Jamesie's diamonds. She never did find the diamonds, but she found something far more valuable: her worth beyond jewels.

"LifePilot," says Jamesie, "has given me a better understanding of my values and actions, and I'm learning to appreciate all the lessons in life, whether they have a positive or negative effect. I look at life in a more positive way and try to pass that on to the people around me, including my staff. I think LifePilot's influence on people is probably much greater than the individual might know. It's hard to be around Peter without his positive attitude rubbing off on you. Whenever something supposedly can't be done, Peter just looks at it and says, 'We'll find a solution.' And you know, nine out of ten times it works."

Write your mission statement:

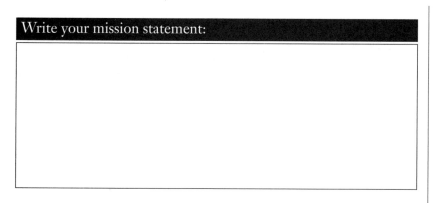

Write Your Biography

Aside from writing your mission statement, another exercise that will help you develop your brand is to write a two- to three-paragraph personal biography. Pretend you are writing it for publication in a prestigious, popular news magazine like *Time*. Strive to make your biography lively and full of interesting details. Accentuate the positives and find ways to show how interesting you are (remember, we are all interesting!).

Write your biography:

Help People Discover Your Depth

The most effective personal branding means taking a deeper look at who you are, where you want to go in life and what you hope to contribute. Exploring the depths of the person you are will help you become the person you want to be. As Praveen Varshney says, "Remain true to your integrity."

It's what I've tried to do throughout my life, and I am very complimented when people sense that authenticity. As Jamesie puts it, "Peter didn't set out to learn to be a stage presenter or motivational expert. He learned to live life. In everything he does, he walks his talk." If that's what others see as my personal brand, I've done something right.

CHAPTER REVIEW

* The Three C's of Personal Branding are Clarity, Constancy and Consistency.

* The first five to seven seconds of meeting someone is a critical time for making a good first impression. It takes another 20 further experiences with somebody to change a first impression.

* Creating your mission statement and biography helps you focus your energy and discover the kernel of your personal brand.

* To be really effective, personal branding must be authentic; walk your talk.

> "A lot of people approach risk as if it's the enemy when it's really fortune's accomplice." *Sting*

> "Most people would rather be certain they're miserable, than risk being happy." *Robert Anthony*

SECRET 12

The Rewards of Risk

Have you ever parked near an airport and watched jumbo jets take off? They are so huge and awkward that flying seems impossible — yet they fly anyway. Similarly, if you watch a bumblebee, you might think, as writer John Maxwell did, that it shouldn't be able to fly. "Because of its size, weight, and total wing span," Maxwell writes, "flying is scientifically impossible. The bumblebee, being ignorant of scientific theory, goes ahead and flies anyway."

Debi Thomas is a world figure skating champion and Olympic bronze medalist who went on to study medicine. "I tell people I'm too stupid to know what's impossible. I have ridiculously large dreams, and half the time they come true."

Her attitude is one you'll frequently find in successful people. They take calculated risks. They refuse to be held back by naysayers, statistics and odds. Fueled by a belief in themselves, they are willing to push the limits and go where no one has ever ventured.

There's a famous scene in the movie *Star Wars* that perfectly illustrates the attitude many successful people have when it comes to taking risks. As Han Solo, the rakish pilot, prepares to take his bucket-of-bolts spaceship on a dangerous escape mission from the dark forces of Darth Vader, the robot C-3PO attempts to tell him the statistical probabilities of a successful escape.

"*Never* tell me the odds," Solo tells the robot. To him, the odds are irrelevant; the power of belief and the will to succeed trump all odds.

I'm not for a minute advocating that you continually fling yourself into wild risks. I *am* saying that it's unlikely you'll achieve your dreams if you never risk anything and remain in a comfort zone all of your life.

"You make your own dream," said John Lennon. "That's the Beatles' story, isn't it? That's Yoko's story. That's what I'm saying now. Produce your own dream...."

Be Honest With Yourself

Sometimes, the advice to "risk all or nothing" rings quite true. After all, you can't leap a 20-foot chasm in two 10-foot jumps. "Our lives improve only when we take chances," says trainer and author Walter Anderson, "and the first and most difficult risk we can take is to be honest with ourselves."

In identifying your values, hopefully you *have* been honest with yourself about what really matters most to you. By writing down your values and goals, you've already taken that important first step to create the kind of life you really want to live. What are you willing to risk to create that life? Are you willing to risk saying no to things you don't value? Are you willing to risk letting go of old patterns that have kept you in place, like a CD stuck on a scratch? Do you really want to spend your life always wondering what might have happened if only you had taken a risk to follow your dreams? "The important thing is this," said Charles Du Bos, French critic, "to be able at any moment to sacrifice what we are for what we could become."

Daring to Meet Your Destiny

Two thousand years ago, the Roman poet Virgil wrote, "Fortune sides with him who dares." When I was 15, I didn't have a clue who Virgil was but the sentiment rang true with me as I got on the bus and left my hometown of Perryvale, Alberta. I was heading for the "big city" of Edmonton to join the Canadian army for a contracted term of at least five years. To a teenage boy, that amount of time seemed like forever but that wasn't going to stop me.

I was scared to leave home, but I was also very curious about the wonderful adventure that lay ahead. My stepfather and my uncles had always talked about the army and the places they had traveled. All of my life, I had read about faraway places with strange sounding names, occupied by exotic-looking people and animals. I said to myself, "This is my chance to break out of Perryvale." My hometown held little potential for me. I was bored with school, and when I weighed my options and looked into the future, it didn't excite me. The army, I felt, was my ticket out of boredom.

Naturally, my mother didn't want me to go, but I needed to convince her. Because I was underage, I needed her to sign for me to join the army. I remember sitting down with Mom and selling her on the idea that I "had" to do this to get a better life. "If you don't sign," I told her, "I'll run away from home and you won't know where I am. Signing for me to join the army is really the best decision because then you'll know where I am, and that I'm getting three square meals a day, clothes and shelter."

The Nobel Prize-winning French writer Andre Gide once said, "One does not discover new lands without consenting to lose sight of the shore for a very long time." I left "the shore" and I don't regret it. If I had heeded my fear of leaving home, my future would have been quite different than the life I live today. Perhaps I would have always wondered what was out there.

The Great Illusion

In their quest for security, some people avoid risk whenever possible, but there are risks in doing and not doing. Security is really just an illusion. True security comes from within; it doesn't depend on external circumstances as much as we'd like to think it does. You can slip in your bathtub as easily as you can die climbing the side of a mountain.

Erik Weihenmayer has successfully climbed all of the world's Seven Summits, which include formidable mountains like Denali, Everest and Aconcagua. That's a remarkable enough achievement for anyone, but especially for a person who can't see. "People think because I'm blind I don't have as much to be afraid of," Weihenmayer says. "That's insane. Look, death is death, if I can see it or not."

Risk is not just for mountain climbers. It exists at every level of our lives, as the following poem reveals:

> To laugh is to risk appearing the fool.
> To weep is to risk appearing sentimental.
> To reach out for another is to risk involvement.
> To expose feelings is to risk exposing your true self.
> To place your dreams before a crowd is to risk ridicule.
> To love is to risk not being loved in return.
> To live is to risk dying.
> To hope is to risk despair.
> To go forward in the face of overwhelming odds
>   is to risk failure.
> But to risk we must, because the greatest hazard in life
>   is to risk nothing.
> The person who risks nothing is one who does nothing,
>   has nothing, is nothing.
> He may avoid suffering and sorrows, but he cannot learn,
>   feel, change, grow, or love.
> Chained by his certitudes, he is a slave — he has forfeited
>   his freedom.
> Only a person who takes risks is free.

Author Unknown

Beyond Fear of Failure

Isn't it interesting that everyone's definition of success is different but everyone's understanding of failure seems the same? But successful people don't always succeed at first, or even at everything.

Successful people are not always right, nor are people who are still striving for success always wrong.

It's easy to look at successful people and ask, "What do they know that I don't know?" I would suggest it's not what people *know* that makes them successful. It's what they *don't* give into — FEAR. Those without fear are rewarded with endless opportunities to gain knowledge and experience. Their willingness to explore helps them discover and act on strategies to achieve their destinies.

I've found that as soon as you overcome fear and start taking steps to achieve goals, your passion for accomplishment begins to grow and the fear diminishes in contrast. The small victories you achieve along the way act as fuel to keep you going. Tom Robbins, in his book *Another Roadside Attraction*, says we often talk about the courage of risking our lives in heroic ways. But real courage, he writes, "is risking something you have to keep on living with, real courage is risking something that might force you to rethink your thoughts and suffer change and stretch consciousness. Real courage is risking one's clichés."

Achieving that kind of courage means you must deal with fear of the unknown and leave safe ground for unknown territory. We all have these fears; the only difference is that some people conquer them.

"Every time I do something new I just pretend that I don't have any audience whatsoever," says David Bowie, who for three decades has been known as one of the most inventive artists in the rock genre. "Once I've done it, *then* I get trepidation."

Musician John Mellencamp says, "What is there to be afraid of? The worst that can happen is you fail. So what? I failed at a lot of things. My first record was horrible."

Sometimes you need to have faith that you can succeed. In his story "Leap of Faith," Craig Larson describes the African Impala, which can jump to a height of more than 10 feet and cover a distance of greater than 30 feet. Despite their remarkable abilities, these animals are easily restricted in three-feet-high pens because they will not jump if they cannot see where their feet will fall. "Faith," writes Larson, "is the ability to trust what we cannot see, and with faith we are freed from the flimsy enclosures of life that only fear allows to entrap us."

Your Risk Tolerance

When you visit a financial planner, you are asked about your tolerance for risk. Are you willing to endure greater risk for higher return on investment? Will you trade high returns for greater security? Are you risk-adverse? Assessing your tolerance for risk shouldn't just be restricted to financial planning. Your attitude toward risk impacts everything you do.

Some people love risk and they embody the motto coined by Jayne Howard: "If you are not living on the edge, you are taking up too much room." Kurt Vonnegut also refers to the value of life on the edge: "I want to stay as close to the edge as I can without going over. Out on the edge you can see all kinds of things you can't see from the center." Other people require so much control in their lives that any risk is not acceptable. Most people are somewhere in between these two extremes. Often, we are willing to take risks in our teens and 20s, but the older we get, the more risk adverse we become. Risk adversity also tends to grow as people acquire more success, more money or more of anything. As Leonardo da Vinci said, "He who possesses most must be most afraid of loss."

That's exactly what singer Peter Gabriel says happened to the band *Genesis* before they broke up. "As the band got more successful," he notes, "it was increasingly difficult to get people to take a risk with something that might jeopardize their livelihood."

But realizing our dreams often means being willing to let go of something. In *Hope for the Flowers*, author Trina Paulus writes, "How does one become a butterfly? You must want to fly so much that you are willing to give up being a caterpillar."

Self-Confidence and Risk

"You can't get distracted when people tell you that your idea is stupid and isn't going to work," advises Amazon founder and CEO Jeff Bezos. "Invention always leads you down a path that people are going to think is weird." According to Bezos, successful entrepreneurs confront criticism and failure with "a unique combination of stubbornness and flexibility."

In short, they believe in themselves. Who knows how much that extra measure of self-confidence tips the odds in their favor and reduces their risk? Here are some other famous people who took risks and pursued their dreams, even though others tried to discourage them:

* Rock Hudson needed 38 takes to successfully complete just one line in *Fight Squadron*, his first movie. He became one of the 20th century's most famous movie stars anyway.

* Walt Disney's first cartoon production company, Laugh-O-Gram, went bankrupt. He went on to build Disneyland anyway.

* The Beatles were rejected by Decca records in 1962. They became the world's most famous rock band anyway.

* Elvis Presley's music teacher in Memphis told him he couldn't carry a tune. He became "the king" anyway.

* Jay Leno applied for a job at Woolworth's but failed the employment test. He became Johnny Carson's successor anyway.

* Billy Crystal was chosen as an original cast member for *Saturday Night Live* but was cut from the cast before the first show aired. He went on to star in highly-successful comedies anyway.

* Barbara Walters was told by Don Hewitt, who later became *60 Minutes* producer, to "stay out of television." She is one of the most famous women on TV anyway.

* Steven Spielberg's mediocre grades meant he could not get into UCLA film school. He made *ET* and *Close Encounters* anyway.

✱ John Grisham's first novel, *A Time to Kill*, was rejected by 16 agents and 12 publishers. He became a best-selling author anyway.

People will always criticize risk takers. In his 1910 speech in Paris, Theodore Roosevelt said, "It is not the critic who counts, nor the man who points out how the strongman stumbled, or where the doer of deeds could have done better. The credit belongs to the man who is actually in the arena, whose face is marred with dust and sweat and blood, who strives valiantly, who errs and comes up short again and again, who knows great enthusiasms, great devotions, and spends himself in a worthy cause, who at best knows achievement and who at worst if he fails at least fails while daring greatly..."

Dare Greatly but Do Your Homework

I take risks, but like most successful risk takers I've learned the value of combining risk with research. When I was negotiating the Century 21 Real Estate franchise rights for Canada, I took a risk that turned out to be one of the best financial moves I've ever made.

We had finished our negotiating and planned to reconvene the next day to conclude the transaction. That evening, I tried to work out the numbers to see just how good this investment could really be. Century 21 had a similar regional franchise agreement that they used with every group. I felt I could not afford to pay them as much as the other regions because my region was different – but how could I explain that and still acquire the rights to what I felt would be the best deal I had ever done? I loved the project but decided there should be an accommodation for the unique geography of the Canadian region.

The next day, I explained to the group that Canada was a very big country — actually bigger than the continental United States. Despite its size, most of the Canadian market was only 4,500 miles long and 100 miles high because that was where most of the population lived. The US had no region that was even near that size. I argued that because of the size of the region, it would be so much more expensive to service it that we could not afford to pay the same fees the other regions paid.

The Century 21 principals bought the argument and I received a one-third discount on the fees to compensate for the size of the country. My high-risk investment of $5,000 became a business generating billions of dollars of sales a year. Many years later, when Century 21 Canada sold, its value was substantially more than any other region in the company system. A lot of the reason for the high value was the extraordinary job done by the management and staff, but it also had much to do with the fact that the discount I negotiated left more on our bottom line and increased our value substantially.

When I first looked at the opportunity to acquire the rights for the franchise, my business partners all had very valid opinions about why it would not work, but none of these opinions were based on facts. I felt I had done my due diligence and had covered all of my questions so, based on my instincts, I went ahead with the acquisition of the Canadian rights. The rest, as they say, is history.

If you feel strongly about an issue and know that you have done your homework, trust your instincts and dare greatly. People love to romanticize about risk takers, so go ahead and let them as long as you know the facts and exactly what is at risk.

One story that always reminds me to look at the whole picture is the tale of three blind men who were led up to an elephant and were asked to determine what an elephant looked like. One of the blind men approached the elephant from the front and came into contact with its trunk. He said, "An elephant is long and skinny like a snake. The next blind man approached the elephant from the side. He reached up under the elephant and touched its belly. "The elephant is like some large balloon that floats in the air," he said. The third blind man approached the elephant from the back and put his arms around the elephant's hind leg. "The elephant is a creature that is built like a pillar reaching up to the sky," he said. Each man had a totally different view of what an elephant looked like. They were all partially correct but none of them had the full picture. The next time you need to make a decision, ask yourself if you have explored the entire elephant.

Failure: Get Past It

The great Irish writer James Joyce said, "A person's errors are his portals of discovery." I've been through plenty of portals of discovery. I used to say I made all my money in real estate and lost it in everything else. But failing isn't a problem in life; it's a natural part of the whole process of learning and growth. How we deal with it is what separates the self-defined winners and losers.

In his book *The Change Makers*, which details the characteristics of great entrepreneurs, author Maury Klein writes, "Like other great people, the entrepreneurs did nearly everything on an enlarged scale, including their gaffes. In many cases, their misjudgements stemmed from the same qualities that characterized their successes. Galvanized by some vision, they threw themselves into the quest, turned a deaf ear to those who said it couldn't be done or warned that it invited disaster, and pounded relentlessly against all obstacles. The joy, after all, was in the doing, even when the doing turned into a grind or turned out badly. Risk and failure are an indelible part of the creative process."

Dale Carnegie was known for his ability to "shut the door on the past with so resolute a slam and with hardly a backward glance." Many people will tell you that I share this trait. I admit, I do tend to have amnesia when it comes to bad news. By refusing to dwell on what has happened, I stay motivated and upbeat. I don't think this makes me a shallow person. I think it makes me positive and committed.

Don't Be Afraid to Laugh

There's a saying by Arthur Koestler: "If the creator had a purpose in equipping us with a neck, he surely meant us to stick it out."

I stick my neck out quite a bit, sometimes with laughable results. "Peter loves to incorporate healthy activities into his life," says my wife Rita. "One day he came home with a pair of rollerblades for each of us. They had rollers the size of tractor tires attached to them! These particular rollerblades, he told me enthusiastically, were for *off-road rollerblading*. He thought it would be fun, but the whole thing looked pretty intimidating to me. I suggested I would give them a try *only* after he had experimented with them. So he eagerly strapped them on and headed out the door. About an hour later he returned, all scratched and bruised and really beaten up. He agreed he should exchange the tractor-tire rollerblades for regular ones."

That's exactly what I did because, as Winston Churchill says, "If you are going through hell, keep going." But I was far from done with rollerblading.

"Then Peter decided he wanted to win an Olympic gold medal," says Rita. "He figured he could do this in rollerblading because he had become pretty good at it. As there was no category in the Olympics for this sport yet, his first goal would be to get them to add rollerblading to the Olympic roster. Then, as soon as this happened, he could go into the over-50 group. He reasoned that there wouldn't be that many over-50 rollerbladers so he'd stand a good chance of winning! In the meantime, he hired a coach for us so we could work on our technique and master the speed. Every day, we'd head out and race down to some secluded area with our coach. Peter eventually developed some pretty major injuries and decided to put his ambition for an Olympic rollerblading medal to bed. My point here is that no task is too great for him to try to achieve. If he fails, that's okay, there's nothing lost. He just moves on to the next deal."

If I had been afraid of failure, think of the fun I would have missed. I encourage you to pursue your potential. At best you'll succeed. At worst, you'll have stories to tell. Some failures may not seem so funny at the time, but the further you move away from them, the more perspective you'll gain and the more you'll learn.

Get Back Up

When I was a boy, I was riding a horse at full gallop along a trail I'd taken many times before. I knew the trail and so did the horse. This particular time, however, I was looking straight ahead when, for some reason, the horse decided to veer abruptly at the fork in the road. I flew over his head, hit the ground and lost consciousness. When I came to, some of the other kids were standing above me. They helped me to my feet and away we went to catch my horse.

Sometimes in life, you'll find yourself tearing straight ahead with all your plans set, when all of a sudden life "turns right" for no apparent reason, just as my horse did. When you fall, as you often will, you've got to pick yourself up and get back at it immediately. It doesn't matter why life turned right or whose fault it was: accept the facts, pick yourself up and get back in the saddle. If you never quit, then you never fail. You only fail when you give up before you've done all you can do to make something a success.

When Enough is Enough

I've said the only time you fail is when you quit, but when you've done your utmost and nothing seems to be working, sometimes you have to cut your losses. Many people, when they find themselves going down the wrong road, have a tendency to try and go faster. But increasing your speed isn't going to get you moving in the right direction. You need to stop, turn around and reassess your aims.

Once I was part of a home construction project that just kept going from bad to worse. Even so, we kept putting in more money. Finally, we had to stop and really consider where we stood. If we kept funding the project, it appeared we could lose a lot more money than we already had. If we cut our losses and changed contractors, it would be difficult and would cost us a lot of money, but the upside was that we could bring on board a new contractor who would be bonded. We would be guaranteed no more losses. We chose to change contractors. Many issues in life are like that.

If a situation or a deal is bad, the first loss is usually the cheapest loss. Take it and move on. Learn from what you've experienced, but don't be afraid to ever risk again.

CHAPTER REVIEW

* Successful people take calculated risks. Fueled by a belief in themselves, they are willing to push the limits and go where no one has ever gone.

* By writing down your values and goals, you've already taken the important first step to create the kind of life you want. Now you must determine what you are willing to risk to create that life.

* As you overcome your fears and start taking steps to achieve your goals, your passion for accomplishment begins to grow and the fear diminishes in contrast.

* Most successful risk takers have learned the value of combining risk with research. Trust your instincts and dare greatly, but always do your homework first.

* When a situation keeps going from bad to worse, know when to cut your losses, regroup and re-strategize.

Secret 13

Your Flight Path is an S Curve

In my late 30s, I worked for a very successful entrepreneur. One day he called all of his managers together to tell us what he'd learned from a Young Presidents' Organization meeting. He was excited to tell us about the S Curve Theory, also known as the Sigmoid Curve Theory. The definition of sigmoid is, in fact, an S-shaped form.

This theory recognizes that we all have certain ebbs and flows to our lives. These patterns of living resemble the shape of an S. During the course of your life, you may go through a series of S Curves. A typical S Curve journey might last from five to seven years. How you handle your S Curves is a critical component of successful living.

The S Curve

To help you understand the way a typical person might move through an S Curve, look at the diagram on the right. Let's say you are beginning a new job. When you first start out, you are at *Point 1* on the lower left of the S Curve. Getting to know the in's and out's of your job can be challenging during the first year. This is represented by *Point 2* at the bottom of the S as it curves downward. At this time, you are still learning the ropes, gaining new skills and getting used to your environment.

As you become more familiar with your job, you increase your efficiency and start to move up the S to *Point 3*, working your way towards the top. It usually takes five to seven years to work your way from the bottom of an S to the top, although some psychologists believe timelines are becoming more compressed

201

due to the information age and trends toward a greater diversity of careers in the course of our lifetimes.

When you reach *Point 4*, the top of the S, you hit a plateau. Some people become overly confident at this time — it's the height of their success, after all. Often, they become so psyched up by that success they fail to notice that the S now has nowhere to go but down, moving toward *Point 5*. This is called the slope of diminishing returns. You can't sit at the top of an S forever. As the song goes, "What goes up, must come down."

Sliding unaware over the top of the S leaves many people wondering, "What happened? Why didn't I see the signs?" This downward slide, however, does not have to become inevitable. When you understand the S Curve Theory and apply it to your life, you begin to sense when you are approaching your crest and the need to take action. The key is to create a new S Curve for yourself before you reach the plateau and begin sliding down.

Take Action

You need to introduce new challenges or opportunities into your life when you sense yourself nearing the peak of your S Curve. If you plan to stay in your present job, you may have to approach your employer and ask for new challenges, whether it's moving to a new area or getting a promotion. At this point, consider what you need very carefully. You may also want to think about moving to a new job or even starting your own company using the experience you've gained.

How S Curves interlink throughout your life

Changing your career, or launching a business, isn't the only way to introduce new S Curves into your life. Buying a new home, moving to another city, starting a family, enrolling in a course of study or taking a trip all qualify to move you over to a new S Curve. You don't need to get a divorce or quit your job, or anything so dramatic — you are going through a natural evolution.

I saw a perfect example of the importance of the S Curve Theory in the life of my sister-in-law, Alice, who had reached a personal plateau. Alice had always had a natural ability to perform and absolutely loved it even though she had never taken any formal classes. Then, I decided to give her a gift in the form of acting classes. This created a whole new dimension of excitement to her life and, with a bit of support from her family, she finished her class and was the star in the grand finale of the class play.

Success on the S Curve

In "The S Curve: What is Wrong with Success?" Rajagopal Sukumar discusses how we can maximize our understanding of the S Curve Theory:

> "By analogy, consider mountain climbing, which is sort of similar to learning new skills. Initially, we start at the bottom with a clear estimate and a timeline to climb the mountain. As we come to grips with the terrain of the mountain, we are able to climb more efficiently and reach the summit. Having reached the summit, we cannot stay there for long, depending on the altitude.
>
> For instance, if we were climbing Mt. Everest, we could be there at the peak only for a few minutes due to atmospheric conditions and human limitations. Descent becomes important pretty soon. But if we are keen mountaineers, we set our sights on the next mountain to climb. In a similar way, when we reach the top of the S Curve of a particular skill, we should start the S Curve of the next important skill. Ultimately, our skill set should look like a mountain range with a lot of mountains (or a lot of S Curves) in it, representing various skills we have learned."

You can apply the S Curve Theory to business life cycles, product cycles, consumer trends and even political cycles. Some people even speculate the S Curve describes the cycle of Mozart's symphony productions, the construction of Gothic cathedrals and the rise of airline traffic. Studying the S Curve will give you new insights into the world around you and your role in it.

CHAPTER REVIEW

* Look back over your life and try to apply the S Curve to the patterns you find there.

* Ask yourself, "Where am I in my current S Curve?"

* Begin planning for your new S Curve before the current one runs out. Use the S Curve Theory to assist you in pre-setting your goals and priorities.

* Recognize that declines in the S Curve are natural patterns. Stay action oriented and focus on your goals to prevent entropy from setting in.

* Remain aware of the five- to seven-year cycle of the S Curve.

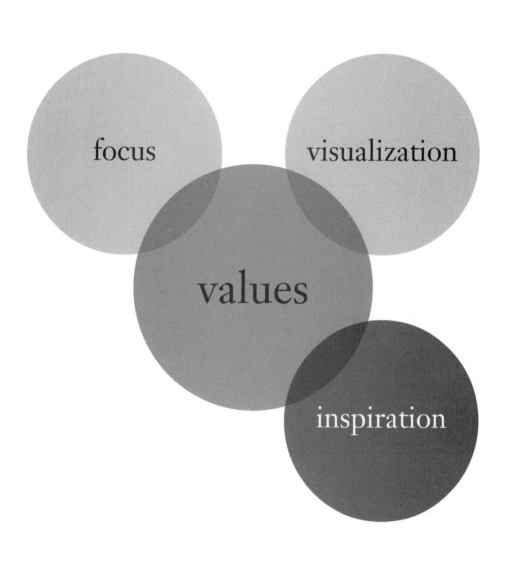

SECRET 14
New Heights of Inspiration

Don't wait for lightning to hit you with a bolt of inspiration. That's great when it happens, but some of the world's most inspired and successful people find ways to inspire themselves.

According to Tom Wujec, author of *Five Star Mind* and *Pumping Ions*, great men and women throughout history have all had their personal inspirational rituals. Beethoven dumped ice water over his head. Brahms shined his own shoes. Kipling apparently wrote only with a certain type of black ink. Charles Dickens slept with his bed pointing north; he believed the Earth's magnetic field stimulated him.

If you don't think you can stand pouring ice water on your head to spark inspiration, I have to say I agree with you. Fortunately, there are easier and more pleasurable ways to get inspired.

"A creative mind-set for one person," writes Wujec, "may be a state of anxiety for another. What stimulates a musician may bore a novelist. In fact, there isn't really a single state of mind — a combination of thoughts and moods — that we could call a creative mind-set. However, every person experiences peak moments when he or she is at a creative peak. Athletes call these peak moments *the zone*. Comedians call it *being on a roll*. Musicians call it *getting in the groove*. Psychologists call it *flow* or *optimal experience*."

Find Your Place

There is a 100-year-old quarry in Victoria, British Columbia that had been dug out and depleted of its stone. Many such quarries are deserted and forgotten; some turn into swimming holes for local kids. But this quarry is different because of the vision of a remarkable family who turned it into one of the world's most celebrated sunken gardens. Today, Butchart Gardens is a 55-acre wonder, featuring flowers and plants from all over the world.

Overlooking the sunken garden is a spot where you can pause and drink in the garden's incredible beauty and serenity. No matter what's going on in my life, when I stand in this spot I feel inspired, and connected to God and the beauty of this Earth.

It's important to have your personal sanctuary, a place where you can go to reflect and feel inspired. Your spot may not be a garden. It may be a riverbank, a beach, a mountaintop, or a Buddhist temple or church. Find *your* spot and try to spend a little time there each year. It's good for your soul.

Live the Learning Lifestyle

Knowledge is the fuel that keeps our inspiration going. Unless you are continually learning new things, you can't really expect to be at your most creative and inspired. Continual learning also keeps our brains limber as we age. It's the old "use it or lose it" axiom. We must avoid at all costs becoming like the juvenile sea squirt that Daniel C. Dennett describes in his book *Consciousness Explained*. According to Dennett, the sea squirt, with only a rudimentary nervous system, meanders through the ocean in search of the right rock or piece of coral to make its home in. When it finds the right spot, it takes root there. Since it doesn't need its brain any longer, it eats it.

Unlike sea squirts, we *need* our brainpower throughout our lives. One of my favorite ways of keeping my brain active and inspired is to read everything I can get my hands on, including three or four newspapers a day, then put into practice the things I've learned that align with my values.

Not only does reading exercise the brain, which is essential in staving off depression, it takes you on explorations into yourself. "A book," wrote Franz Kafka, "must be the axe for the frozen sea inside us."

Doing puzzles also keeps the brain active. In 1994, *Life* magazine told the story of a group of nuns aged 80 to 100. These women all shared very alert minds and exhibited no signs of senility. They attributed this to the fact that they all did puzzles every day. What they were actually doing was creating connections in the neural pathways of their brains, something neurobiologists refer to as "use-dependent plasticity."

Keep your mind limber, no matter what age you are. When you don't force your mind into new areas of exploration, you actually create ruts in your brain. The only difference between a rut and a grave is the length and depth of the hole.

Wring the Most Out of Life

When I visualize the way I want to live my life, I picture myself taking up a face cloth — we used to call them flannels in England — dipping it in water, soaking it up and squeezing every last drop out of it. I want to experience *everything*. During my lifetime I've climbed the pyramids, driven a Formula One race car, jumped out of an airplane, flown a helicopter, crossed Alligator Alley in Florida on a jet boat, visited the Taj Mahal, scuba dived in Fiji with just a rope separating me from the sharks, dived to 850 feet in a submarine, and raced motorcycles.

If a random idea comes to mind, don't dismiss it out of hand just because it doesn't fit with your standard view of the world. Write it down and think about it. Be willing to clean out the stereotypes in your mind to make room for these wild ideas to take root.

It's not just wild adventures that stimulate me. Whenever I see people really enjoying themselves, I want to find out why. In my view, the best way to do that is to experience it for myself. "We were in Sun Valley with some friends for a ski holiday," my wife Rita remembers. "After a full day of skiing, we were all hanging out in our chalet just before dinner. Our friends took out a deck of cards and started playing. They apparently do this every night around this time. Peter turned to me, horrified, and said 'How come we don't play cards every night?' He then made immediate plans to incorporate this into our daily schedules. On our first day at home we sat down, played cards for less than five minutes, and he announced that he would prefer reading to playing cards. But, you know, he had to try it!"

Collect Pictures of Your Future

When you see pictures in books and magazines that inspire you, cut them out and keep them where you can look at them on a regular basis. Sometimes these pictures will take you to places you find inspiring; sometimes they will fuel your dreams. For example, if your dream is to visit Spain, collect enticing travel brochures. Do you want to get in better shape? Find a picture of someone who looks great. I think you get the idea!

A woman I work with spends every New Year's Day cutting out pictures of things, travel experiences and people she wants to enter her life during the coming year. She then pours some left-over eggnog and creates a collage. She says she's no longer surprised when her visions become reality.

Color Outside the Lines

Talk to people outside your usual circle of friends, acquaintances and co-workers. Ask for their opinions, especially when they know nothing about what you do in life. Do things you've never done before but always wanted to do, whether it's taking an art class or learning how to drive a stock car. By coloring outside the lines, you may just create your masterpiece rather than just filling in someone else's vision of what life should look like.

Discover the Value in "Accidents"

Some of the most famous inventions in history have been the result of accidents. Laurens Van der Post says, "I remembered a story of how Bach was approached by a young admirer one day who asked, 'Papa Bach, how do you manage to think of all these new tunes?' 'My dear fellow,' Bach said, 'I have no need to think of them. I have the greatest difficulty not to step on them when I get out of bed in the morning and start moving around my room.'"

"Over the years," says artist Sean Landers, "I have learned to put myself in a position where accidents can happen and where I can take advantage of small mysteries. This is a strange process of discovery. I know my initial idea is merely a point of departure, never the end."

Set Inspirational Goals

Some people feel they are at their most inspired when they are under pressure. From what we know about the effects of stress on the body, it's true that pressure may stimulate a temporary high that results in an inspired state. Many people need deadlines to stimulate inspiration and creativity. Novelist Rita Mae Brown says, "A deadline is negative inspiration. Still, it's better than no inspiration at all."

Take Time Out

One day, two men were splitting wood. One man was a 6'6", 250-pound lumberjack in great physical shape. The other was a 130-pound nerd, all skin and bones. Both men began splitting wood at about the same time. They worked until coffee break, at which point the nerd quit splitting and took his break while the lumberjack just kept on splitting. The same thing happened at lunchtime, and again during the afternoon break. This went on for two weeks. The big lumberjack noticed that, despite his longer hours of work, he wasn't far ahead of the nerd. He worked extra hard into the nights while the nerd left at 6:00 p.m. each evening. After three weeks of working, the lumberjack saw that the piles of split wood were about even between the two men.

By the end of the fourth week, it was really obvious the nerd had the advantage. One morning just before he left to have coffee, the lumberjack angrily accosted him. "I cannot understand why you have more wood split than I do," he sputtered. "You are smaller than I am, and you don't have the strength that I have." The nerd answered, "Ah yes, my friend, but you never stop to sharpen your axe!" This story is a good reminder that we all need time off from work to think and refresh our creativity. Remember, you can only make so much money with your hands. It is unlimited how much you can make with your brain.

Spend Time with Inspiring People

All kinds of people inspire me, including my grandchildren. Being with children can help you to reconnect with the kid in yourself, to play again, and to think out of the box.

Jennifer Carol, a talented news anchor who had put her career on hold to raise her family, had an epiphany during her first LifePilot workshop. She emerged from the workshop determined to create a LifePilot program for her two children, Jessica and Austin, but what she created is now inspiring other children as well. Jennifer has written a children's book called *Cool 2 BEE You* and launched a website for kids, *www.cool2beeyou.com*.

"I have discovered my voice through a bumblebee named Bigsbee," says Jennifer, who describes herself as a desperate housewife turned enlightened infopreneur. "Together we hope to inspire people to *bee-gin* with a dream, *bee-lieve* in themselves so that they can *bee-come* all they can *bee* and discover their own brilliance." Her goal is to appear on the Oprah show. I believe she will.

Revisit Your Dreams

Childhood dreams don't die — they just go on holiday. I like to revisit some of mine now and again, sometimes with hilarious results.

"One day I received a call from Peter's assistant," remembers Rita. "She announced that Peter had just received a massive whip he'd ordered from some infomercial. She laughed and suggested I should thank her for the warning. When Peter arrived home, he couldn't get his new whip out quick enough. He said that when he was a kid he had seen cowboys use these whips and he had always wanted to master the skill. After accidentally whipping himself and a few household articles, he decided it was better to practice this skill outside. He eventually got the technique down pretty good with very little damage, other than the loss of our entrance flower garden."

Switch Gears

Meredith Thring, author of *How to Invent*, says an essential characteristic of the creative state is the ability to switch off the critical parts of ourselves that inhibit inspiration.

Albert Einstein knew the power of doing this. Although he kept a regular work schedule, he also made time to switch off his "critical faculty" to take long walks on the beach or retreat to his bedroom so he could listen to what was happening inside his head.

"If my work isn't going well," he said, "I lie down in the middle of a workday and gaze at the ceiling while I listen and visualize what goes on in my imagination."

Keep an Idea Book

Sometimes we get inspirational thoughts and vow to commit them to memory. Unfortunately, these thoughts are often so ephemeral that they don't stay in our memories very long. Keep a small notebook with you and write down these thoughts as they occur to you. Look back over them whenever you need some inspiration.

Trigger Inspiration

A personal trigger is a biofeedback technique you can use to take you back to a time when you felt totally inspired or creative. Many hypnotherapists use personal triggers to help their clients quit smoking, lose weight or reduce anxiety. You can use personal triggers to stimulate inspiration.

First decide what personal trigger you want to use. Many people use the gesture of touching the index finger and thumb together. The gesture you choose doesn't matter, but it must be something you can do without embarrassment in a public place. When you touch your fingers together, this acts as a physical signal or trigger that tells your mind it's time to return to a place of inspiration.

Now, relax and close your eyes. Think of a time when you felt particularly inspired. Try to fill the memory in with as much detail as you can. How did you feel when you were casting about for inspiration? What did it feel like when that "aha" moment came to you? As soon as this memory and feeling crystallizes in you, touch your thumb and forefinger together. Do this any time you want to recreate the feeling.

Model Thinking

Model your thinking on people you find inspiring. How would they bring more inspiration and creativity into their lives? (Actually, this works with just about anything, not just inspiration.) When you pretend to be that person and imitate their way of being, you communicate their talents to your subconscious. If you do this enough, the process becomes your own. You can't and shouldn't imitate another person forever. Eventually, however, their strengths will become part of you.

Tune it In, Turn it Up

"Some people find it easier to picture the stream of inspiration as being like radio waves of all sorts being broadcast at all times," writes Julia Cameron in *The Artist's Way*. "With practice, we learn to hear the desired frequency on request. We tune in to the frequency we want. Like a parent, we learn to hear the voices of our current brainchild among the other children's voices."

* Don't wait for lightning to strike. The world's most inspired people find ways to inspire themselves.

* Find a personal sanctuary where you can go to reflect and feel inspired.

* Continual learning encourages creativity and inspiration, and keeps the brain limber as we age.

* If a random idea comes to mind, don't dismiss it out of hand. Write it down and think about it. Be willing to clean out your mental stereotypes.

* Collect pictures, photographs, poems, lyrics, quotes and newspaper or magazine articles that inspire you. These things should reinforce your values, constantly motivate you to achieve your dreams and demonstrate that your dreams can become reality.

* Talk to people outside your usual circle to collect new ideas, views and experiences.

* Spend time with people who inspire you, or try to think of what they might do to bring inspiration into their lives.

* Keep a small notebook with you and write down inspirational thoughts before you forget them.

* Use personal triggers to stimulate inspiration.

SECRET 15

Music to Live a Great Life By

M usic is such a vital source of inspiration, I think it deserves its own chapter in this book. As Shakespeare wrote in *The Twelfth Night*, "If music be the food of love, play on."

In my experience, music is a critical tool in reaching new heights of happiness and success. It's the soundtrack to our lives and its effect on the mind, body and soul is profound. Music boosts brainpower, affects focus, soothes senses, increases endurance and enhances creativity.

"Music is a means of rapid transportation," says John Cage, one of America's greatest musical innovators, noted for his often-bizarre experimentations with sound and even silence.

I'd have to agree with Cage. Whenever I play "The Power of Love," I am immediately transported back to the first time I met my wife. This became our song. All of the love, laughter and emotion of young love comes back to me clearly each time I hear this song.

When I play a song called "Slowly" by Webb Pierce, I'm 10 years old again, riding my bike home from school and singing at the top of my voice as I come over the hill. When I hear "The Great Pretender" by Tony Williams and The Platters, I'm a 16-year-old in Allison, Ontario, standing at a jukebox in a restaurant where I'm hanging out with my buddies.

The fact that music so easily awakens our memories signals its power. But its power is not only based on its ability to transport us to the past. As we navigate through life, music has the power to transport us to new parts of ourselves, deeper levels of consciousness and new heights of learning. Sometimes it takes us there at rapid velocity; sometimes it waltzes us there. It doesn't matter how we get there — the point is we *do* get there.

Some of history's greatest successes have credited music with stimulating their imaginations and boosting brainpower. Albert Einstein saw music as an integral part of his genius. "If I were not a physicist," he said, "I would probably be a musician. I often think in music. I live my daydreams in music. I see my life in terms of music."

Former US President Bill Clinton says, "Music has had a powerful influence on my life, helping me to mix practice and patience with creativity. The most enjoyable activity of my presidency was the opportunity to meet the musical greats of America." Music so profoundly influenced Clinton that his presidential library opened an exhibit called "A World of Music" featuring the music he loves and its impact on his life.

My own life has been played out against a soundtrack that includes everything from country music (the only music on the radio in Alberta when I was a kid) to rock, pop and jazz. My tastes have run the gamut, from The Mamas and the Papas to Dire Straits, Roberta Flack, Freddie Mercury, The Pointer Sisters, U2 and even the Culture Club. Amidst all of that, the artist who always reigned supreme for me is Elvis. If he's singing a rockin' tune, he gets me rockin.' If he's crooning a bluesy song, I feel bluesy.

"...it was like he came along and whispered some dream in everybody's ear, and somehow we all dreamed it," says Bruce Springsteen.

Over the years, I have collected thousands of CDs. I listen to them whenever I can — when I'm driving, when I need to relax, and when I crave a pick-me-up. When I'm riding my exercise bike, I notice how fast my workouts go by if I'm listening to music. When I need to focus, I like to have jazz playing in the background. As I intensify my focus, the music fades. Then, as I come back down from this extreme focus, the music becomes prominent again.

The Sound Evolution

There's no doubt music has the power to change lives, but its amazing impact hardly began with Elvis. Throughout history, music has shaped our lives and the world in which we live. Scientists have discovered bone flutes, jaw harps and percussive instruments dating back to the time of the Neanderthals. In a paper published in *Science*, Patricia Gray, head of the Biomusic program at the National Academy of the Sciences, proposes that music came into this world long before the human race ever did.

Gray came to that conclusion after noting in her research that humpback whales use the same techniques as humans in composing songs. They use similar rhythm and length variations. As well, the whales sing in key, and appear to rhyme. Gray speculates whales might use rhymes for the same reasons we do: as devices to help them remember.

"The fact that whale and human music have so much in common even though our evolutionary paths have not intersected for 60 million years," writes Gray, "suggests that music may predate humans — that rather than being the inventors of music, we are latecomers to the musical scene."

Greek philosophers Socrates and Plato believed music was essential to our souls. Plato saw musical training as a more powerful instrument than any other in the integration of the human being. "Music is a moral law," he wrote. "It gives a soul to the universe, wings to the mind, flight to the imagination, a charm to sadness, gaiety and life to everything. It is the essence of order, and leads to all that is good, just, and beautiful, of which the invisible, but nevertheless, dazzling, passionate, and eternal form."

From the ancient Greeks to the Beatles to the band Green Day, music has defined us and moved us forward. During the 1960s, music became a driving force behind revolutions in human rights, the women's movement, anti-war protests and more. Even in the midst of war — specifically Vietnam — music helped people articulate their feelings and escape from the harsh reality. "The best music," says Bruce Springsteen, "is essentially there to provide you with something to face the world with."

If music has the power to change the world, think of the power it possesses to create change in individuals. "Music is the shorthand of emotion," wrote Russian novelist Leo Tolstoy. Today, more than ever, we know that to be true — and it's helping us access higher states of consciousness.

It's What You Feel

As teenagers, most of us would have found life without music unbearable, but somehow, as we move further into adulthood, many of us let music slip away. Other sounds intrude: traffic, conversation, criticism, office machines, appliances, the drone of computers and the interruptions of cell phones. We forget about music and, in the process, we forget some of the vital gifts music teaches us about living. We forget how, as Samuel Butler said, "[Living] must be composed by ear, feeling and instinct, not by rule."

When we lose music, we lose a vital connection to our own rhythm and bypass the incredibly positive effects it can have on our focus, motivation and creativity. For instance, some researchers, like Daniel Levitin, have found listening to familiar music activates neural structures deep within the ancient primitive regions of the brain, the *cerebellar vermis*.

"For music to so profoundly affect this gateway to emotion, it must have some ancient and important function," says Levitin, a McGill university professor and record producer who has conducted research with musicians such as Paul Simon and Eric Clapton.

Luciano Pavarotti may believe "you don't need any brains to listen to music," but scientific research shows that's not true. Carol Krumhansl of Cornell University demonstrated that music directly affects our brain's limbic system (sometimes called "the old mammalian brain"), which controls our emotions.

In a 1997 study, Krumhansl and her team played a number of musical pieces that expressed fear, sadness, happiness and tension. As each volunteer listened to the music, the team recorded heart rates, blood pressure, respiration and other indicators. They found music with a fast beat in a major key brought about all the physical changes associated with happiness in listeners. In contrast, a slow beat and minor key led to sadness.

Music's effect on us starts early. "Infants as young as two months will turn toward consonant, or pleasant sounds and away from dissonant ones," says Norman M. Weinberger in his *Scientific American* article, "Music and the Brain."

"And when a symphony's denouement gives delicious chills, the same kinds of pleasure centers of the brain light up as they do when eating chocolate, having sex or taking cocaine."

Taj Mahal, one of the most celebrated figures in late-20th-century blues, says, "In the end, ultimately, the music plays you, you don't play the music."

Music Exercises the Brain

When asked about how he developed the theory of relativity, Albert Einstein said, "It occurred to me by intuition, and music was the driving force behind that intuition. My discovery was the result of musical perception."

A number of studies show learning and performing music boosts brainpower by strengthening synapses between brain cells. In fact, in brain scans conducted on volunteers during musical performances, almost the entire cerebral cortex is active.

Can we become geniuses like Einstein by tuning in to music? That topic has elicited a great deal of debate since studies in the 1990s linked listening to Mozart with increased special IQ.

In 1993, researchers at the University of California at Irvine found college students who listened to Mozart's *Piano Sonata K. 448* for ten minutes prior to taking a spatial IQ test scored eight points higher than those who did not. This phenomenon was dubbed The Mozart Effect after the results of the study were published in *Nature* magazine in 1993. Since then, the Irvine study has yielded some big headlines, but critics now say the original study didn't live up to the hype surrounding it.

While the original study was conducted only on college students, a flurry of books and articles promoted Mozart for everyone from babies to business people despite the fact that babies had never been studied, nor had business people.

Was it all a dream? No, but it appears to have been over-hyped. But regardless of the validity of the Mozart Effect, plenty of anecdotal and actual evidence exists to show that music does play a positive role in our lives. "Even a little training can quickly alter the brain's reactions," says Norman W. Weinberger, referring to a 2004 study at McMaster University which recorded brain responses to piano, violin and pure tones in four- and five-year-old children.

If you really want to tune into the power of music to improve your brain's functioning powers, learn to play. "The very best engineers and technical designers in the Silicon Valley industry are, nearly without exception, practicing musicians," says Grant Venerable in his book *The Paradox of the Silicon Savior*.

Music Promotes Healing

The Egyptians, Greeks, and Romans and other ancient cultures described music as a healing medium. In the 20th century, the famous nurse Florence Nightingale recognized the healing influence of certain kinds of music on patients."

In fact, during World War II, musicians went to hospitals to play for veterans suffering physical and emotional trauma. Soon the hospitals began hiring musicians. Music has continued to be used by the medical profession to promote healing, curb pain and ease anxiety during medical procedures.

Dentists frequently offer patients headphones and a selection of music during everything from tooth extraction to root canals. Doctors are even using music to rehabilitate stroke patients through Melodic Intonation Therapy. They have noted that stroke patients who have lost their ability to speak retain the ability to sing. Instead of struggling to talk, patients sing what they want to say.

Music Affects Our Physiology

A number of studies show the heart rate is responsive to the pace, tempo, volume and frequency of music. Music can even affect our blood pressure. Dr. Shirley Thompson, an associate professor of epidemiology at the University of South Carolina School of Public Health, reports excessive noise may raise blood pressure by as much as 10 percent. The reverse also appears to be true. People with hypertension use music to bring their blood pressure readings down.

Music also influences body temperature. According to Don Campbell, author of *The Mozart Effect*, "Transcendent music can flood us with warmth. Loud music with a strong beat can raise our body heat a few degrees, while soft music with a weak beat can lower it. Music does this by influencing blood circulation, pulse rate, breathing, and sweating."

The level of stress hormones in the blood declines significantly in those listening to relaxing, ambient music. Sometimes this music can overcome the need for medication. University of Illinois researchers found in a study of 256 office workers that listening to music of their own choice soothed frayed nerves, drowned out distracting noise, boosted mood, and significantly enhanced office performance.

One can only wonder what Ludwig van Beethoven would have thought of all of these studies and experiments. It was Beethoven, after all, who said, "Music is a higher revelation than all wisdom and philosophy. Music is the electrical soil in which the spirit lives, thinks and invents."

Bring Music Into Your Life

✴ Re-energize your music collection. Ask friends and family — especially people whose tastes you admire — for their ideas.

✴ Experiment with the way different types of music affect you. What boosts your mental energy, lifts your creativity, or soothes you into relaxation?

✴ Play music while you are exercising. You'll be amazed at how much this boosts your endurance and reduces the boredom factor.

✴ When you want to relax, opt for music with a slow tempo.

✴ Launch into your day with music that energizes you. What lifts your mood and makes you feel like getting out of bed?

✴ When you need a boost, listening to familiar melodies can take you back to a time when you were happy.

✴ If the sounds of nature soothe you, bring them indoors to your sound system. "When I hear music," wrote Henry David Thoreau, "I fear no danger. I am invulnerable. I see no foe. I am related to the earliest times, and to the latest."

Chapter Summary

* Music boosts brainpower, affects our ability to focus, soothes our senses, increases endurance and enhances creativity.

* Some researchers have found listening to familiar music activates neural structures deep within the ancient primitive regions of the brain.

* Learning and performing music increases brainpower by strengthening synapses between brain cells.

* Music is used by the medical profession to promote healing, curb pain, and ease anxiety during procedures. It affects the heart rate, blood pressure, body temperature, level of stress hormones, and mood.

* Bring music into your life to inspire you, relax or to give you a much-needed energy boost.

Secret 16

The Magic of Mentorship

Mentoring is one of the oldest forms of influence. Scholars have noted that mentors were commonplace in Africa, long before the beginnings of ancient Greek civilization. But it wasn't until Odysseus came along that mentoring had a formal name in Western civilization.

Like many great leaders, Odysseus, the hero of the Trojan Wars whose epic adventures have been recounted in Homer's *Ulysses*, had a wise teacher. That teacher's name was said to be Mentor. According to myth, the goddess Athena would take on Mentor's form for the purpose of giving counsel to Odysseus. When Odysseus left on his travels, he entrusted the care of his son Telmachus to Mentor. From that point on, Mentor's name came to depict a wise and trusted counselor.

Through the ages, successful men and women have experienced the power of mentorship to gain knowledge. They have relied on mentors to help open important doors to the future. Our culture is filled with stories of famous mentoring relationships, both factual and fictitious. The story of King Arthur and Merlin is a classic example. When Arthur was just a boy, Merlin became his mentor and helped him develop his strengths. Merlin also arranged opportunities for Arthur to secure the kingship, including the challenge of the sword in the stone. Later, Merlin created the legendary round table by which Arthur governed.

The mentoring relationship was the basis of Mitch Albom's book *Tuesdays with Morrie*, about his relationship with his old college

229

professor Morrie Schwartz. When Albom found out Schwartz was dying of Lou Gehrig's disease, he reunited with his professor and met with him every Tuesday to discuss everything from work to forgiveness to love.

There are other such famous relationships. Frodo had Gandalf, Robin had Batman, Alexander the Great had Aristotle, Jung had Freud, Gail Sheehy had Margaret Mead, and Helen Keller had Anne Sullivan.

Most of us can identify someone who has had a positive, significant impact on our lives. Mentors can be friends, relatives, co-workers, teachers, as well as historic or contemporary personalities. Most often, a mentor is a more experienced or older person who acts as a role model, compatriot, challenger, guide or cheerleader.

Writer Thomas Wolfe's mentor not only made him feel he could become great; he was there when greatness seemed a long way off. "I was sustained by one piece of inestimable good fortune," says Wolfe. "I had for a friend a man of immense and patient wisdom and a gentle but unyielding fortitude. I think that if I was not destroyed at this time by the sense of hopelessness which this gigantic labor has awakened in me, it was largely because of the courage and patience of this man. I did not give in because he would not let me give in."

Who Would You Choose?

Most of us have heard the adage, "When the student is ready the teacher will appear." Back when I started my first company, my lawyer wisely told me I needed to appoint some directors who could give the company wisdom, direction and strategy, but I was 28 years old and hadn't met enough people at that time who I felt could give me the advice I needed.

The answer came to me one day as I browsed through a book of black and white portraits by the renowned photographer Yousuf Karsch. In the book were beautiful pictures of John F. Kennedy,

Martin Luther King Jr., Indira Gandhi and Ernest Hemingway. The personalities of these great leaders seemed to leap right off the pages at me. I thought, "These people can become my directors; they have a lot of wisdom and can advise me on what I need to do."

I cut their photos out of the book, framed them, and studied them by reading everything I could find about them. For years, these portraits hung on my wall. When I needed advice, I would ask myself, "What would my mentors do?" In time, I came to refer to these distinguished people as my "virtual mentors."

JFK was a great business advisor. He was charismatic, assertive, outgoing and fair-minded. He struck me as the consummate dealmaker — a man with the ability to articulate his dreams and motivate others to turn those dreams into action.

Martin Luther King Jr. was the person who could tell me what was right and wrong: he was a wonderful decision maker. I admired King's total dedication to achieving his goals. I saw him as strong and just. Interestingly, Martin Luther King's mentor was Mahatma Gandhi. In 1950, Dr. King toured India, following a path to the towns and villages where Gandhi had spent time. He read about Gandhi, reflected on his philosophies and talked to people who had followed Gandhi. "To other countries I come as a tourist," King said upon his arrival there, "but to India, I come as a pilgrim." He discovered firsthand what Gandhi had achieved and how he had achieved it. Then he took the concept of nonviolence and applied it to the American civil rights movement.

Another Gandhi — Indira Gandhi, prime minister of India — was my virtual spiritual mentor. She was the daughter of Jawaharlal Nehru, who had been mentored by Mahatma Gandhi. I saw her as a woman who led her country with passion, vision and humanity. She pursued her goals without trampling on others to do so. This is something I have been firm about in my own career. In my business dealings, I believe in the power of win-win — both sides need to feel they have received benefit.

Ernest Hemingway became my rogue advisor. If I needed an excuse to have a little fun I would be sure to ask Ernest. He pursued a lifestyle most people just dream about. He approached life with daring and gusto, and translated those experiences into some of the greatest writings of the 20th century.

Virtual mentors can help you access the wisdom of the ages. To identify and learn about your virtual mentors, comb the Internet, bookstores or libraries for biographies of people you admire. Learn how they conquered their challenges. Try to identify the key things they did to achieve their dreams. The more you learn about your virtual mentors, the more wisdom you will draw from them.

My friend Alfredo J. Molina drew on the wisdom of virtual mentors as he built Molina Fine Jewelers in Phoenix. He looked to jewelry icons like Winston, Cartier, Faberge and Tiffany. Alfredo would ask himself, "What would Harry Winston do in this situation?"

"I still refer to my virtual mentors today," says Alfredo, "and you know, it's funny, even the people around me know about this. One time I was on a phone call and had to make a decision. My public relations assistant was in the room. When I got off the phone, she asked me, 'Would Harry Winston do this?'"

One of my favorite stories about Alfredo involves Harry Winston. Winston was known as the king of diamonds. He loved them so much he always carried a diamond with him. People came to expect this from him, and often, at parties and other gatherings, they would come over to see which diamond he happened to be carrying that day.

One day, Alfredo and I were in Beverly Hills, walking down Rodeo Drive. We ran into another jeweler Alfredo knew and stopped to chat. To my surprise, Alfredo pulled out of his pocket the 76.45 Archduke Joseph Diamond, named for the Archduke of Austria. Now, this diamond is the 12th largest perfect white diamond in the world, and there was Alfredo showing it to his associate in a Beverly Hills store.

"Peter couldn't believe it," Alfredo remembers. "He asked me, *Why do you do that?* Ten minutes later, we went into the premises of another jeweler, and a Prince of Saudi Arabia walked in looking for something unique. I just happened to have this stone in my pocket."

While no sale was made that day, Alfredo *was* able to meet the prince and make a valuable connection. "Peter was shocked," he laughs. "Ten minutes earlier he had been telling me how silly I was!" From a virtual mentor like Harry Winston, Alfredo had learned, among other things, to always be ready for opportunity.

Once you've selected your virtual mentors, try to find a photo of each of them you can frame. Having images of these influential people on your walls will remind you why you chose them. Plus, you'll feel more connected to them when you need their virtual advice.

From Virtual to Visible

Virtual mentors will sustain you through many of life's challenges, but you may reach a point where you crave more reciprocal relationships with your mentors. In addition to your virtual "Board of Directors," identify five people you would like to mentor you.

One of my mentors is Ken Marlin. Ken describes himself as a "people builder who gets a real thrill out of motivating people to move up the ladder and achieve their potential." Hopefully, Ken could hear the influence he's had on my life emerging when he attended a recent LifePilot workshop.

Ken was my general manager at First Investors Corporation, a company he helped found and grow. After leaving First Investors, Ken started Marlin Travel in a basement in Edmonton, Alberta. The business blossomed to 320 agencies and became Canada's best-known travel brand before it was sold to Thomas Cook Travel in 1998.

Through the years, Ken has been very generous in sharing his time and wisdom with me. Now in his 80s, he is still full of energy and devotes himself to mentoring and teaching the Marlin Method of investing and financial management to rising executives and entrepreneurs.

"Peter was a willing student," says Ken. "He would say, 'Ok, I did what you said. Now what? What's next?' He was disciplined and very willing to absorb knowledge because he wasn't a know-it-all — he was a know-nothing!"

Ken was born in Wosley, Saskatchewan in 1923. He came from a family of six. The 1920s were very tough years in the economy. By age 12, Ken was working hard. "I didn't think I was just a kid," he remembers. Then Ken's Dad died when Ken was 15. His mother took charge and Ken learned from her "management style," which he later passed on to his employees and the people he mentored.

"She had the ability to direct us without being bossy," he recalls. "She explained and motivated us to do what needed to be done."

Ken has led a fascinating and diverse life. The knowledge he passed to me didn't just come from a boardroom: it came from his work in the fields, as a telegrapher on the railways (he learned Morse code and still talks to other telegraphers in Morse today), as a house builder, and as an outstanding salesperson. He sold refrigerators and vacuums door-to-door for Electrolux (yes, Electrolux once sold refrigerators!), and learned a host of sales strategies he later told me about.

Later, Ken met Stan Melton, Ralph Forrester and Don Cormie as they were about to form a "little company" called First Investors Corporation. Anyone who knows Ken knows First Investors might never have become the success it was without his hard work and innovative input. He credits his success at First Investors to his almost crusade-like belief that people can achieve financial freedom by learning to save money. He firmly believes in the words of James J. Hill, founder of the Great Northern Railroad: "The test is simple and infallible. Are you able to save money? If so, the seed of success is in you." He set a goal to become a millionaire by age 40 and he achieved his goal.

When I went to work at First Investors and met Ken, I took to him right away. He taught me so many things, including how to set goals, stay focused, and channel my enthusiasm into results.

Ken always tells the story of the day I barged through the door of his house at 6 a.m. like I owned the place. "I was in the bathroom shaving," Ken recalls. "Peter just came right in, sat down on the toilet seat and made himself at home. He had some new idea — he always had ideas — and he was going to tell me that idea no matter what time it was."

Ken's wife Helen came into the bathroom and asked me if I could put my idea on hold while Ken finished shaving.

Ken was always available to me. Instead of telling me what to do, he would encourage me to come up with my own answers. At one point, I was sent to another city to investigate why the office there wasn't making money and why some funds were mysteriously missing. After investigating, I decided to fire the manager. My next move was to tell Ken what I had done to solve the problem. "So now what are you going to do?" Ken asked. He made sure I knew I wasn't going anywhere until a new manager was found. It took me three months, but I solved the problem. In allowing me the space to tackle this problem on my own, and to see it through, Ken taught me lessons that still influence me today.

"The dream," says recently retired anchor Dan Rather, "begins with a teacher who believes in you, who tugs and pushes and leads you to the next plateau, sometimes poking you with a sharp stick called 'truth.'"

How to Choose Your Mentors

Here are some well-tested guidelines for selecting your mentors:

* Ideally, your mentors should share your values and possess qualities or areas of expertise you would like to see in yourself.

* Whenever possible, choose mentors who are about 15 years older than you. This allows for enough of an age difference that competition and ego are not issues. Another advantage of selecting older mentors is they have already navigated many of the aspects of life you are now just beginning to explore.

* Your mentors should not be in competition with you or need anything you've got.

* A mentoring relationship should be positive. Mark Twain advised, "Keep away from people who try to belittle your ambitions. Small people always do that, but the really great make you feel that you, too, can become great." That doesn't mean a mentor should always be gentle.

* Your mentors should be people you respect and with whom you can talk openly.

* Your mentors should be willing to share their networks with you.

* Your mentors should have time to spend with you.

* Not every mentoring relationship is forever. Sometimes, certain people have an important role to play in your life for only a select period of time. Be grateful for what you have learned and let your mentors know how much you appreciate what they have offered you.

Mentors for the Diversity of Your Life

Not every mentor can address every area of your life. I have had mentors for various areas of my life: in business, in fitness and even in my love of Harley Davidsons.

Some mentors come into your life only for a very short time and teach you lessons that stay with you. When I was a very young man in the Soldier Apprentice Training Program of the Canadian Army, I arrived at Camp Borden ready to serve my apprenticeship. We were based a few miles from Barrie, Ontario where all the girls were. As a teenager, that was an important thing for me. One Saturday, while on a weekend pass, I found myself wandering into a used car lot where I saw a small black Austin car that took my breath away. It was perfect, with four seats and low gas consumption. I decided to buy it so I sat down with the manager to conduct my first meaningful transaction.

The car cost $300 and I only had $50. "No problem," the manager told me. "$50 is enough to start." By then, I had all kinds of pictures in my head of me having fun with my new car. He brought out the papers for me to sign to borrow the other $250 from him. When it came time to sign, he asked me where I worked. I told him I was a soldier stationed at Camp Borden. At that point, his entire demeanor changed. He took the papers back. "I didn't know you were a soldier," he said. "I cannot offer you any financing."

Naturally, I was distraught. Nothing I could do or say could change his mind. I left and hitchhiked right back to camp. I went into my barracks and sat on my bed. I must have looked very dejected because Duty Sergeant Vart asked me, "Why are you back at camp when you have a weekend pass?" I told him the woeful story of the car. He left and came back a few minutes later. "I'm off duty," he said. "I'm driving back to Barrie so come on and we'll have a talk with the manager of the used car lot. I'll see if I can put in a good word for you."

At that point, I would have grasped at any straw. I thought I had exhausted every avenue, so I really had nothing to lose. When we got to the car lot, Sergeant Vart told me to wait in the car. He went in to talk to the manager. Finally, he came out and told me the man had changed his mind. I went in and the manager had all the papers ready to sign. "I'll make an exception in your case," he told me.

I drove that car for over a year and I cannot tell you how much happiness it gave me. One day after I had paid the car off — ahead of time! — I received a letter and a copy of the agreement in the mail. When I read over the agreement, I saw there were actually two agreements. The first agreement had my signature on it, and the second one had the signature of Sergeant Jack Vart. Until that moment, I had no idea Sergeant Vart had actually provided his personal guarantee that I would pay for the car. He had assumed all the risk. I still get goose bumps thinking how Sergeant Vart trusted me enough to put himself on the line for me — and not even tell me he did it.

Sergeant Vart didn't lead me through a formal mentoring program, but he was a mentor all the same. His generosity and belief in me forever changed my life and how I treated other people. If I can help someone through an act of trust then I thank God for the opportunity. You can change a life with an act of kindness.

Sometimes people like Sergeant Vart serendipitously appear in your life. Other times, you might find yourself consciously sitting down and trying to select your mentors.

My wife Rita initially had a difficult time choosing her mentors. "I'm a bit of a perfectionist and could never find anyone who I thought I might want to emulate," she says. "It took me some time to realize you can pick a mentor based on what they excel at because no one is perfect."

Rita's list of mentors seems endless. "It's so great having people who know a lot more about some of my passions than I do and are willing to share them with me," she says.

To give you an idea of just how diverse your own mentor list can be, here's a look at some of Rita's mentors:

> "My mother is my overall inspirational mentor. She goes to church every day, exercises six days a week, is very careful about what she eats, and hugs everybody she can.

At 83 years old, she has no aches and pains, has more energy than most 50-year-olds, and lives a life based on love. Who wouldn't want to be just like her? My sister, Mary Ann Smithwick, is my spiritual advisor as she is the epitome of holiness. If I have questions that relate to my spiritual life or how to handle a difficult situation, she's my perfect advisor. My precious grandson Trent Norris is my 'see life through a child's eye' mentor. I love my discussions with Trent. His innocence and insights on life are pretty amazing.

Jamesie Bower is my 'everything' mentor. She always seems to know everything about everything and is wise beyond her years. Lou La Freniere is my mentor who keeps me positive. No matter what she has to deal with, her cup is always half full not half empty, and she's forever grateful for what she has. Erin Holm is a trained professional chef, loves to cook healthy, pure food and sends me her new creations regularly. Julie Molnar is my traveling mentor. She is as passionate about travel as I am, takes copious notes on every area she visits, and loves to share. Penny Galarneau is my design mentor. She could turn a barn into a palace!"

Who are the people who inspire you? What do you want to learn from them? As you can see from Rita's mentors, you may need or want all kinds of mentors in your life for the diversity of wisdom they can offer you.

How to Meet Your Mentors

Many successful people are willing to act as mentors. It is their way of giving back some of the generous advice they've received on their paths to success. They know what it's like to start out, and they are willing to share their knowledge. The best will also share their networks.

Some mentoring relationships develop almost organically, but when that avenue isn't open to you, one of the best ways to find a mentor is by looking around at people you admire. Check your network. Is there someone you've met who you would like to learn from?

Many organizations link retired professionals with people seeking mentorship. Chambers of commerce and boards of trade may offer this as part of their membership benefits packages. Groups such as the Young Entrepreneurs' Organization and the Young Presidents' Organization also offer valuable mentorship programs.

My advice is to request a meeting with your mentor of choice and ask if he or she would consider mentoring you. Tailor the delivery and detail of your proposal to how well you know the person. Tell them why you chose them and what you hope to gain. Be clear about your focus so they can be clear about what they can honestly contribute. As with most proposals, the worst they can say is no. Even then, they'll likely be flattered.

Remember, mentoring is a give-and-take relationship. It's important to be an active participant in the process, to come to your meetings prepared and to follow up on what you and your mentor discussed. When you can, find opportunities to contribute value to your mentors. "Successful people are always looking for opportunities to help others," says motivational expert Brian Tracy. "Unsuccessful people are always asking, 'What's in it for me?'"

Becoming a Mentor: Giving Back

Winston Churchill once said, "We make a living by what we get, but we make a life by what we give." This quote perfectly captures the attitudes of most people who decide to share their knowledge by mentoring.

I like to think of success as an elevator. Once you've taken the elevator to the top, be sure to send it down again to help the next person on his or her way up. This is really what mentorship is — helping someone else by sharing your experience and connections. One of my greatest pleasures has been to mentor others and give back something of what I've experienced. Mentoring also helps me reflect on my life and what I've learned.

Rather than deplete my energy, I find mentoring to be very energizing. Not only do I pass on my knowledge, I also learn from the person I am mentoring. In this regard, I think of the words of Buddha, who said, "Thousands of candles can be lighted from a single candle and the life of the candle will not be shortened."

I no longer have time for a great deal of one-on-one mentoring. My way of giving back is through books like this and through the LifePilot workshops we deliver worldwide. Even so, I've done my share of one-on-one mentoring. In my experience, being a good mentor requires interest, patience, time, and confidence that you have something to offer. Most importantly, you need to do it because you are sincerely interested in helping another person reach his or her goals.

Chapter Review

* Choose different mentors throughout your life to reflect where you are, where you want to be and what you want to learn.

* Your mentors can be virtual or real.

* Ideally, you should have two to three mentors, up to a maximum of five.

* Your mentors should be at least 15 years older than you.

* Your mentors should be people you trust and feel comfortable talking to.

* Your mentors should be people you respect, not just people who are successful by other people's definitions.

* Your mentors don't have to live in the same city as you do as long as they are committed to providing you with some of their time. Fortunately, email and Internet make this easier than ever.

* Your mentors should always share your values.

"Life can be seen through your eyes but it is not fully appreciated until it is seen through your heart." *Mary Xavier*

"As we express our gratitude, we must never forget that the highest appreciation is not to utter words, but to live by them." *John Fitzgerald Kennedy*

SECRET 17

Appreciate the View

Charles Plumb, a US Naval Academy graduate, was a jet fighter pilot in Vietnam. After 75 combat missions, his plane was destroyed by a surface-to-air missile. Plumb parachuted into enemy hands. He spent the next six years in a Vietnamese prison. He now tells his story to people throughout the United States.

One day, he and his wife were sitting in a restaurant when a man at another table said, "You're Plumb! You flew jet fighters in Nam from the carrier, *Kitty Hawk*. You were shot down!"

"How in the world did you know that?" asked Plumb.

"Oh, I was the one who packed your parachute," the man replied.

Plumb gasped in surprise and gratitude. "Yep, I guess it worked!" the man laughed.

"It sure did work," Plumb said. "If your chute hadn't worked, I wouldn't be here today."

That night, Plumb thought a lot about the man who had packed his parachute. He kept wondering what the man might have looked like in uniform. "I wondered how many times I might have passed him on the *Kitty Hawk*. I wondered how many times I might have seen him and not even said good morning, how are you or anything, because you see, I was a fighter pilot and he was just a sailor."

He thought of the many hours the man had spent at a long wooden table in the bowels of the ship, meticulously weaving the shrouds and folding the silks of each chute. Did he realize he held a man's life in his hands each time he packed a chute?

Now Plumb, a motivational speaker, asks his audiences, "Who's packing your chute?" Showing appreciation, he feels, brings magic and blessings into the lives of those we meet.

The Pleasures of Appreciation

One of my greatest lessons in the power of appreciation came to me one year near Thanksgiving when I received a card from a fellow named Bill. The card said, "Dear Peter, I just want you to know that I appreciate having you in my life." Receiving that card was one of the many moments in my life when I've felt truly humbled. I decided to pass that feeling on to others, so today I always carry note cards with me wherever I go. When I have a few spare moments, I'll write a note to someone I appreciate and mail it off.

Appreciation is energy. When you direct that energy, you begin to affect the world around you and the people you encounter. I truly believe that when you send out positive vibrations, you receive the same back from others.

Tell the World

Every human being needs to feel appreciated. Since we are unable to read each other's minds, as much as we would like to, we need to actively show people how much we appreciate them. Showing appreciation passes positive energy from one person to another. It can positively affect someone's day, week or entire life.

An example of this is the story of a man who used to walk to work each morning past a jewelry shop that had a large clock in the window. The man always checked his watch against the clock in the window. One day, as he was going to work, he did his usual stop and checked the clock. As he stood there, the owner of the shop came out and asked him why he looked in the window every morning. Was there something that he wanted to buy? The man said no, this was not the reason he stopped and looked into the window.

"I'm the person who blows the noon whistle in town each day," he told the shopkeeper. "Every morning I check my watch against the clock in the window to make sure my watch is correct."

The jeweler couldn't believe his ears. He said to the man, "I set my clock in the window each day by the noon whistle."

This story not only reminds me of how interconnected we all are, but of the many people who do small things every day that we set our lives by. They deserve our appreciation. How many times have we heard about people in the depths of despair who find their lives unexpectedly changed because of the kind words of a stranger? What about people who felt inspired to achieve remarkable goals because a stranger showed appreciation? As an unknown author wrote so poignantly, "To the world you may be just somebody, but to somebody you may just be the world."

If I Knew

Showing kindness and appreciation to strangers is important. Even more important is showing appreciation to people we love. There's a heartfelt poem about appreciation called "If I Knew." When I read it out loud during LifePilot workshops, it always affects people deeply. This poem has circulated on the Internet in the years since September 11 as a tribute to those who died that tragic morning.

As one of the many people who have unexpectedly and tragically lost someone I loved, this poem has special meaning for me. Its lesson is this: Don't wait to tell the people in your life how much they matter to you. Don't wait for the right time to magically reveal your feelings. Create the moment yourself. Someone in your life will be very happy you did.

If I Knew

If I knew it would be the last time
That I'd see you fall asleep,
I would tuck you in more tightly
and pray the Lord, your soul to keep.

If I knew it would be the last time
that I see you walk out the door,
I would give you a hug and kiss
and call you back for one more.

If I knew it would be the last time
I'd hear your voice lifted up in praise,
I would videotape each action and word,
so I could play them back day after day.

If I knew it would be the last time,
I could spare an extra minute
to stop and say "I love you,"
Instead of assuming you would *know* I do.

If I knew it would be the last time
I would be there to share your day,
Well, I'm sure you'll have so many more,
so I can let just this one slip away.

For surely there's always tomorrow
to make up for an oversight,
and we always get a second chance
to make everything just right.

There will always be another day
to say "I love you,"
And certainly there's another chance
to say, "Anything I can do?"

But just in case I might be wrong,
and today is all I get,
I'd like to say how much I love you
and I hope we never forget.

Tomorrow is not promised to anyone,
young or old alike,
and today may be the last chance
you get to hold your loved one tight.

So if you're waiting for tomorrow,
why not do it today?
For if tomorrow never comes,
you'll surely regret the day,

That you didn't take that extra time
for a smile, a hug, or a kiss
and you were too busy to grant someone,
what turned out to be their one last wish.

So hold your loved ones close today,
and whisper in their ears,
Tell them how much you love them
and that you'll always hold them dear.

Take time to say, "I'm sorry,"
"Please forgive me," "Thank you," or "It's okay,"
and if tomorrow never comes,
you'll have no regrets about today.

Author Unknown

Your Appreciation List

Create a list of the people you appreciate and the reasons why. List major figures in your life *and* the people who offered you small kindnesses. They may be people you know — or people you've never spoken to. Perhaps a particular musician has enhanced your enjoyment of life. Maybe the old man who stops to say hello and pat your dog always makes your day a little brighter.

List the people you appreciate:	...and the reasons why:

Once you've written down your list, you may want to find ways to tell these people how much you appreciate them and why. Most importantly, take time to let the people you love know how much they mean to you. Find ways to "wow" them with kind words and pleasant surprises — and by spending time with them. For instance, when my wife Rita has been away, one of the ways I show my appreciation for her is to always pick her up at the airport, no matter what time it is. I do this because I value her in my life and want to be sure she knows this.

Being away from people you love often makes you appreciate them even more. You realize how much you miss them and can't wait to see them again. Recently, I returned from Switzerland and stopped in to see my daughter, her husband and my grandchildren. My grandson came running toward me, shouting my name with such passion and longing I felt bad I had been away for so long. Though it was only a couple of months, it must have seemed like forever to him. At that moment, he showed me his unbridled appreciation, and I showed my appreciation for him a few days later when we travelled to our annual family vacation. "When we express appreciation to young people," says writer Josh McDowell, "we give them a sense of significance." What could be more important?

Wherever I go, I carry photos of the people who matter most to me — including my wife, my children Todd and Liane, and my grandchildren — so I can continue to appreciate them and visualize them when I'm gone. I reflect on the good times we've had together and it makes me smile.

Appreciate Yourself

Now it's time to take a few moments to appreciate yourself. Browse the list on the following page and use the chart provided there to identify your best qualities. Think about which aspects of your character really shine. What positive things would others say about you? If you aren't sure, you may want to ask a few of the people who are closest to you about your best qualities. When you know your best qualities, you can play your best cards. You can also use this list to remind yourself of your value, instead of always relying on others for recognition.

A Yale University study found the two most important words in the English language are thank you. Sadly, these words are often a rarity. "Many people," writes Robert K. Cooper in *The Other 90%: How to Unlock Your Potential for Leadership and Life*, "have come to tolerate the absence of respect and to expect poor recognition, or none at all, for the efforts they make. One of the main reasons why people end relationships in life or work is that they receive limited, if any, genuine praise or recognition for their contributions."

"Take a few moments to remember the best respect and recognition you ever received — a time when you made an effort and someone else noticed and genuinely acknowledged you, saying something like, 'thanks for what you did. I saw you making this (specific) effort. You made a difference.'"

Examples of Positive Qualities

Ambitious	Focused	Patient
Artistic	Forgiving	Peaceful
Calm	Friendly	Perceptive
Caring	Funny	Persistent
Charismatic	Generous	Playful
Charitable	Gentle	Practical
Compassionate	Helpful	Precise
Conscientious	Honest	Rational
Controlled	Imaginative	Reliable
Courageous	Independent	Reserved
Creative	Inspirational	Resilient
Daring	Intelligent	Responsible
Dedicated	Intuitive	Sensitive
Determined	Kind	Serious
Diplomatic	Loving	Studious
Energetic	Motivating	Thorough
Enthusiastic	Open	Thoughtful
Fair	Optimistic	Trusting
Fearless	Organized	Vivacious
Flexible	Outgoing	Youthful

List your best qualities:

Saying thank you, according to motivational writer Melody Beattie, "unlocks the fullness of life. It turns what we have into enough, and more. It turns denial into acceptance, chaos to order, confusion to clarity. It can turn a meal into a feast, a house into a home, a stranger into a friend. Gratitude makes sense of our past, brings peace for today, and creates a vision for tomorrow."

Take time to list the things you are grateful for. As with your appreciation list, update this list regularly to remind yourself of the good things in your life that inspire, support and sustain you.

List the things you feel grateful for:	

CHAPTER REVIEW

* Create a list of all the people you appreciate and why.

* Take time to acknowledge the people you appreciate.

* Appreciate yourself. Create a list of your strengths and positive qualities.

* Talking and writing about what you are grateful for amplifies your happiness.

* List the things you are grateful for — and update your list regularly to remind yourself of the good things in your life that inspire, support and sustain you.

> "You have to leave the city of your comfort and go into the wilderness of your intuition. What you'll discover will be wonderful. What you'll discover is yourself." *Alan Alda*
>
> "Intuition is the highest form of knowing." *Albert Einstein*

SECRET 18

Listen to Your Instincts

Some people live purely by logic. They evaluate the pros and cons of every situation and plot their way through life as carefully as a bomb expert in a minefield. Other people leap through those same minefields without thinking about the dangers. The most successful people I know gather the information they need, but ultimately, they trust the power of their intuition to guide them. When someone is successful we often hear it said that the person has a "sixth" sense or an "uncanny ability." To me, it just means these people have learned to heed their instincts.

We've all had times when we've sensed something without knowing why. A person or a situation may put our stomachs in knots or, on a more positive note, cause butterflies of anticipation when we see them. Often, we call these reactions "gut feelings" and we dismiss them because we don't understand them. But recent scientific breakthroughs demonstrate that so-called "sixth sense" may not be as mystical as we once thought.

That Gut Feeling

Candace Pert, author of *Molecules of Emotion: The Science Behind Mind-Body Medicine*, used to believe, like almost everyone else, that emotions reside in the brain. But during the past 20 years of research, Pert has discovered that the brain and the body are intimately connected. In fact, they constantly communicate through the language of biochemicals. In other words, the head really can talk to the heart and gut.

253

These biochemicals are called neuropeptides and their receptors are located throughout our bodies in our immune, neural, hormonal and gastrointestinal systems, including our organs, spinal cords and body tissues. This means emotional memory is stored throughout the body. Our "gut feelings" really do have a scientific basis. However, there's no denying that "following our neuropeptides" just doesn't have the same resonance as "following our hearts" or "trusting our guts."

Our heart- and gut-generated instincts are the radar systems of the unconscious, working in tandem with our other senses. It's when we ignore these important instincts and rely only on logic that we miss incredible opportunities or allow dubious people to fly under our radar.

Just as we listen to our guts for hunches and vague feelings of warning, we listen to our hearts to access our deepest emotions involving love, passion and nurturing. "The workings of the human heart are the profoundest mystery of the universe," said writer Charles W. Chestnut.

Keep Instinct in Sight

Some scientists also believe that instinct involves "mind sight," the ability to see and register changes in our environment on a subconscious level. This, according to Ronald Rensick of the University of British Columbia, may be why, when we are looking at something and it changes without our knowledge, we know something has been altered, even though we cannot identify what that change is.

Rensick showed 40 subjects a series of photographic images flickering on a computer screen. Each image was revealed for just seconds, and followed by a blank gray screen. Sometimes Rensick's researchers would change the image, sometimes they wouldn't. When the image was changed, about a third of Rensick's subjects had a strong gut feeling that the image had been altered but they couldn't say how or visualize it. "I think this effect explains a lot of the belief in a sixth sense," says Rensick. "Mind sight could well be an alerting system."

In his bestseller *Blink: The Power of Thinking Without Thinking*, author Malcolm Gladwell explores the power of so-called gut feelings and snap decisions. "I believe," Gladwell writes, "that the task of making sense of ourselves and our behavior requires that we acknowledge there can be as much value in the blink of an eye as in months of rational analysis."

Inside Intuition

Gary Klein Ph.D., chairman and chief scientist of Klein & Associates, trains senior executives in decision-making. Klein says 90 percent of the critical decisions we make are actually based on intuition, which he sees as an essential skill for survival and success. He feels intuition is not a magical sixth sense; it is a natural extension of the experiences we have accumulated.

Klein, a cognitive psychologist, has spent 15 years studying professionals who must make quick — often life or death — decisions on a regular basis. His interviews have included firefighters, senior executives, emergency medical staff, soldiers and others. These quick-thinking professionals, Klein shows, have learned to recognize clues and patterns that enable them to get a fast take on situations, head off problems, and rapidly create solutions.

"Experienced decision makers see a different world than novices do," says Klein, "and what they see tells them what they should do. Ultimately, intuition is all about perception."

Klein's findings demonstrate gut instinct is at its height when people are under stress — when they don't have all the necessary information and they need to make a decision immediately.

Years ago, when I worked in the Alberta bush as an on-site safety attendant, I encountered a stressful incident that required my gut instincts to kick in. The company I worked for fully expected me to uphold their stellar safety record, so armed only with a St. John's Ambulance course, I went to work. It all went smoothly until one day a worker got a steel splinter stuck in his eyeball. What to do? I had only a first aid kit and no access to emergency rooms. My first aid course hadn't included any lessons on how to remove splinters from eyeballs. Thinking fast, I searched the kit and found a plastic loop. I hooked it around the splinter and pulled. The piece of steel slid out. I packed the eye with gauze and sent the worker off to the nearest hospital, miles away. It was only afterwards that I questioned how I had found the ability to act decisively under intense pressure.

We can rely on our learning and experience to make decisions, but when those elements are lacking, we sometimes need to go on gut instinct as I did that day. Klein says gut instinct basically relies on "four sources of power" that astute decision makers tend to use when they must make decisions under pressure: intuition, mental simulation, metaphor and storytelling.

Klein advises people to banish vague fears, such as "It may be a mistake," and instead try to "see yourself in a specific scenario. Ask yourself concrete questions about the possible outcome: 'What's the worst that could happen? What would I do then? Could I live with that?'"

Let go of the idea of the perfect answer, he says. You're not a fortune teller. You can't calculate all the risks. "The harder a decision is to make," he says, "the closer the outcomes are to each other, and the less it matters."

Intuition: Listening to your intuition or gut feelings can help you make fast assessments of situations. Psychologist Carl Jung placed intuition among the four functions of consciousness, along with thinking, feeling and sensation. Klein says the rational mind, which tends to list pros and cons, can stifle intuition. Stay open to what your body is trying to tell you.

Mental Simulation: Klein sees mental simulation as a tool that helps us discern the patterns, similarities and differences that exist between the present and the past. He describes it as the ability to imagine people and objects consciously and to transform those people and objects through several stages, eventually picturing them in a different way than at the start. This helps us translate old knowledge to new situations quickly. People who engage in mental simulation are able to quickly try out their options in their minds before making decisions.

Metaphor: Klein has also discovered that although fast decision-makers may appear to magically come up with answers, they are actually accessing metaphors, often at deeper levels of consciousness. A metaphor is a figure of speech in which a word or phrase for one kind of object or action is used in place of another to suggest a likeness or analogy between them. A person who is adept at thinking in metaphor may look at a problem and try to find a likeness or analogy to a situation they've experienced in the past. In their search for fast solutions, they typically don't reinvent the wheel — they apply the knowledge they already have.

Storytelling: Klein says storytelling helps us to bring together our experiences in a way that is easy to access. Storytelling also makes it easy to share our experiences with others. I've always collected inspirational stories. Not only do they teach and entertain me, they also help me readily remember important lessons and experiences.

Watch the Masters

To learn more about the role of intuition in business, Peter Noordink, a PhD. candidate at the University of Queensland's School of Business, interviewed 27 expert traders and found 40 percent of decisions made by stockbrokers were based on "gut feelings."

"One floor trader told me that when traders are on the exchange floor they have about three seconds to make a major decision," Noordink says, "they don't have enough time to be rational; they can do that kind of analysis before the trade. But when you are in the thick of making decisions you have to do it based on your intuition."

Noordink compared the decisions made by stockbrokers and traders to crossing a road. "Do you calculate distances or speeds of vehicles before you cross the road, or do you simply 'feel' whether it is okay to cross? Most people use the second [option], and make it across 99.9 percent of the time."

Weston Agor, a management professor of the University of Texas, found that of the 2,000 managers he tested, higher-level managers had the top scores in intuition. When making decisions, they typically first took in all the relevant information and data available to them. However, when the data conflicted or was incomplete, these managers relied on intuition to reach their conclusions.

Douglas Dean of the New Jersey Institute of Technology studied the relationship between business success and intuition. He discovered 80 percent of executives whose companies' profits had more than doubled in the past five years demonstrated "above-average precognitive powers."

Here are some interesting stories about a few of the top minds in business and their so-called hunches or gut feelings. Intuition is, of course, important no matter which sector you work in, but many people find it fascinating when juxtaposed against the seemingly strict rationalism of business:

* Robert Lutz, former president of Chrysler, had a "feeling" that a high-priced sports car could help revive the public's interest in the company. Against everyone's advice, he launched the Viper, which went on to lead Chrysler's resurgence in the auto market.

* Rod Aissa, vice president for talent development and casting for MTV, was home from work one day with strep throat when he saw a rerun that featured the home of Ozzy Osbourne and his family. He immediately thought "they would make great TV" so he set up a dinner with Sharon Osbourne, the kids, and two

MTV executives to watch the family interact. When he met the Osbournes, he felt in his gut that his concept for a TV show about the family would fly. It certainly did.

* Conrad Hilton was known to have relied on gut feelings in his business decisions. Many of the people who knew him called these gut feelings "Connie's hunches." A classic example of this was when he submitted a sealed bid on a piece of New York real estate he evaluated at $159,000. Satisfied, he went to sleep but awoke with the figure $174,000 stuck in his mind. The feeling was so strong that he changed his bid to $174,000. His was the highest bid — the closest bid to his was $173,000! Hilton later sold the property for several million dollars. His gut instinct paid off again.

* Richard Branson, the mastermind of Virgin Airways, is another strong believer in intuition. "I never get the accountants in before I start up a business," he says. "It's done on a gut feeling..."

* If Fred Smith had heeded the "C" grade he got on the college paper which detailed his idea for an overnight delivery service, he would never have launched Federal Express. Instead, he went with his gut.

* Howard Schultz was in Milan, Italy, when he realized that the leisurely caffeine-and-conversation café model would work in the United States too. Market research said Americans would never pay $3 for a cup of coffee, but Schultz had a gut feeling that his concept of Starbucks would work. Americans did indeed pay Starbuck's price for a cup of coffee.

Sense a Winning or Losing Game

In recent studies, researcher Antoine Bechara and his colleagues asked participants to play a game that involved choosing cards from several decks. Unbeknownst to the players, the decks had been rigged to provide either modest payoffs and losses, or large payoffs and losses. The researchers found that as the participants played, they quickly formed hunches about which deck to use. That is, their bodies registered increased arousal if they reached to draw from a risky deck. The players were at a loss to explain how they so quickly decided to draw from the less risky decks. Players who were not able to use this intuitive information, or who disregarded it, fared less well than those who went with their guts.

"I think the mind is more powerful than we realize. Ninety percent of what we know is subconscious," says Alfredo J. Molina, chairman and CEO of Molina Fine Jewelers of Phoenix. Alfredo was born in Cuba, where children are normally given a protective saint whose name they are born under. Alfredo's is Saint Lazarus, whose number is 17. Not surprisingly, 17 became Alfredo's lucky number, a signpost he's watched for and been guided by throughout his life.

In 1992, he was searching for a property on which to locate his appointment-only salon. He looked for several years and then he found it — a property with a 4,500 square foot building located at Camelback and 32nd, the ideal Phoenix address. The building even had a walk-in vault.

Alfredo discovered the property was being held by the Resolution Trust Corporation (RTC), an organization created by Congress to liquidate the assets of failed savings and loan (S & Ls) associations and pay insured depositors. He contacted the property manager who told him the property would go to sealed bid but couldn't say when. Alfredo tried to find out as much as he could through his network but he had no luck. So he called the property manager every Tuesday and Thursday. This went on for many months. Then one day Alfredo called the property manager and was told the property had been sold.

Frustrated and "hot under the collar," Alfredo decided to complain. Then one day he received a call and learned the property would be resold under sealed bid. Alfredo submitted a bid and waited, and waited. The RTC was days behind schedule. Finally, he learned that because he and the closest bidder were within 10 percent of each other's bids, the property had to go back to sealed bid under RTC rules.

"I knew I'd get one shot at this," Alfredo remembers. "I didn't want to overbid and I didn't want to underbid. I went through a drawer of old files on properties I had to get an idea of the kind of offer to make. In the file I found a letter from the real estate agent to the RTC stating that when properties were being sold under sealed bids, they typically were selling for *17 percent* over market value."

Alfredo immediately recognized his lucky number 17.

To make a long story short, he estimated the amount he would pay, then added 17 percent for luck. The sealed bid was due at 1700 hours and the answer was due at 1700 hours on the 17th of the month. But the 17th of the month passed with no word from the RTC. Alfredo called and was told, "Mr. Molina, we're doing calculations and we can't discuss this with you."

"I said, 'Well, can you at least tell me how many offers there were?'" The answer came back: 17 offers.

"I got off the phone and one of the women who works with me was there. I said, 'We got it.' She said, 'How do you know?'" So Alfredo told her about how the number 17 kept appearing throughout the entire process. Sure enough, when he called the RTC on Monday, they said, "You should be very happy." His was the winning bid. Today, Molina Fine Jewelers is housed in a world-class building on the corner of Camelback and 32nd in Phoenix, just as Alfredo always envisioned it would be.

Too often we fail to pay attention to the subtle signs all around us that guide our way. We discount them in favor of so-called rational analysis. But not everything of value can be explained rationally. By trusting his gut intuition, and paying attention to the signs many of us are too busy to observe, or too logical to give credence to, Alfredo Molina realized his dream.

Believe Your Body

Scientific research into the inner workings behind the "sixth sense" may remove some of the mystery from our lives, but it also empowers us with the knowledge that our hunches have far more validity than we once assumed. By listening to our bodies — to our gut feelings, heart stirrings and mindsight — we gain deeper insight into the world around us and a powerful intuitive ability to navigate through the fog when logic fails us.

CHAPTER REVIEW

* Strong intuition can give you a "sixth sense" for opportunity and a "gut feeling" when something is not quite right.

* Carl Jung placed intuition among the four functions of consciousness, along with thinking, feeling and sensation.

* Research has identified that emotional memory centers are located throughout our bodies, even in our organs, colon and tissues, and the spinal cord.

* People who work in demanding professions that require fast thinking have learned to intuitively sort through patterns of experience to come up with solutions.

* Studies show high performers have developed the best intuition.

* Intuition is a powerful tool for steering us through the fog of chaos.

* Though some of us appear to be born with more access to our intuition than others, it can be developed with practice.

> "Beware the barrenness of a busy life." *Socrates*
>
> "The greatest weapon against stress is our ability to choose one thought over another." *William James*

SECRET 19

Conquer Stress to Reach Success

S tress is epidemic in our society. One fourth of all the drugs prescribed in the United States go to the treatment of it. While many people believe stress is a normal and necessary part of a successful lifestyle, I feel that stress — when it isn't offset by healthy lifestyle techniques — is detrimental to your success and your longevity.

When your brain perceives an experience as stressful, some interesting things happen. First, your body goes on alert and sends in an army of responders, including stress hormones. In the short term, this is a wonderful thing because it helps prime you for the moment when "fight or flight" may be necessary. That's great when you are preparing to flee a mountain lion, but many people with extended and high levels of stress spend most of their time in office buildings and living rooms where no dangerous predators exist.

"In many ways," says Emeran A. Mayer, M.D, of the UCLA School of Medicine in California, "the stress response of an organism can be understood in analogy to the response of a nation confronted with an actual or perceived threat to its stability. As we are all too familiar, such a threat will result in the activation of a series of preprogrammed civilian (economic, security) and military measures, optimizing the chances of the nation to overcome or avoid the threatening situation. On the one hand, the readiness to quickly mount such a response is paramount to the long-term survival of the nation; on the other hand, the longer this response has to be maintained, the greater the toll will be on other functions of the society."

The Load You Carry

How we cope with stress is influenced by genetics, experiences, and behavior. Recent research shows chronic stress may accelerate cell aging and alter the immune system. Dealing with stress is an important part of aging successfully.

Doctors refer to your accumulation of stress as your allostatic load. The higher the allostatic load you carry, the bigger the price your body pays for remaining in an extended state of stress. Here's what happens when you are under stress:

* Your body releases more glucose to improve your memory and sharpen your senses. In the short-term, that's fine but when stress is prolonged, your body sends out the extra glucose your muscles need to help you fight or take flight. When glucose levels in the brain decrease, your memory and learning abilities are negatively impacted.

* Your adrenal glands start pumping out glutocorticoids. That's good in the short term, but over an extended period this response weakens the immune system.

* Your thyroid helps maintain your body's energy levels. When you are under stress, it surges to give you an intense burst of energy. If the stress remains constant this can lead to fatigue, anxiety and sleep problems.

* Athletes will tell you the release of endorphins gives you a healthy high. They are also natural painkillers, but extended stress kicks endorphin release into overdrive. You may become overly agitated and miss vital warning signs to slow down, including headaches, backaches, muscular aches and pains, and more.

* Stress hormones slow the development of neurons, and even kill them. This can eventually lead to a reduction in the size of

your hippocampus. To show you how dramatic this is, strokes, long-term depression and trauma have also been shown to reduce the size of the hippocampus. People with Alzheimer's tend to have smaller hippocampuses.

* To get more oxygen moving through your body, your heart rate, breathing rate and blood pressure increase under stress. This puts increased pressure on your body's vital systems. Non-essential systems go on hiatus, including your immune system, your digestive system and your sex drive.

* Stress contributes to high cholesterol levels. Whereas primitive humans needed the energy provided by cholesterol, in modern humans excess cholesterol gets stuffed into our arteries instead.

* In anticipation of your body being wounded, your blood vessels constrict and your blood-clotting ability increases. If your arteries are already clogged with cholesterol, you become a prime candidate for stroke or heart attack.

* Under chronic stress, your body produces too much cortisol and adrenalin. Cortisol provides high levels of energy during important periods but scientists have found that extended periods of cortisol in the body weakens bones, damages nerve cells in the brain, and can weaken the body's defense system against disease. Cortisol over-abundance has also been linked to weight gain.

Deal with It and Be Done

Over an extended period, your body can become addicted to stress. While the responses your body generates feel good in the short term, over the longer term, instead of de-stressing when you need it most, you may tend to find new ways to try to generate the stress high. Stress addiction may be thrilling but it can be deadly.

"It is an ironic habit of human beings to run faster when we have lost our way," says existential therapist Rollo May. When you're dealing with stress, it's important to stop running and review the LifePilot basics of living in alignment with your values. This will provide you with a structure that will help reduce your stress.

Getting up in the morning with a fully-planned day is a great stress reliever. This keeps me focused. Once my top priorities are done, I can relax a bit with the good feeling that I have accomplished what I set out to do. I always leave room in my day for fitness, family and things that increase my happiness quotient.

In this way, I avoid procrastination and worry, which are huge stress inducers. As my friend Alfredo Molina says, "Worry is the misuse of imagination." Ninety percent of the things you worry about never come true in the first place, and the other 10 percent are things you can't do anything about.

Don't Carry Anyone's Monkeys

You've heard about people who carry monkeys on their backs. These monkeys are their *problems*. They are tenacious and clinging. Their weight is a burden that's hard to shake off. I believe monkeys also sit on shoulders! There's strategy in this — when they sit on shoulders, it's easier for them to jump onto unsuspecting people who get too involved in the problems of others.

Have you ever noticed how people will lean in close to share their problems with you? "Can I talk to you?" they ask, moving closer. Naturally, you lean in to listen. At this moment, *their* monkeys jump to *your* shoulders.

Now, I'm not saying you shouldn't listen to others' problems or try to help, but be aware of becoming too involved. Some people thrive on other people's problems; as a result, they have limited energy to devote to finding solutions to their own issues. When someone leans in close to share a problem, remember that you have your own monkeys to carry. My advice is to show empathy, help if you are able, but don't take on their problems as your own. I try to empower people to come up with their own solutions by asking, "What do *you* think you should do?" Often, they *know* the solution; they just need someone to help coax that solution to the surface.

Health and Fitness

Many of you will not want to hear this, but you need to hear it anyway: eating well and getting exercise is key to stress reduction and extending your life span. Exercise increases energy, regulates biorhythms, improves sleep and helps control weight. When you are in good physical shape, your body is more resistant to the erosion of stress. You look healthier and toned, which in turn helps you feel better about yourself. Exercise has also been shown to prevent and curb depression, accordingly to the 1996 US Surgeon General's *Report on Physical Activity and Health*.

I work out daily because health is a priority for me. I don't just stick to the same routine year after year; I always look for new ways to keep myself interested in fitness. For instance, I might try new exercise techniques like working out with tension bands or wearing a heart monitor during my workout sessions. My wife Rita and I also plan fun activities that include fitness. Next year, for example, we plan to take a biking vacation as part of our goal to incorporate more physical exercise into our lives.

Earlier in the book you read about how Villages Pizza owner John Papaloukas dropped from 500 pounds to just over 300 pounds. John identified health as one of his core values and brought it into alignment with his other values. He set diet and exercise goals to achieve that remarkable weight loss. Today, John moves faster, feels better and has his stress under control. He lives by his values and works off his stress through exercise instead of eating.

Bev McClung, who I've known for years, spends up to two hours walking every morning. This busy chief financial officer and grandmother says walking helps her prepare for her day, and is one of her best inspirational times.

You Might As Well Laugh

The old saying "he who laughs, lasts" is gaining increasing credibility today as research shows how important humor is to stress reduction. But we still don't laugh enough. According to the *Discovery Health* website, "By the time a child reaches nursery school, he or she will laugh about 300 times a day. Adults laugh an average of 17 times a day." A University of Maryland Medical Center study found people with heart disease were 40 percent less likely to laugh in a variety of situations compared to people of the same age without heart disease.

"Without humor one's thought processes are likely to become stuck and narrowly focused, leading to increased distress," according to the Association for Applied and Therapeutic Humor.

So what is the connection between laughter and stress reduction? John Morreall, a professor of religion, has been studying humor for more than 25 years. He believes that the first human laughter might have begun as a reaction of relief at the passing of danger. Research today seems to support this theory. Some researchers see laughter as a "safety valve" that shuts off the flow of stress hormones that constrict blood flow and suppress our immune systems.

Give yourself permission to laugh. Rediscover your laughter triggers. Rent old Monty Python movies. Welcome people into your life who know how to have fun. Tell yourself that it's ok to act silly from time to time.

Realize even the most stressful situations have elements of humor. Once, when I was going through a particularly uncomfortable time and feeling a bit sorry for myself, I said to my wife, "Honey, if I lost all of my money, do you think you would still love me?" to which she immediately replied, "Of course I would love you, honey — I would miss you but I would love you." I had to laugh.

Sleep Away Stress

Whoever said, "Growl all day and you'll feel dog tired all night" knew a thing or two about the connection between stress and sleep. The two go hand in hand: when you don't get enough sleep, your stress level increases.

In surveys conducted by the National Sleep Foundation from 1999 to 2004, researchers found at least 40 million Americans suffer from over 70 different sleep disorders, and 60 percent of adults report having sleep problems a few nights a week or more. Most of these problems are undiagnosed and untreated.

Even a seemingly minor reduction in sleep can have profound effects. When University of Pennsylvania sleep researchers studied the effects of sleep deprivation, they discovered that subjects who slept four to six hours a night for 14 nights in a row showed significant deficits in cognitive performance. Amazingly, they also found that this amount of sleep deprivation was the equivalent of not sleeping for up to three days in a row. Interestingly, the subjects weren't even aware of the effects. They reported feeling only mildly sleepy and had no idea how impaired they really were.

I know many CEOs, including Donald Trump, say they don't need much sleep. That may be true for them, but most adults need about eight hours a night to perform at peak levels.

In the August 2004 issue of the journal *Sleep*, Dr. Timothy Roehrs of the Sleep Disorders and Research Center at Henry Ford Hospital in Detroit published one of the first studies to measure the effect of sleepiness on decision-making and risk-taking.

Dr. Roehrs and his researchers paid sleepy and fully-alert subjects to complete a series of computer tasks. At random times, the subjects were given a choice to take their money and stop, or to keep going with the potential of either earning more money or losing it all if their work was not completed within an unspecified remainder of time.

According to Dr. Roehrs, the alert subjects were sensitive to the amount of work required to finish the tasks. They understood the risk of losing their money if they didn't finish. The sleepy subjects, however, either quit the tasks prematurely or risked losing everything by attempting to finish the task for more money, even when the odds were about 100 percent they wouldn't be able to complete the task.

When you don't get enough sleep, your body acts in the same way as it does when it responds to stress.

Incorporate sleep into your LifePilot success plan. Begin seeing it as an essential part of your overall wellbeing instead of a nuisance that takes away from your ability to do more. Here are some other sleep tips:

* Maintain a regular sleep and waking schedule.

* Don't drink caffeine for four to six hours before bed.

* Don't smoke, especially near bedtime or if you awaken in the night.

* Avoid alcohol and heavy meals before sleep.

* Get regular exercise.

* Minimize noise, light and excessive hot and cold temperatures in the room where you sleep.

* Because researchers have found that constantly hitting the snooze button may impact our all-important REM sleep, which typically occurs near the end of our sleep cycles, try to awaken without an alarm clock, or put the clock across the room and sleep until you have to get up.

* If you suffer from a persistent sleep disorder, see your physician. Many communities have sleep disorder clinics that specialize in diagnosis and treatment.

Get in Your Best Zone

One day, I felt my staff needed some inspiration, so I asked them if they'd like to go skydiving. Amazingly, they all said yes. That shows you what a bunch of keeners they were. My son and daughter joined us too. We spent about three hours in training before the instructor felt we were ready to jump. "Who wants to jump first?" he asked. My son Todd put up his hand. He had a fantastic dive and came back very enthusiastic. I volunteered to be next, so up

I went. I started chatting with the pilot, and before I knew it, he said, "We're in our zone; you better get ready to jump."

I checked my chute as he flipped open the door. "Get into position," he said. For all of you non-jumpers, the "position" is where you actually step out of the plane at about 3,000 feet and put your left foot on the pedal outside. Then you place your hands on the strut directly in front of you. Your right foot just hangs out there, blowing in the wind.

Once I was in position, the pilot said, "You're looking good. Have a good jump." I just stared at him, smiled and froze. This is when you're supposed to push off and fall backwards, away from the airplane. Since I didn't show any signs of fear, the pilot couldn't see that I was actually in a panic situation. He looked at me again for what seemed like an eternity, then in a normal voice he said, "Go ahead, jump" — with a little more emphasis on the word "jump." I just smiled and hung on for dear life. At that point he realized I was paralyzed and couldn't let go. He gave me an angry look and barked at the top of his voice, "JUMP!" That scared me enough to let go and jump.

Everything worked beautifully and automatically. As I floated downward, I found I could actually steer the parachute. The next few seconds were absolutely unbelievable. As I rapidly descended, I looked down. I could see the airport a long way over to my right. I tried to steer that way, but I did not make any progress. Then I began to understand. While I was frozen on the wing, the plane had been continuing its circuit, and I had jumped out of the intended flight path.

I would be very happy if the next episode of my adventure hadn't happened. As I was plummeting, I looked down at the beautiful farms below, and suddenly realized I had steered myself directly into a pig farm. I landed up to my knees in pig manure. Then I had to gather up my smelly parachute and walk as best as I could through the pig farm, over half a mile back to the airport and my fellow paratroopers.

Life is full of surprises. When you do new and exciting things you should always be prepared to go through some stress and a little pig manure. Just treat it as part of the adventure. That was one of the lessons I learned from this jump. The other was this: when you're in the right zone, let go!

What Zone Are You In?

Often, when we're heavily stressed it's as though we're in the wrong flight zone. We all have different zones we move in and out of; the trick is being in the *right* zone at the *right* time to achieve the *right* outcome.

I've found that I operate mostly in what I call Zone One — a state of being very active, almost hyper-alert, with my radar always on. Usually, operating in this zone works well for me. I get things done, I'm aware and I maintain a high level of energy. But once in a while, Zone One is a dangerous place to be.

One of the worst places for this, I've found, is in airports. For me, there's something about these places that turns hyper-awareness into just plain hyper. I find it very easy to get caught up in some of the ridiculous situations that occur when I'm traveling. Agitation sets in and it's downhill from there.

After a particularly bad session in an international airport where our bags went missing and no one seemed to care, I almost lost it. At that point I decided I absolutely had to learn how to de-stress and cope with whatever issues would arise. As it turns out, I had taken a self-hypnosis course from Dr. Lee Pulos, a friend and a fantastic teacher. He taught me how to take myself "down" into what I now refer to as my Zone One, Zone Two and Zone Three states of being:

Zone One — I'm fully alert – my normal condition
Zone Two — I'm slowing down considerably
Zone Three — I'm deeply relaxed, almost comatose.

I now go into Zone Three as soon as I get to the airport and Rita handles the travel logistics. This works perfectly. In fact, it works so well that I now go into Zone Three in line-ups and anytime I feel open to stress. I don't want to stay in Zone Three — that wouldn't be productive — but I go there when I need to bring my stress levels down.

It's been a long time since I've let an airport stress me out. Actually, I'm a thousand times better than I used to be. If you have the opportunity, take a self-hypnosis course and learn more about how to control your brainwaves — it is really excellent.

Zoning In On Brainwaves

I later discovered that my zones are similar to the zones that scientists use to categorize brainwave patterns: Gamma, Beta, Alpha, Theta and Delta. These brainwaves are produced by very low voltages which help transmit messages along neurons.

Gamma Zone (30+ hertz) Gamma waves are the fastest brainwaves. They are linked to complex brain functions such as storing memory or concentrating. University of Wisconsin researchers recently studied 10 Zen Buddhist monks, along with a control group of eight students who had been trained in the very basics of meditation. While the monks meditated they produced Gammas waves that were very high in amplitude with long-range Gamma synchrony — their brainwaves moved in almost perfect unison with each other. The students' Gamma waves were far weaker than the monks. Trained musicians also show superior levels of Gamma synchrony when listening to music, and are able to achieve calm but intense focus.

Beta Zone (13 to 30 hertz) This zone represents our day-to-day awake state where we are alert and learning. High levels of environmental and work pressures can accelerate brainwaves to the high end of the Beta scale. People who are exposed to high levels of noise, or who work in noisy environments, often exhibit mid- to high-level Beta frequencies. Being in the Beta zone uses

Gamma brainwave
Ultra-alert

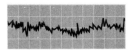

Beta brainwave
Alert/working

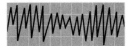

Alpha brainwave
Relaxed/reflecting

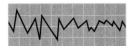

Theta brainwave
Sleep or daydreaming

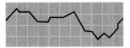

Delta brainwave
Deep, dreamless sleep

high amounts of energy. Prolonged, consistent Beta levels may lead to exhaustion and breakdown.

Alpha Zone (9 to 13 hertz) The Alpha zone is associated with increased serotonin production, calmness and a heightened sense of awareness. It's the ideal state for learning because the brain is relaxed but aware. Many people achieve this state through meditation and relaxation combined with deep breathing. Certain types of musical rhythms, such as music by Bach and Vivaldi, and New Age music, can also help you reach this state.

Theta Zone (4 to 9 hertz) is often associated with dreaming (REM) sleep or deep daydreaming. Indian or Aboriginal shamanic drumbeats or the chanting of Tibetan monks may cause your waves to drop into the Theta range. This, in turn, would alter your state of consciousness. Interestingly, Theta waves are not common in the EEGs (electroencephalographs) of normal awake adults, but they are the predominant rhythm in young children.

Delta Zone (.5 to 4 hertz) Awake adults do not generally enter this zone, although many practitioners of yoga and meditation claim it is possible to train our minds to journey into the Delta state. Delta waves are also associated with deep, dreamless sleep. In this state, our bodies essentially hibernate. Delta waves never drop to zero — that would make us dead!

Learning about brainwaves reinforced for me the idea that when you can't adapt conditions to you, you need to adapt to conditions. "The perfect no-stress environment is the grave," writes Greg Anderson in *The 22 Non-Negotiable Laws of Wellness*. "When we change our perception, we gain control. The stress becomes a challenge, not a threat. When we commit to action, to actually doing something rather than feeling trapped by events, the stress in our life becomes manageable."

The world seems to move faster every day and demands pile up — this won't stop. It's up to you to make changes in your life so stress doesn't become a bad habit and eventually cause serious health issues. By changing your outlook, you'll begin to enjoy life more — and you might even save your life.

Chapter Review

* Explore which situations always make you feel stressed.

* Expect chaos and navigate through by using your values.

* Eat healthy foods, stay fit and sleep well.

* Don't procrastinate; deal with your challenges sooner rather than later to decrease worry and anxiety.

* Weed things out of your schedule that don't fall into alignment with your values, goals and priorities.

* Practice getting in the right "zone."

* Control what you can — let go of what you can't control.

* Do something every day that makes you feel good about yourself and your life.

279

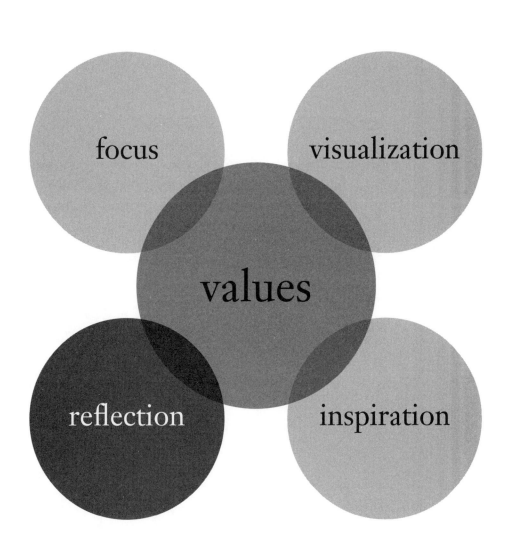

> "REFLECTION, n. An action of the mind whereby we obtain a clearer view of our relation to the things of yesterday and are able to avoid the perils that we shall not again encounter."
> *Ambrose Bierce*

SECRET 20
Look Back to Move Ahead

Decades after I first immigrated to Canada from England, I still reflect on the adventure of traveling to a new country and standing on the deck of the *Queen Mary* with my Mom, looking out at the ocean. The ship's motors churned up the water furiously, leaving behind a "road" of white wake. To my seven-year-old eyes, this "road" appeared to stretch all the way to the horizon. I stood there holding my Mom's hand for what seemed like hours. I felt so confident in the future, so safe and secure, yet at the same time so full of trepidation — *what would my new home be like, who would I meet, what new friends would I make?* I still feel wonderful when I think back on that time.

The philosopher Socrates said, "The unexamined life is not worth living." I agree it's important for you to examine your life from time to time, and reflect on the fantastic experiences you've had. In difficult times, you can quickly "go there" in your imagination. I often think back to my *Queen Mary* experience. I recall attending a bank meeting when I was having serious financial challenges. When the lawyers became particularly obnoxious, I let my mind drift back to the time I stood on the deck of the ship with my Mom. I'm sure those lawyers were wondering why I sat there so calmly, with a smile on my face.

Reflection Brings You Closer to Success

In particular, reflecting on your successes is an important aspect of learning and growing. You'll gain the strength and confidence to inspire you to greater heights. One night I was driving home from an amazing sales call in my 1963 Mercury S-55, with my radio blaring. I was on top of the world because, not only did I make a sale to one family, they had invited their neighbors into their kitchen and I had sold mutual funds to them too! As I was driving, I wasn't thinking too much about the road or my speed — I was reflecting on my success.

All of a sudden, I heard the scream of sirens behind me. I pulled over and a tall policeman walked up to my window. "Where do you think you're going in such a hurry?" he asked me. Well, that was all the encouragement I needed. I *had* to tell him my good news! "I was on this sales call and, wouldn't you believe it, I didn't just sell one…" He stopped me in the middle of my stream of talk. "Go on, get out of here!" he said. I drove off slightly slower, but still on top of the world. Even now, years later, when I'm in the middle of a deal, I often reflect back on that night with a smile.

"We often become so focused on our negatives that we lose sight of the positive aspects of ourselves," writes Gary Buffone, PhD. in his book, *The Myth of Tomorrow*. "Our filter becomes clogged with negative thoughts, strangling the perceptions that encourage, support, and inspire our confidence."

To feel good about ourselves, Buffone advises, "we must take time to appreciate our strengths and assets, and recognize what is working and going well in our lives. When time is short, gratitude grows. Our mortality begs us to be kind."

Find some quiet time and write down your successes from the past year. Don't just focus on career matters or how much money you've earned. One man attending a LifePilot workshop was unable to find any successes to reflect upon. His business was in deep trouble and that colored his entire outlook. Encouraged to look deeper, he *did* acknowledge that he had learned to ride a horse that year.

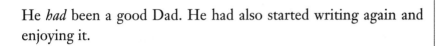

He *had* been a good Dad. He had also started writing again and enjoying it.

"The hardest arithmetic to master is that which enables us to count our blessings," writes Eric Hoffler in *Reflections on the Human Condition*. I agree, but sometimes it seems easier to count blessings in the lives of other people. Ask yourself, "If I were a friend to myself, what would I view as successes in my life?" If you are still having trouble identifying your successes, ask people who you like and trust to tell you what they think your successes have been.

Set aside a regular time to update your list. Sundays are often quiet reflective days for many people. By adding to your list on a regular basis, you'll be amazed at the change that will come over your life. Because of your new focus on "finding successes," you'll begin to see accomplishments where you previously saw failures, your self-esteem will grow and you'll attract more success into your life.

"And as we let our own light shine, we unconsciously give other people permission to do the same," says Nelson Mandela. "As we are liberated from our fears, our presence automatically liberates others."

List your successes:	8.
1.	9.
2.	10.
3.	11.
4.	12.
5.	13.
6.	14.
7.	15.

Reflect or Ruminate?

Carl Jung firmly believed that we need to confront ourselves through reflection. "That which we do not confront ourselves with," he said, "we will meet as fate." That said, it's important to make the distinction between reflecting and ruminating. Recent studies by Paul Trapnell and Jennifer Campbell at Ohio State University show that people typically engage in two different types of self-analysis: self-reflection and self-rumination.

"Maybe you personally know people who spend a lot of time analyzing themselves," writes Alain Morin in the *Science & Consciousness Review*. "They seem to constantly be 'beating around the bush,' re-evaluating themselves, always questioning their behavior and appearance, being unsure of themselves, nervous, etc. This is self-rumination: anxious attention paid to the self, where the person is afraid to fail and keeps wondering about his/her self-worth."

"Then maybe you have other acquaintances who are also highly self-aware," Morin continues "but instead of being anxious about themselves, they have wisdom — they know themselves very well, are the 'contemplating' types, feel secure, have depth, and are philosophical about their shortcomings. This is self-reflection: a genuine curiosity about the self, where the person is intrigued and interested in learning more about his or her emotions, values, thought processes, attitudes, etc."

According to Morin, self-reflection represents a higher form of consciousness which makes it possible for us to "become the object of our own attention and to acknowledge our own existence."

"Without continuous personal development," says leadership development expert Eli Cohen, "you are now all that you will ever become, and hell starts when the person you are, meets the person you could have been."

So use reflection to take the wisdom from your past and engrave it on your present and future. By doing so, you bring yourself closer to becoming the amazing person you were meant to be.

Chapter Review

* Self-awareness and self-analysis are the cornerstones of emotional intelligence.

* Reflection isn't about dwelling in the past — it's a bridge between our experiences and our learning.

* To reflect is to review, understand, discover and examine our lessons, and apply them towards creating a positive future.

* Reflection is also a way to celebrate the achievement of your goals. Revisiting these achievements is a great pick-me-up on a bad day and a pleasurable exercise on a good day.

> "One can never consent to creep when one feels an impulse to soar." *Helen Keller*

Secret 21

Enjoy the Flight of Your Life

When you bring LifePilot into your life and begin to live by your values, you'll feel more in balance and in control of your destiny. Once you've learned to soar, you can hardly return to the ground. You have an obligation to yourself to create and live the life you desire. The time to do that is now. As Mark Twain said, "Twenty years from now you will be more disappointed by the things you didn't do than by the ones you did do."

Dare to Make a Difference

Part of creating the life you desire is daring to make a difference in the world by doing what you feel passionate about. According to Patanjali, a philosopher who lived in 2nd century BC, "When you work only for yourself, or for your own personal gain, your mind will seldom rise above the limitations of an undeveloped personal life. But when you are inspired by some great purpose, some extraordinary project, all your thoughts break your bonds: your mind transcends limitations, your consciousness expands in every direction, and you find yourself in a new, great and wonderful world. Dormant forces, faculties and talents become alive, and you discover yourself to be a greater person by far than you ever dreamed yourself to be."

There's a story that illustrates well the power and potential each of us has to make a difference in the world. One day a man was walking along the seashore. He noticed that during the night, thousands of starfish had washed up on the beach. Thoroughly enjoying the morning sun and cool sea air, the man strolled for miles along the sand. Far off in the distance, he saw a small figure dancing. The man felt joyous that someone was celebrating life in such a grand and uninhibited manner. As he drew closer, however, it became apparent that perhaps the person was not dancing but repeatedly performing some ritual.

Approaching the small figure, the man noticed it was a young girl methodically picking up starfish from the shore and tossing them back into the surf.

The man paused for a moment, puzzled, and then asked, "Why are you throwing those starfish into the water?"

"If I leave these starfish on the beach," the girl replied, "the sun will dry them and they will die. So I'm throwing them back into the ocean because I want them to live."

The man was silent for a moment, impressed with the child's thoughtfulness. Then he motioned at the miles and miles of beach and said, "There must be millions of starfish along here! How can you possibly expect to make a difference?"

The girl pondered the man's words for a moment. Then she slowly reached down, carefully picked up another starfish and gently placed it in the surf. She turned to the man and said, "It makes a difference to *that* starfish."

Changing a Life

I began the LifePilot process with the notion of changing one life for the better — my own. When I saw the difference living by my values made, I decided to share the ideas with others in the hope they would also find more fulfillment, balance and happiness.

As I said in the beginning of this book, these ideas are not mine alone. Throughout the ages, successful men and women have discovered and flight-tested these philosophies. One of these great thinkers, Socrates, said, "I cannot teach anybody anything, I can only make them think." I hope *LifeManual* will inspire you to think about the life you really want to live.

The unknown author of the following poem perfectly sums up my thoughts about the meaning of success. The secret is inside each of us if we take the time and have the will to discover it.

Dream Big

If ever there was a time to dare to make a difference,
to embark on something worth doing, it is now.
Not for any grand cause necessarily —
but for something that tugs at your heart,
something that's your aspiration,
something that's your dream.

You owe it to yourself to make your days count.
Have fun. Dig deep. Stretch. DREAM BIG.
Know though, that things worth doing seldom come easily.
There will be good days. And there will be bad days.
There will be times when you want to turn around,
pack it up, and call it quits.
Those times tell you that you are pushing yourself,
that you are not afraid to learn by trying.

Persist.
Because with an idea, determination,
And the right tools, you can do great things.
Let your instincts, your intellect,
and your heart guide you.

Trust.
Believe in the incredible power of the human mind.
Of doing something that makes a difference.
Of working hard. Of laughing and hoping.
Of lazy afternoons. Of lasting friends.
Of all the things that will cross your path this year.
The start of something new
brings the hope of something great.
Anything is possible.
There is only one you.

And you will pass this way only once.
Do it right. Just do it!

Remember, the key to achieving your dreams is to navigate by your values, set your goals and stay focused on what you desire. Along the way, seek inspiration, express gratitude, engage in reflection — and enjoy the flight of your life.

293

Bibliography

Adrienne, Carol, *The Purpose of Your Life*, Eagle Brook, New York, NY, 1998

Albom, Mitch, *Tuesdays with Morrie*, Doubleday Books, New York, NY, 1997

Allenbaugh, Eric, PhD., *Wake-Up Calls: You Don't Have to Sleepwalk Through Your Life, Love, or Career!*, Simon and Schuster, New York, NY, 1992

Anderson, Greg, *The 22 Non-Negotiable Laws Of Wellness*, HarperCollins, New York, NY, 1995

Armstrong, Lance with Jenkins, Sally, *It's Not About the Bike*, Penguin Publishing Group, New York, NY, 2001

Arruda, William, "The Three C's of Personal Branding," *Brandchannel.com*, 2002

Assaraf, John, *The Street Kid's Guide to Having it All*, LongStreet Press, Athens, GA, 2003

Bayles, David and Orland, Ted, *Art and Fear: Observations on the Perils (and Rewards) of Artmaking*, Continuum Press, New York, NY, 2002

Bennet, Bo, *Year to Success*, Archieboy Holdings, Sudbury, MA, 2004

Breen, Bill, "What's Your Intuition," *Fast Company*, September 2000

Britten, Rhonda, *Fearless Living: Live without Excuses and Succeed Beyond Your Dreams*, Hodder Headline, Australia, 2001

Buffone, Gary, PhD., *The Myth of Tomorrow*, McGraw-Hill, New York, NY, 2003

Butler, Brett, *Knee Deep In Paradise*, Hyperion, New York, NY, 1996

Caine, Mark, *The S-man: A Grammar of Success*, Houghton Mifflin Co., Boston, MA, 1961

Cameron, Julia, *The Artist's Way: A Spiritual Path to Higher Creativity*, Penguin Books, New York, NY, 1992

Campbell, Don, *The Mozart Effect: Tapping the Power of Music to Heal the Body, Strengthen the Mind, and Unlock the Creative Spirit*, Quill/HarperCollins, New York, NY, 1997

Cappon, Daniel, "The Anatomy of Intuition," *Psychology Today*, May/June 1993

Cassel R.N.; Costello; B.R.; and Pullar, B.M., "Where Today is Tomorrow in Health: Comparing Two Worlds of Feelings Using Biofeedback," Cassell Research Institute, *Education*, 1993

Clark, Glenn, *The Man Who Tapped the Secrets of the Universe*, Macalaster Park Publishing Co., Waynesboro, VA, 1982

Collins, Ingrid, *A Year of Spirituality*, MQ Publications Ltd., London, UK, 2003

Collins, Jim, *Good to Great*, HarperBusiness, New York, NY, 2001

Cooper, Robert K., *The Other 90%: How to Unlock Your Vast Potential for Leadership & Life*, Crown Business, New York, NY, 2001

Covey, Stephen, *7 Habits of Highly Effective People*, Simon and Shuster, New York, NY, 2003

Dennett, Daniel C., *Consciousness Explained*

Deutschman, Alan, "Making Change," *Fast Company*, May 2005

Dobbs, David, "Headlines," *Scientific American Mind*, Volume 16, Number 1, 2005

Dyer, Wayne W., *Wisdom of the Ages*, HarperCollins, New York, NY, 1998

Eade, Diane M., "Goal Planning: Strategies for a Balanced Life," *Clinician Reviews*, 1995

Ellis, Keith, *The Magic Lamp: Goal Setting for People Who Hate Setting Goals*, Three Rivers Press, New York, NY, 1998

Epstein, Mark, "Opening Up to Happiness," *Psychology Today*, July-August, 1995

Feldman, Christine, *Silence: How to Find Inner Peace in a Busy World*, Rodmell Press, Berkeley, CA, 2001

Gawain, Shakti, *Creative Visualization*, New World Library, San Farael, CA, 1995

Gladwell, Malcolm, *Blink: The Power of Thinking Without Thinking*, Little, Brown and Company, New York, NY, 2005

Gladwell, Malcolm, *The Tipping Point*, Little Brown and Company, New York, NY, 2002

Green, Joey, *The Road to Success is Paved with Failure*, Little, Brown and Company, New York, NY, 2001

Hill, Napoleon and Ritt, Michael, *Keys to Positive Thinking*, Penguin Group, New York, NY, 1998

Hill, Napoleon, *Think and Grow Rich*, Wilshire Book Company, New York, NY, 1999

Holmes, Ernest S., *Creative Mind*, Dodd, Mead & Company, New York, NY, 1999

Johnston, Theresa, "Love is the basis of our practical reasoning, philosopher says in Tanner Lectures," *Stanford Report*, April 20, 2004

Katz, Stan J. and Liu, Aimee E., "Success in the Land of the Less," *Psychology Today*, January 1992

Kelly, Matthew, *The Rhythm of Life*, Simon & Schuster, New York, NY, 2004

Klein, Gary and Weick, Karl E., "Decisions: Making the Right Ones. Learning from the Wrong Ones," The Conference Board Inc., 2005

Klein, Maury, *The Change Makers*, Henry Holt & Company, New York, NY, 2003

Krech, Gregg, "Naikan: Gratitude, Grace and the Japanese Art of Self-Reflection," Stone Bridge Press, Berkeley, CA, 2002

Krumhansl, Carol, "Effects of Perceptual Organization and Musical Form on Melodic Expectancies," Joint International Conference on Cognitive and Systematic Musicology, 1996

Lague, Louise, "Reinvention Strategy," *Oprah.com*, January 2001

Larson, Craig, "Leap of Faith," *Concentric.net*, 2000

Leslie, Mitchell, "The Vexing Legacy of Lewis Terman," *Stanford Magazine*, 2004

Litman, Mark and Jason, Oman, *Conversations with Millionaires: What Millionaires Do to Get Rich, That You Never Learned About in School!*, CWM Publishing, New York, NY, 2001

Marinoff, Lou, PhD., *Therapy for the Sane: How Philosophy Can Change Your Life*, Bloomsbury, New York, NY, 2003

Matys, Monica, "'Music for the Brain' Could Be a Stress-Buster," *CTV*, 2002

Mayer, Emeran A., M.D., "The Neurobiology of Stress and Emotions," *Participate/Digestive Health Matters*, UCLA Mind Body Collaborative Research Center, UCLA School of Medicine, CA, Winter 2001

Merrill, Roger A., and Merrill, Rebecca R., *Life Matters: Creating a Dynamic Balance of Work, Family, Time and Money*, McGraw-Hill, Columbus, OH, 2003

Merzenich, Michael, PhD., "Neural Origins of Higher Brain Functions: Origins of, and Remediation of Human Neurological Dysfunction and Disability," UCSF Neuroscience program, 1998

Montoya, Peter and Vandehey, Tim, *The Brand Called You*, Personal Branding Press, Santa Ana, CA, 2003

Morin Alain, "Do you Self-reflect or Self-ruminate?" *Science & Consciousness Review*, No.1, December 2002

Mueller, Roy, "Music and the Brain," *Hand to Hand*, a quarterly publication of the Association of Children's Museums, Washington, DC, Fall 2001

National Sleep Association, "Ten Tips for Better Sleep," *health.discovery.com*, 2005

Newens, Hoa, "The Power and Techniques of Focusing," *www.aikidoinstitute.com*, 1999

Paulus, Trina, *Hope for Flowers*, Paulist Press, USA, 1992

Pearsall, Paul, PhD., *Toxic Success: How to Stop Striving and Start Thriving*, Inner Ocean Publishing, Inc., Makawao, Maui, Hawaii, 2004

Pearson, Will; Hattikudur Mangesh; and Hunt, Elizabeth, eds., *Mental_Floss Presents: Condensed Knowledge: A Deliciously Irreverent Guide to Feeling Smart Again*, Harper Collins, New York, NY, 2004

Pelzer, Dave, *Help Yourself*, Dutton Books, New York, NY, 2000

Pert, Candace, *Molecules of Emotion: The Science Behind Mind-Body Medicine*, Scribner, New York, NY, 1999

Platkin, Charles Stuart, *Breaking the Pattern: The 5 Principles You Need to Remodel Your Life*, Penguin Group, New York, NY, 2005

Poulos, John Allen, *A Mathematician Reads The Newspaper*, Penguin Books, New York, NY, 1996

Ratey, John, M.D., and Johnson, Catherine, PhD., *Shadow Syndromes*, Pantheon Books, a division of Random House, Inc., New York, NY, 1997

Richardson, Cheryl, *Stand Up for Your Life*, The Free Press, New York, NY, 2002

Rilke, Ranier Maria, *Letters to a Young Poet*, trans. by Joan M. Burnham, New World Library, New York, NY, 1992

Roberts, Kevin, *Lovemarks: The Future Beyond Brands*, PowerHouse Books, New York, NY, 2004

Roehrs, Timothy, M.D., "Why Sleep is Important and What Happens When You Don't Get Enough," *Sleep*, August 2004

Ryan, M.J., *Trusting Yourself*, Broadway Books, New York, NY, 2004

Scheinfeld, Robert, *The Invisible Path to Success*, Hampton Roads Publishing Company, Inc., Charlottesville, VA, 1998

Shanor, Karen Nesbitt, PhD., ed., *The Emerging Mind*, Renaissance Books, Los Angeles, California, 1999

Simons, Daniel J., "Current Approaches to Change Blindness," Harvard University, Cambridge, MA, USA, 2000

Sukumar, Rajagopal, "The S Curve: What is Wrong with Success?," *itotd.com*, 2004

Thring, Meredith W., and Laithwaite, Eric, *How to Invent*, Macmillan, London, UK 1977

Trump, Donald, *How to Get Rich*, Random House, New York, NY, 2004

University of Queensland Online, "Stockbrokers & Traders Guided by 'Gut Feelings,'" Thursday, September 30, 2004

Tracy, Brian, *Create Your Own Future: How to Master the 12 Critical Factors of Unlimited Success*, Wiley Books, New York, NY, 2005

Tracy, Brian, *Focal Point*, American Management Association, New York, NY, 2002

US Surgeon General, *Mental Health: A Report of the US Surgeon General*, US Department of Health and Human Services, 1999

US Surgeon General, *Report on Physical Activity and Health*, US Department of Health and Human Services, 1996

Van Dongen, Hans P.A., PhD. et al., "The Cumulative Cost of Additional Wakefulness: Dose-Response Effects on Neurobehavioral Functions and Sleep Physiology From Chronic Sleep Restriction and Total Sleep Deprivation," *Sleep*, March 2005

Venerable, Grant, "The Paradox of the Silicon Savior," as reported in "The Case for Sequential Music Education in the Core Curriculum of the Public Schools," New York, NY, 1989

Weinberger, Norman M., "Music and the Brain," *Scientific American*, November 2004

Wieder, Marcia, *Making Your Dreams Come True*, Harmony Books, New York, NY, 1999

Wujec, Tom, *Five Star Mind*, Doubleday, New York, NY, 1995

Zaleznik, Abraham, "Managers and Leaders: Are They Different?" *Harvard Business Review*, 2004

Zoglio, Suzanne, Ph.D., "Living Full—Living True: The Authentic Life," *Soulfulliving.com*, January-March 2005

Acknowledgements

I would like to acknowledge the following people for their encouragement, inspiration and expertise in the writing of *LifeManual: A Proven Formula to Create the Life You Desire*. First, I want to acknowledge my son Todd Thomas in whose memory this book has been written. He has been the angel and guiding light of this project. I also want to express my thanks to my wife, Rita Thomas. She has been a constant source of inspiration and insight in the success of LifePilot and the writing of this book.

I am grateful to Kerry Slavens for her editorial assistance, research and passion for the project. I also want to thank the following people for sharing their stories and wisdom with me: Jamesie Bower, Kevin Foster, Dr. Steven Funk, Dr. Gary Hall, Mark Horne, Michelle Farver-Luedtke and Vance Luedtke, Ken Marlin, Nancye Miller, Beverly McClung, Alfredo J. Molina, Dru Narwani, John Papaloukas, Brian Scudamore, Dr. Kumar Shivdasani, Praveen Varshney and Cheryl Wheeler.

I want to thank the many people and organizations who have hosted and supported LifePilot workshops, and those who have attended the workshops. Special thanks to Bill Swinimer, Ellie Byrd, Tracey Gurton, Norm Friend, Mike Desjardins, Michelle Lemons-Poscente, Paul Robshaw and John Assaraf.

Your support and enthusiasm has been a great inspiration. Thanks to that support, we at LifePilot are continuing to fulfill our dream of donating funds to organizations that assist people with mental health disorders. For further information about the charities we support, please visit *www.lifepilot.org*.

LifeManual draws on many inspiring stories I have heard over the years. Wherever possible, I have credited the source, but in some cases, I have been unable to trace the source of the original story. I would be pleased to receive any information regarding the proper identification of sources.

About the Author

Peter H. Thomas is one of North America's most recognized motivational speakers and business visionaries. Peter's exceptional career has spanned more than three decades in the investment and real estate fields. He was founder and Chairman of Century 21 Real Estate for Canada, which at the time of its sale was the largest real estate network in the country. His company Thomas Pride International developed the Four Seasons Resort and Hotel in Scottsdale, Arizona. Peter also served as the Chairman and CEO for 11 years for the company now known as Sterling Centrecorp, a major North American public real estate company specializing in managing and developing shopping centers all over North America.

Inspired by a Young Presidents' Organization seminar he attended decades ago, Peter learned the power of living and setting priorities in alignment with his values. After the suicide of his son Todd in 2000, Peter developed the LifePilot program to assist people to navigate their way toward more meaningful lives, and to raise funds for mental health charities.

Today, Peter serves as a World Presidents' Organization Director and as International Chairman of the Board of Trustees of the Young Entrepreneurs' Organization. *LifeManual* is Peter's fourth publication. He is also the author of several books, including the best-selling *Never Fight with a Pig: A Survival Guide for Entrepreneurs*, which details the lessons learned during his rise to business success, and *Windows of Opportunity: 21 Steps to Successful Selling*. Peter also produced *The Peter Thomas Sales Course*, an audio sales training program.

Peter is committed to a life of health, happiness and personal freedom. He lives in Switzerland with his wife Rita.

empty sack — sacks or containers unique to
guru - full cups   story
                              store as a
   faith -   containers

Story Listening - importance of
" To be a person is to have a story to tell.
                              Isak Dinesen
Much clothed in.
    Story
11th century
It is like cleaning out your
   closet + organizing it to better
serve your life."